Puppet 3 Cookbook

Build reliable, scalable, secure, and high-performance
systems to fully utilize the power of cloud computing

John Arundel

BIRMINGHAM - MUMBAI

Puppet 3 Cookbook

First published: October 2011

Second published: August 2013

Production Reference: 1190813

Published by Packt Publishing Ltd.
Livery Place
35 Livery Street
Birmingham B3 2PB, UK.

ISBN 978-1-78216-976-5

www.packtpub.com

Cover Image by Asher Wishkerman (wishkerman@hotmail.com)

Credits

Author
John Arundel

Reviewers
Dhruv Ahuja
Carlos Nilton Araújo Corrêa
Daniele Sluijters
Dao Thomas

Acquisition Editor
Kartikey Pandey

Lead Technical Editor
Madhuja Chaudhari

Technical Editors
Anita Nayak
Larissa Pinto

Project Coordinator
Kranti Berde

Proofreader
Lawrence A. Herman

Indexers
Hemangini Bari
Monica Ajmera Mehta

Graphics
Ronak Dhruv

Production Coordinator
Kyle Albuquerque

Cover Work
Kyle Albuquerque

About the Author

John Arundel is a devops consultant, which means he solves difficult problems for a living. (He doesn't get called in for easy problems.)

He has worked in the tech industry for 20 years, and during that time has done wrong (or seen done wrong) almost everything that you can do wrong with computers. That comprehensive knowledge of what not to do, he feels, is one of his greatest assets as a consultant. He is still adding to it.

He likes writing books, especially about Puppet (*The Puppet 3 Beginner's Guide* is available from the same publisher). It seems that at least some people enjoy reading them. He also provides training and coaching on Puppet, which it turns out is far harder than simply doing the work himself.

Off the clock, he can usually be found driving a Land Rover up some mountain or other. He lives in a small cottage in Cornwall and believes, like Cicero, that if you have a garden and a library, then you have everything you need.

You can follow him on Twitter at `@bitfield`.

My thanks go to Rene Lehmann, Cristian Leonte, German Rodriguez, Keiran Sweet, Dean Wilson, and Dan White for their help with proofreading and suggestions. Special thanks are due to Lance Murray and Sebastiaan van Steenis, who diligently read and tested every chapter, and provided invaluable feedback on what did and didn't make sense.

About the Reviewers

Dhruv Ahuja is a Lead Engineer at a managed hosting provider. He specializes in infrastructure solutions design and configuration, with a keen eye on achieving mechanical sympathy. His first brush with Puppet was in 2011 when he developed a solution on dynamically scaling compute nodes for a multi-purpose grid platform. He also holds a master's degree in Advanced Software Engineering from King's College London, and won the Red Hat UK Channel Consultant of the Year award in 2012 for delivering progressive solutions. A long history in conventional software development and traditional systems administration equip him with aptness in both areas, and he bridges many infrastructural gaps in a well-delimited way. In this era of infrastructure as code, he believes that declarative abstraction is essential for a maintainable systems life-cycle process.

Carlos N. A. Corrêa is an IT Operations manager and consultant, and is also a Puppet enthusiast and an old-school Linux hacker. He has a Master's Degree in Systems Virtualization and holds CISSP and RHCE certifications. Backed by a 15-year career on systems administration, Carlos leads IT Operations teams for companies both in Brazil and Africa. He is also a part-time professor for graduate and undergraduate courses in Brazil. Carlos co-authored several research papers on network virtualization and OpenFlow, presented on peer-reviewed IEEE and ACM conferences worldwide.

I thank God for all the opportunities of hard work and all the lovely people I always found on my way. To the sweetest of them all, my wife Nanda, I give thanks for all the loving care and support that pushes me forward. And to my parents, Nilton and Zélia, for being such a big inspiration for all the things that I do.

Daniele Sluijters is a student of Informatics and has been working as a systems operator for a few years. Initially it all started out as a hobby, but eventually it turned into both his field of study and work. His primary focus in both work and study for the past years have been large(r) networks made up of mostly Unix systems offering services to the world disclosed over the internet and how to manage and secure both the systems, the services they provide, and the networks they use. He has also worked on the book Zabbix Network Monitoring Essentials, Munin Plugin Starter

www.PacktPub.com

Support files, eBooks, discount offers and more

You might want to visit www.PacktPub.com for support files and downloads related to your book.

Did you know that Packt offers eBook versions of every book published, with PDF and ePub files available? You can upgrade to the eBook version at www.PacktPub.com and as a print book customer, you are entitled to a discount on the eBook copy. Get in touch with us at service@packtpub.com for more details.

At www.PacktPub.com, you can also read a collection of free technical articles, sign up for a range of free newsletters and receive exclusive discounts and offers on Packt books and eBooks.

http://PacktLib.PacktPub.com

Do you need instant solutions to your IT questions? PacktLib is Packt's online digital book library. Here, you can access, read and search across Packt's entire library of books.

Why Subscribe?

- ▸ Fully searchable across every book published by Packt
- ▸ Copy and paste, print and bookmark content
- ▸ On demand and accessible via web browser

Free Access for Packt account holders

If you have an account with Packt at www.PacktPub.com, you can use this to access PacktLib today and view nine entirely free books. Simply use your login credentials for immediate access.

Table of Contents

Preface   **1**

Chapter 1: Puppet Infrastructure   **7**
  Introduction   **7**
  Installing Puppet   **8**
  Creating a manifest   **10**
  Managing your manifests with Git   **11**
  Creating a decentralized Puppet architecture   **14**
  Writing a papply script   **16**
  Running Puppet from cron   **18**
  Deploying changes with Rake   **22**
  Bootstrapping Puppet with Rake   **26**
  Automatic syntax checking with Git hooks   **29**

Chapter 2: Puppet Language and Style   **33**
  Introduction   **34**
  Using community Puppet style   **34**
  Checking your manifests with puppet-lint   **36**
  Using modules   **38**
  Using standard naming conventions   **42**
  Using inline templates   **44**
  Iterating over multiple items   **45**
  Writing powerful conditional statements   **47**
  Using regular expressions in if statements   **49**
  Using selectors and case statements   **50**
  Using the in operator   **53**
  Using regular expression substitutions   **54**

Chapter 3: Writing Better Manifests — 57

Introduction	58
Using arrays of resources	58
Using definitions	59
Using dependencies	61
Using tags	65
Using run stages	68
Using node inheritance	71
Passing parameters to classes	73
Using class inheritance and overriding	75
Writing reusable, cross-platform manifests	79
Getting information about the environment	81
Importing dynamic information	83
Passing arguments to shell commands	84

Chapter 4: Working with Files and Packages — 87

Introduction	87
Making quick edits to config files	88
Using Augeas to automatically edit config files	89
Building config files using snippets	91
Using ERB templates	94
Using array iteration in templates	96
Using GnuPG to encrypt secrets	98
Installing packages from a third-party repository	103
Building packages automatically from source	106
Comparing package versions	108

Chapter 5: Users and Virtual Resources — 111

Introduction	112
Using virtual resources	112
Managing users with virtual resources	115
Managing users' SSH access	118
Managing users' customization files	121
Efficiently distributing cron jobs	126
Using schedules to limit when resources can be applied	129
Using host resources	132
Using multiple file sources	133
Distributing directory trees	135
Cleaning up old files	137

Auditing resources 139

Temporarily disabling resources 140

Chapter 6: Applications 143

Introduction 143

Managing Apache servers 144

Creating Apache virtual hosts 145

Creating Nginx virtual hosts 150

Managing MySQL 153

Managing Ruby 158

Chapter 7: Servers and Cloud Infrastructure 165

Introduction 165

Building high-availability services using Heartbeat 166

Managing NFS servers and file shares 171

Using HAProxy to load-balance multiple web servers 174

Managing firewalls with iptables 178

Managing EC2 instances 188

Managing virtual machines with Vagrant 193

Chapter 8: External Tools and the Puppet Ecosystem 199

Introduction 200

Creating custom facts 200

Adding external facts 202

Setting facts as environment variables 205

Importing configuration data with Hiera 206

Storing secret data with hiera-gpg 210

Generating manifests with puppet resource 213

Generating manifests with other tools 214

Testing your manifests with rspec-puppet 218

Using public modules 221

Using an external node classifier 223

Creating your own resource types 226

Creating your own providers 228

Creating your own functions 231

Chapter 9: Monitoring, Reporting, and Troubleshooting 235

Introduction 235

Doing a dry run 236

Logging command output 237

Logging debug messages 239

Generating reports   **240**

Producing automatic HTML documentation   **242**

Drawing dependency graphs   **245**

Understanding Puppet errors   **248**

Inspecting configuration settings   **251**

Index   **253**

Preface

A revolution is underway in the field of IT operations. The new generation of configuration management tools can build servers in seconds and automate your entire network. Tools such as Puppet are essential to take full advantage of the power of cloud computing, and build reliable, scalable, secure, high-performance systems.

This book takes you beyond the basics and explores the full power of Puppet, showing you in detail how to tackle a variety of real-world problems and applications. At every step, it shows you exactly what commands you need to type and includes complete code samples for every recipe.

It takes the reader from rudimentary knowledge of Puppet to a more complete and expert understanding of Puppet's latest and most advanced features, community best practices, writing great manifests, scaling and performance, and how to extend Puppet by adding your own providers and resources.

This book also includes real examples from production systems and techniques that are in use in some of the world's largest Puppet installations. It will show you different ways to do things using Puppet and point out some of the pros and cons of these approaches.

The book is structured so that you can dip in at any point and try out a recipe without having to work your way through from cover to cover. You'll find links and references to more information on every topic, so that you can explore further for yourself. Whatever your level of Puppet experience, there's something for you, from simple workflow tips to advanced, high-performance Puppet architectures.

I've tried hard to write the kind of book that would be useful to me in my day-to-day work as a devops consultant. I hope it will inspire you to learn, to experiment, and to come up with your own new ideas in this exciting and fast-moving field.

What this book covers

You'll find the following chapters in this book:

Chapter 1, Puppet Infrastructure, shows how to set up Puppet for the first time, including instructions on installing Puppet, creating your first manifests, using version control with Puppet, building a distributed Puppet architecture based on Git, writing a script to apply Puppet manifests, running Puppet automatically, using Rake to bootstrap machines and deploy changes, and using Git hooks to automatically syntax-check your manifests.

Chapter 2, Puppet Language and Style, covers aspects of writing good Puppet code, including using Puppet community style, checking your manifests with `puppet-lint`, structuring your manifests with modules, using standard naming and style conventions, using inline templates, using iteration, conditional statements, and regular expressions, using selectors and case statements, and string operations.

Chapter 3, Writing Better Manifests, goes into detail on specific features of Puppet that you can use to improve your code quality and usability, including arrays, definitions, ordering your resources with dependencies, inheriting from nodes and classes, passing parameters to classes, overriding parameters, reading information from the environment, writing reusable manifests, and using tags and run stages.

Chapter 4, Working with Files and Packages, deals with some of the most common sysadmin tasks, including managing config files, using Augeas, generating files from snippets and templates, managing third-party package repositories, using GnuPG to encrypt secret data in Puppet, and building packages from source.

Chapter 5, Users and Virtual Resources, explains what virtual resources are and how they can help you manage different combinations of users and packages on different machines, and shows you how to use Puppet's resource scheduling and auditing features.

Chapter 6, Applications, focuses on some specific applications that you may need to manage with Puppet, including complete recipes for Apache and Nginx, MySQL, and Ruby.

Chapter 7, Servers and Cloud Infrastructure, extends the power of Puppet to manage virtual machines, both on the cloud and on your desktop, with recipes for Vagrant and EC2 instances. It also shows you how to set up load balancing with HAProxy, firewalls with `iptables`, network filesystems with NFS, and high-availability services with Heartbeat.

Chapter 8, External Tools and the Puppet Ecosystem, looks at some of the tools that have grown up around Puppet, including Hiera, Facter, and `rspec-puppet`. It also introduces you to some advanced topics including writing your own resource types, providers, and external node classifiers.

Chapter 9, Monitoring, Reporting, and Troubleshooting, covers ways that Puppet can report information about what it's doing, and the status of your system. This includes reports, log, and debug messages, dependency graphing, testing and dry-running your manifests, and a guide to some of Puppet's more common error messages.

What you need for this book

To run the examples in this book, you will need a computer with Ubuntu Linux 12.04 and an Internet connection.

Who this book is for

The book assumes that the reader has a little experience of Linux systems administration, including familiarity with the command line, file system, and text editing. No programming experience is required.

Conventions

In this book, you will find a number of styles of text that distinguish between different kinds of information. Here are some examples of these styles, and an explanation of their meaning.

Code words in text, database table names, folder names, filenames, file extensions, pathnames, dummy URLs, user input, and Twitter handles are shown as follows: "You can check your manifests for style guide compliance using the `puppet-lint` tool."

A block of code is set as follows:

```
node 'cookbook' {
  cron { 'randomised cron job':
    command => '/bin/echo Hello, world >>/tmp/hello.txt',
    hour    => '*',
    minute  => random_minute(),
  }
}
```

When we wish to draw your attention to a particular part of a code block, the relevant lines or items are set in bold:

```
newparam(:path) do
  validate do |value|
    basepath = File.dirname(value)
    unless File.directory?(basepath)
      raise ArgumentError , "The path %s doesn't exist" % basepath
    end
  end
end
```

Any command-line input or output is written as follows:

```
ubuntu@cookbook:~/puppet$ papply
Notice: Hello, I was included by your ENC!
Notice: /Stage[main]/Admin::Helloenc/Notify[Hello, I was included by your
ENC!]/message: defined 'message' as 'Hello, I was included by your ENC!'
Notice: Finished catalog run in 0.29 seconds
```

New terms and **important words** are shown in bold. Words that you see on the screen, in menus or dialog boxes for example, appear in the text like this: "clicking the **Next** button moves you to the next screen".

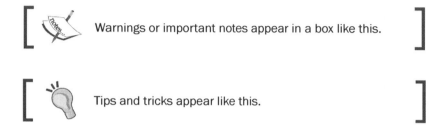

Warnings or important notes appear in a box like this.

Tips and tricks appear like this.

Reader feedback

Feedback from our readers is always welcome. Let us know what you think about this book—what you liked or may have disliked. Reader feedback is important for us to develop titles that you really get the most out of.

To send us general feedback, simply send an e-mail to feedback@packtpub.com, and mention the book title via the subject of your message.

If there is a topic that you have expertise in and you are interested in either writing or contributing to a book, see our author guide on www.packtpub.com/authors.

Customer support

Now that you are the proud owner of a Packt book, we have a number of things to help you to get the most from your purchase.

Downloading the example code

You can download the example code files for all Packt books you have purchased from your account at http://www.packtpub.com. If you purchased this book elsewhere, you can visit http://www.packtpub.com/support and register to have the files e-mailed directly to you.

Errata

Although we have taken every care to ensure the accuracy of our content, mistakes do happen. If you find a mistake in one of our books—maybe a mistake in the text or the code—we would be grateful if you would report this to us. By doing so, you can save other readers from frustration and help us improve subsequent versions of this book. If you find any errata, please report them by visiting `http://www.packtpub.com/submit-errata`, selecting your book, clicking on the **errata submission form** link, and entering the details of your errata. Once your errata are verified, your submission will be accepted and the errata will be uploaded on our website, or added to any list of existing errata, under the Errata section of that title. Any existing errata can be viewed by selecting your title from `http://www.packtpub.com/support`.

Piracy

Piracy of copyright material on the Internet is an ongoing problem across all media. At Packt, we take the protection of our copyright and licenses very seriously. If you come across any illegal copies of our works, in any form, on the Internet, please provide us with the location address or website name immediately so that we can pursue a remedy.

Please contact us at `copyright@packtpub.com` with a link to the suspected pirated material.

We appreciate your help in protecting our authors, and our ability to bring you valuable content.

Questions

You can contact us at `questions@packtpub.com` if you are having a problem with any aspect of the book, and we will do our best to address it.

1
Puppet Infrastructure

Computers in the future may have as few as 1,000 vacuum tubes and weigh only 1.5 tons.

—Popular Mechanics, 1949

In this chapter, we will cover:

- ▶ Installing Puppet
- ▶ Creating a manifest
- ▶ Managing your manifests with Git
- ▶ Creating a decentralized Puppet architecture
- ▶ Writing a papply script
- ▶ Running Puppet from cron
- ▶ Deploying changes with Rake
- ▶ Bootstrapping Puppet with Rake
- ▶ Automatic syntax checking with Git hooks

Introduction

Some of the recipes in this book represent best practices as agreed upon by the Puppet community. Others are tips and tricks which will make it easier for you to work with Puppet, or introduce you to features that you may not have been previously aware of. Some recipes are shortcuts that I wouldn't recommend you use as standard operating procedure, but may be useful in emergencies. Finally, there are some experimental recipes that you may like to try, but are only useful or applicable in very large-scale infrastructures or otherwise unusual circumstances.

My hope is that, by reading through and thinking about the recipes presented here, you will gain a deeper and broader understanding of how Puppet works and how you can use it to improve your infrastructure. Only you can decide whether a particular recipe is appropriate for you and your organization, but I hope this collection will inspire you to experiment, find out more, and most of all have fun using Puppet!

Linux distributions

Because Linux distributions, such as Ubuntu, Red Hat, and CentOS differ in the specific details of package names, configuration file paths, and many other things, I have decided that for reasons of space and clarity the best approach for this book is to pick one distribution (Ubuntu 12.04 Precise) and stick to that. However, Puppet runs on most popular operating systems, so you should have very little trouble adapting the recipes to your own favored OS and distribution.

Puppet versions

At the time of writing, Puppet 3.2 is the latest stable version available, and consequently I have chosen that as the reference version of Puppet used in the book. The syntax of Puppet commands changes often, so be aware that while older versions of Puppet are still perfectly usable, they may not support all of the features and syntax described in this book.

Installing Puppet

If you already have a working Puppet installation, you can skip this section. If not, or if you want to upgrade or re-install Puppet, we'll go through the installation process step by step.

I'm using an Amazon EC2 cloud instance to demonstrate setting up Puppet, though you may prefer to use a physical server, a Linux workstation, or a virtual machine such as Vagrant, VMWare, or VirtualBox (with Internet access). I'll log in as the ubuntu user and use sudo to run commands that need root privileges (the default setup on Ubuntu).

On EC2 Ubuntu images, the ubuntu user is already set up with the sudo permissions to run any commands as root. If you're using a different Linux distribution or you're not on EC2, you'll need to configure this yourself in the /etc/sudoers file.

Getting ready...

To prepare the machine for Puppet, we need to set its hostname.

1. Set a suitable hostname for your server (ignore any warning from sudo):

```
ubuntu@domU-12-31-39-09-51-23:~$ sudo hostname cookbook
ubuntu@domU-12-31-39-09-51-23:~$ sudo su -c 'echo cookbook
   >/etc/hostname'
sudo: unable to resolve host cookbook
```

2. Log out and log back in to check the hostname is now correctly set:

```
ubuntu@cookbook:~$
```

3. Find out the local IP address of the server:

```
ubuntu@cookbook:~$ ip addr show |grep eth0
    inet 10.96.247.132/23 brd 10.96.247.255 scope global eth0
```

4. Copy the IP address of your server (here it's 10.96.247.132) and add this to the /etc/hosts file so that it looks something like this (use your own hostname and domain):

```
10.96.247.132 cookbook cookbook.example.com
```

How to do it...

Puppet packages for most Linux distributions, including Ubuntu, are available from Puppet Labs. Here's how to install the version for Ubuntu 12.04 Precise:

1. Download the Puppet Labs repo package:

```
ubuntu@cookbook:~$ wget http://apt.puppetlabs.com/puppetlabs-
   release-precise.deb
```

2. Install the repo package:

```
ubuntu@cookbook:~$ sudo dpkg -i puppetlabs-release-precise.deb
Selecting previously unselected package puppetlabs-release.
(Reading database ... 33975 files and directories currently
   installed.)
Unpacking puppetlabs-release (from puppetlabs-release-
   precise.deb)
Setting up puppetlabs-release (1.0-5)
```

3. Update your APT configuration:

```
ubuntu@cookbook:~$ sudo apt-get update
```

 If you're not using Ubuntu 12.04 Precise, you can find out how to add the Puppet Labs repos package to your system here:

http://docs.puppetlabs.com/guides/
puppetlabs_package_repositories.html

4. Install Puppet:

```
ubuntu@cookbook:~$ sudo apt-get -y install puppet
```

 If you're on Mac, you can download and install suitable DMG images from Puppet Labs available at:

```
https://downloads.puppetlabs.com/mac/
```

If you're using Windows, you can download MSI packages from the Puppet Labs website available at:

```
https://downloads.puppetlabs.com/windows/
```

5. Run the following command to check that Puppet is properly installed:

```
ubuntu@cookbook:~$ puppet --version
3.2.2
```

If the version of Puppet you've installed is not exactly the same, it doesn't matter; you'll get whatever is the latest version made available by Puppet Labs. So long as your version is at least 3.0, you should have no trouble running the examples in this book.

If you have an older version of Puppet, you may find that some things don't work or work differently to the way you'd expect. I recommend that you upgrade to Puppet 3.x or later if at all possible.

Now that Puppet is set up, you can use it to make some configuration changes by creating a manifest. We'll see how to do this in the next section.

Creating a manifest

If you already have some Puppet code (known as a Puppet manifest), you can skip this section and go on to the next. If not, we'll see how to create and apply a simple manifest.

How to do it...

Follow these steps:

1. First, let's create a suitable directory structure to keep the manifest code in:

```
ubuntu@cookbook:~$ mkdir puppet
ubuntu@cookbook:~$ cd puppet
ubuntu@cookbook:~/puppet$ mkdir manifests
```

2. Within your puppet directory, create the file manifests/site.pp with the following contents:

```
import 'nodes.pp'
```

3. Create the file `manifests/nodes.pp` with the following contents (use your machine's hostname in place of `cookbook`):

```
node 'cookbook' {
  file { '/tmp/hello':
    content => "Hello, world\n",
  }
}
```

4. Test your manifest with the `puppet apply` command. This will tell Puppet to read the manifest, compare it to the state of the machine, and make any necessary changes to that state:

```
ubuntu@cookbook:~/puppet$ sudo puppet apply manifests/site.pp

Notice: /Stage[main]//Node[cookbook]/File[/tmp/hello]/ensure:
  defined content as '{md5}a7966bf58e23583c9a5a4059383ff850'

Notice: Finished catalog run in 0.06 seconds
```

5. To see if Puppet did what we expected (create the file `/tmp/hello` with the contents **Hello, world**), run the following command:

```
ubuntu@cookbook:~/puppet$ cat /tmp/hello
Hello, world
```

Managing your manifests with Git

It's a great idea to put your Puppet manifests in a version control system such as Git or Subversion (I recommend Git) and give all Puppet-managed machines a checkout from your repository. This gives you several advantages:

▶ You can undo changes and revert to any previous version of your manifest

▶ You can experiment with new features using a `branch`

▶ If several people need to make changes to the manifests, they can make them independently, in their own working copies, and then merge their changes later

▶ You can use the `git log` feature to see what was changed, and when (and by whom)

Getting ready...

In this section we'll import your existing manifest files into Git. If you have created a `puppet` directory in the previous section, use that, otherwise use your existing manifest directory.

I'm going to use the popular GitHub service as my Git server. You don't have to do this, it's easy to run your own Git server but it does simplify things. If you already use Git and have a suitable server, feel free to use that instead.

Note that GitHub currently only offers free repository hosting for public repositories (that is, everyone will be able to see and read your Puppet manifests). This isn't a good idea if your manifest contains secret data such as passwords. It's fine for playing and experimenting with the recipes in this book, but for production use, consider a private GitHub repo instead.

Here's what you need to do to prepare for importing your manifest:

1. First, you'll need Git installed on your machine:

   ```
   ubuntu@cookbook:~/puppet$ sudo apt-get install git
   ```

2. Next, you'll need a GitHub account (free for open-source projects, or you'll need to pay a small fee to create private repositories) and a repository. Follow the instructions at github.com to create and initialize your repository (from now on, just "repo" for short). Make sure you tick the box that says, **Initialize this repository with a README**.

3. Authorize your SSH key for read/write access to the repo (see the GitHub site for instructions on how to do this).

How to do it...

You're now ready to add your existing manifests to the Git repo. We're going to clone the repo, and then move your manifest files into it, as follows:

1. First, move your puppet directory to a different name:

   ```
   mv puppet puppet.import
   ```

2. Clone the repo onto your machine into a directory named puppet (use your own repo URL, as shown on GitHub):

   ```
   ubuntu@cookbook:~$ git clone
     git@github.com:bitfield/cookbook.git puppet
   Cloning into 'puppet'...
   remote: Counting objects: 3, done.
   remote: Total 3 (delta 0), reused 0 (delta 0)
   Receiving objects: 100% (3/3), done.
   ```

3. Move everything from puppet.import to puppet:

   ```
   ubuntu@cookbook:~$ mv puppet.import/* puppet/
   ```

4. Add and commit the new files to the repo, setting your Git identity details if necessary:

   ```
   ubuntu@cookbook:~$ cd puppet
   ubuntu@cookbook:~/puppet$ git status
   ```

```
# On branch master
# Untracked files:
#   (use "git add <file>..." to include in what will be
  committed)
#
#       manifests/
nothing added to commit but untracked files present (use "git
  add" to track)
ubuntu@cookbook:~/puppet$ git add manifests/
ubuntu@cookbook:~/puppet$ git config --global user.name "John
  Arundel"
ubuntu@cookbook:~/puppet$ git config --global user.email
  "john@bitfieldconsulting.com"
ubuntu@cookbook:~/puppet$ git commit -m "Importing"
[master a063a5b] Importing
Committer: John Arundel <john@bitfieldconsulting.com>
2 files changed, 6 insertions(+)
create mode 100644 manifests/nodes.pp
create mode 100644 manifests/site.pp
```

5. Finally, push your changes back to GitHub:

```
ubuntu@cookbook:~/puppet$ git push -u origin master
Counting objects: 6, done.
Compressing objects: 100% (4/4), done.
Writing objects: 100% (5/5), 457 bytes, done.
Total 5 (delta 0), reused 0 (delta 0)
To git@github.com:bitfield/cookbook.git
    6d6aa51..a063a5b  master -> master
```

How it works...

Git tracks changes to files, and stores a complete history of all changes. The history of the repo is made up of commits. A commit represents the state of the repo at a particular point in time, which you create with the `git commit` command and annotate with a message.

You've added your Puppet manifest files to the repo and created your first commit. This updates the history of the repo, but only in your local working copy. To synchronize the changes with GitHub's copy, the `git push` command pushes all changes made since the last sync.

There's more...

Now that you have a central Git repo for your Puppet manifests, you can check out multiple copies of it in different places and work on them, before committing your changes. For example, if you're working in a team, each member can have her own local copy of the repo and synchronize changes with the others via GitHub.

Now that you've taken control of your manifests with Git, you can use it as a simple, scalable way to distribute manifest files to lots of machines. We'll see how to do this in the next section.

Creating a decentralized Puppet architecture

Some systems work best when they're decentralized. The Mafia is a good example, although, of course, there is no Mafia.

A common way to use Puppet is to run a Puppet Master server, which Puppet clients can then connect to and receive their manifests. However, you don't need a Puppet Master to use Puppet. You can run the `puppet apply` command directly on a manifest file to have Puppet apply it:

```
ubuntu@cookbook:~/puppet$ puppet apply manifests/site.pp
Notice: Finished catalog run in 0.08 seconds
```

In other words, if you can arrange to distribute a suitable manifest file to a client machine, you can have Puppet execute it directly without the need for a central Puppet Master. This removes the performance bottleneck of a single master server, and also eliminates a single point of failure. It also avoids having to sign and exchange the SSL certificates when provisioning a new client machine.

There are many ways you could deliver the manifest file to the client, but Git (or any version control system) does most of the work for you. You can edit your manifests in a local working copy, commit them to Git, and push them to a central repo, and from there they can be automatically distributed to the client machines.

Getting ready

If your Puppet manifests aren't already in Git, follow the steps in *Managing your manifests with Git*.

You'll need a second machine to check out a copy of your Puppet repo. If you're using EC2 instances, create another instance, and call it something like `cookbook2`.

How to do it...

Follow these steps:

1. Check out your GitHub repo on the new machine:

   ```
   ubuntu@cookbook2:~$ git clone
     git@github.com:bitfield/cookbook.git puppet
   Cloning into 'puppet'...
   remote: Counting objects: 8, done.
   remote: Compressing objects: 100% (5/5), done.
   remote: Total 8 (delta 0), reused 5 (delta 0)
   Receiving objects: 100% (8/8), done.
   ```

2. Modify your `manifests/nodes.pp` file, as follows:

   ```
   node 'cookbook', 'cookbook2' {
     file { '/tmp/hello':
       content => "Hello, world\n",
     }
   }
   ```

3. Run the following command:

   ```
   ubuntu@cookbook2:~/puppet$ sudo puppet apply manifests/site.pp
   Notice: /Stage[main]//Node[cookbook2]/File[/tmp/hello]/ensure:
   defined content as '{md5}a7966bf58e23583c9a5a4059383ff850'
   Notice: Finished catalog run in 0.05 seconds
   ```

How it works...

We've created a new working copy of the Puppet repo on the new machine:

```
ubuntu@cookbook2:~$ git clone git@github.com:bitfield/cookbook.git puppet
```

However, before we can run Puppet, we have to create a node declaration for the `cookbook2` node:

```
node 'cookbook', 'cookbook2' {
   . . .
}
```

Now, we apply the manifest:

```
ubuntu@cookbook2:~/puppet$ sudo puppet apply manifests/site.pp
```

Puppet finds the node declaration for `cookbook2` and applies the same manifest that we used before on `cookbook`:

```
Notice: /Stage[main]//Node[cookbook2]/File[/tmp/hello]/ensure:
  defined content as '{md5}a7966bf58e23583c9a5a4059383ff850'
```

There's more...

Having scaled your Puppet infrastructure from one machine to the other, you can now extend it to as many as you like! All you need to do is check out the Git repo on a machine, and run `puppet apply`.

This is a great way to add Puppet management to your existing machines without lots of complicated setup, or using an extra machine to serve as a Puppet Master. Many of my clients have switched to using a Git-based infrastructure because it's simpler, easier to scale, and easier to maintain.

A refinement which you might like to consider is having each machine automatically pull changes from GitHub and apply them with Puppet. Then all you need to do is push a change to GitHub, and it will roll out to all your Puppet-managed machines within a certain time. We'll see how to do this in the following sections.

Writing a papply script

We'd like to make it as quick and easy as possible to apply Puppet on a machine, so I usually write a little script that wraps the `puppet apply` command with the parameters it needs. And to deploy the script where it's needed, what better tool than Puppet itself?

How to do it...

Follow these steps:

1. In your Puppet repo, create the directories needed for a `puppet` module:

    ```
    ubuntu@cookbook:~/puppet$ mkdir modules
    ubuntu@cookbook:~/puppet$ mkdir modules/puppet
    ubuntu@cookbook:~/puppet$ mkdir modules/puppet/manifests
    ubuntu@cookbook:~/puppet$ mkdir modules/puppet/files
    ```

2. Create the file `modules/puppet/files/papply.sh` with the following contents (change the path `/home/ubuntu/puppet` to where your Puppet repo is located). The `sudo puppet apply` command should all be on one line:

```
#!/bin/sh
sudo puppet apply /home/ubuntu/puppet/manifests/site.pp
  --modulepath=/home/ubuntu/puppet/modules/ $*
```

3. Create the file `modules/puppet/manifests/init.pp` with the following contents:

```
class puppet {
  file { '/usr/local/bin/papply':
    source => 'puppet:///modules/puppet/papply.sh',
    mode   => '0755',
  }
}
```

4. Modify your `manifests/nodes.pp` file as follows:

```
node 'cookbook' {
  include puppet
}
```

5. Apply your changes:

```
ubuntu@cookbook:~/puppet$ sudo puppet apply manifests/site.pp
  --modulepath=/home/ubuntu/puppet/modules
Notice: /Stage[main]/Puppet/File[/usr/local/bin/papply]
  /ensure: defined content as '{md5}
    171896840d39664c00909eb8cf47a53c'
Notice: Finished catalog run in 0.07 seconds
```

6. Test that the script works:

```
ubuntu@cookbook:~/puppet$ papply
Notice: Finished catalog run in 0.07 seconds
```

Now whenever you need to run Puppet, you can simply run `papply`. In future, when we apply Puppet changes, I'll ask you to run `papply` instead of the full `puppet apply` command.

How it works...

As you've seen, to run Puppet on a machine and apply a specified manifest file, we use the `puppet apply` command:

```
puppet apply manifests/site.pp
```

When you're using modules (such as the puppet module we just created) you also need to tell Puppet where to search for modules, using the `modulepath` argument:

```
puppet apply manifests/nodes.pp --
  modulepath=/home/ubuntu/puppet/modules
```

In order to run Puppet with the root privileges it needs, we have to put `sudo` before everything:

```
sudo puppet apply manifests/nodes.pp --
   modulepath=/home/ubuntu/puppet/modules
```

Finally, any additional arguments passed to `papply` will be passed through to Puppet itself, by adding the $* parameter:

```
sudo puppet apply manifests/nodes.pp --
   modulepath=/home/ubuntu/puppet/modules $*
```

That's a lot of typing, so putting this in a script makes sense. We've added a Puppet `file` resource that will deploy the script to `/usr/local/bin` and make it executable:

```
file { '/usr/local/bin/papply':
  source => 'puppet:///modules/puppet/papply.sh',
  mode   => '0755',
}
```

Finally, we include the `puppet` module in our node declaration for `cookbook`:

```
node 'cookbook' {
  include puppet
}
```

You can do the same for any other nodes managed by Puppet.

Running Puppet from cron

You can do a lot with the setup you already have: work on your Puppet manifests as a team, communicate changes via GitHub, and manually apply them on a machine using the `papply` script.

However, you still have to log into each machine to update the Git repo and re-run Puppet. It would be helpful to have each machine update itself and apply any changes automatically. Then all you need to do is to push a change to the repo, and it will go out to all your machines within a certain time.

The simplest way to do this is with a cron job that pulls updates from the repo at regular intervals and then runs Puppet if anything has changed.

Getting ready...

You'll need the Git repo we set up in *Managing your manifests with Git* and *Creating a decentralized Puppet architecture*, and the `papply` script from *Writing a papply script*.

You'll also need to create an SSH key that each machine can use to pull changes from the Git repo. To create this, follow these steps:

1. Run the following command to generate the keyfile:

    ```
    ubuntu@cookbook:~/puppet$ ssh-keygen -f ubuntu
    Generating public/private rsa key pair.
    Enter passphrase (empty for no passphrase):
    Enter same passphrase again:
    Your identification has been saved in ubuntu.
    Your public key has been saved in ubuntu.pub.
    The key fingerprint is:
    ae:80:48:1c:14:51:d6:b1:73:4f:60:e2:cf:3d:ce:f1 ubuntu@cookbook
    The key's randomart image is:
    ```

    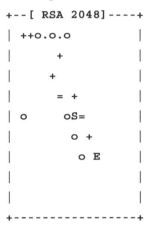

    ```
    +--[ RSA 2048]----+
    |  ++o.o.o        |
    |      +          |
    |      +          |
    |      = +        |
    | o    oS=        |
    |      o +        |
    |       o E       |
    |                 |
    |                 |
    +-----------------+
    ```

2. Print the contents of the `ubuntu.pub` file:

    ```
    ubuntu@cookbook:~/puppet$ cat ubuntu.pub
    ssh-rsa AAAAB3NzaC1yc2EAAAADAQABAAABAQC8EsdLAZHIg1nnMzJuIQ5jEcFL1W
    I5AVhml6Z3Gw4zc4xw6F1Citomc+3DexcaD+y3VrD3WEOGcXweCsxJF0EGyJoc4RbP
    AJaP3D4V/+9FQVZcH90GukasvtIrfJYy2KFfRBROKtrfckMbBlWF7U2U+FwaalMOtg
    LzZeECSDU4eYuheN3UVcyg9Zx87zrLYU5EK1JH2WVoZd3UmdH73/rwPJWtSEQ3xs9A
    2wMr0lJsCF4CcFCVwrAIoEf5WzIoHbhWyZaVyPR4gHUHd3wNIzC0rmoRiYwE5uYvVB
    ObLN10uZhn7zGPWHEc5tYU7DMbz61iTe4NLtauwJkZxmXUiPJh ubuntu@cookbook
    ```

Copy this and add it to your GitHub repo as a deploy key (refer to the GitHub site for instructions on how to do this). This will authorize the key to clone the Puppet repo from GitHub.

How to do it...

Follow these steps:

1. Move the public key file into your `puppet` module:

   ```
   ubuntu@cookbook:~/puppet$ mv ubuntu.pub
       modules/puppet/files/ubuntu.pub
   ```

2. Keep the private key file somewhere separate from your Puppet repo (you'll distribute this via some other channel to machines which need to check out the repo).

3. Create the file `modules/puppet/files/pull-updates.sh` with the following contents:

   ```
   #!/bin/sh
   cd /home/ubuntu/puppet
   git pull && /usr/local/bin/papply
   ```

4. Modify the file `modules/puppet/manifests/init.pp` to look like this:

   ```
   class puppet {
     file { '/usr/local/bin/papply':
       source => 'puppet:///modules/puppet/papply.sh',
       mode   => '0755',
     }

     file { '/usr/local/bin/pull-updates':
       source => 'puppet:///modules/puppet/pull-updates.sh',
       mode   => '0755',
     }

     file { '/home/ubuntu/.ssh/id_rsa':
       source => 'puppet:///modules/puppet/ubuntu.priv',
       owner  => 'ubuntu',
       mode   => '0600',
     }

     cron { 'run-puppet':
       ensure  => 'present',
       user    => 'ubuntu',
       command => '/usr/local/bin/pull-updates',
       minute  => '*/10',
       hour    => '*',
     }
   }
   ```

5. Run Puppet:

```
ubuntu@cookbook:~/puppet$ papply
Notice: /Stage[main]/Puppet/Cron[run-puppet]/ensure: created
Notice: /Stage[main]/Puppet/File[/usr/local/bin/pull-
   updates]/ensure: defined content as
      '{md5}20cfc6cf2a40155d4055d475a109137d'
Notice:
   /Stage[main]/Puppet/File[/home/ubuntu/.ssh/id_rsa]/ensure:
      defined content as '{md5}db19f750104d3bf4e2603136553c6f3e'
Notice: Finished catalog run in 0.27 seconds
```

6. Test that the new SSH key is authorized to GitHub correctly:

```
ubuntu@cookbook:~/puppet$ ssh git@github.com
PTY allocation request failed on channel 0
Hi bitfield/cookbook! You've successfully authenticated, but
   GitHub does not provide shell access.
Connection to github.com closed.
```

7. Check that the `pull-updates` script works properly:

```
ubuntu@cookbook:~/puppet$ pull-updates
Already up-to-date.
Notice: Finished catalog run in 0.16 seconds
```

How it works...

Up to now, you've been using your own SSH credentials to access GitHub from the managed machine (using SSH agent forwarding), but that won't work if we want the machine to be able to pull updates unattended, while you're not logged in. So we've created a new SSH keypair and added the public part of it as a deploy key on GitHub, which gives repo access to anyone who has the private half of the key.

We've added this private key as the `ubuntu` user's default SSH key:

```
file { '/home/ubuntu/.ssh/id_rsa':
  source => 'puppet:///modules/puppet/ubuntu.priv',
  owner  => 'ubuntu',
  mode   => '0600',
}
```

This enables the `ubuntu` user to run `git pull` in the `puppet` directory. We've also added the `pull-updates` script, which does this and runs Puppet if any changes were pulled:

```sh
#!/bin/sh
cd /home/ubuntu/puppet
git pull && papply
```

We deploy this script to the box with Puppet:

```
file { '/usr/local/bin/pull-updates':
  source => 'puppet:///modules/puppet/pull-updates.sh',
  mode   => '0755',
}
```

Finally, we've created a cron job that runs `pull-updates` at regular intervals (every 10 minutes, but feel free to change this if you need to):

```
cron { 'run-puppet':
  ensure  => 'present',
  command => '/usr/local/bin/pull-updates',
  minute  => '*/10',
  hour    => '*',
}
```

There's more...

Congratulations, you now have a fully-automated Puppet infrastructure! Once you have checked out the repo on a new machine and applied the manifest, the machine will be set up to pull any new changes and apply them automatically.

So, for example, if you wanted to add a new user account to all your machines, all you have to do is add the account in your working copy of the manifest, and commit and push the changes to GitHub. Within 10 minutes it will automatically be applied to every machine that's running Puppet.

That's very handy, but sometimes we'd like to be able to apply the changes to a specific machine right away, without waiting for them to be picked up by the cron job. We can do this using the Rake tool, and we'll see how to do that in the next section.

Deploying changes with Rake

Rake is a useful tool from the Ruby world which you can use to help automate your Puppet workflow. Although there are lots of other ways to run commands on remote servers, this happens to be the one I use, and it's easily extensible to whatever you need it to do.

The first helpful thing we can have Rake perform for us is log into the remote machine and run the `pull-updates` script to apply any new Puppet manifest changes. This is fairly simple to do, as you'll see in the following sections.

Getting ready

You may already have Rake installed (try running `rake`), but if not, here's how to install it:

1. Run the following command:

   sudo apt-get install rake

How to do it...

Perform the following steps:

1. In your Puppet repo, create the file, `Rakefile` with the following contents. Replace `ssh...` with the correct `ssh` command line for you to log into your server:

   ```
   SSH = 'ssh -A -i ~/git/bitfield/bitfield.pem -l ubuntu'

   desc "Run Puppet on ENV['CLIENT']"
   task :apply do
     client = ENV['CLIENT']
     sh "git push"
     sh "#{SSH} #{client} pull-updates"
   end
   ```

2. Add, commit, and push the change to the Git repo:

   ```
   ubuntu@cookbook:~/puppet$ git add Rakefile
   ubuntu@cookbook:~/puppet$ git commit -m "adding Rakefile"
   [master 63bb0c1] adding Rakefile
   1 file changed, 8 insertions(+)
   create mode 100644 Rakefile
   ubuntu@cookbook:~/puppet$ git push
   Counting objects: 31, done.
   Compressing objects: 100% (22/22), done.
   Writing objects: 100% (28/28), 4.67 KiB, done.
   Total 28 (delta 1), reused 0 (delta 0)
   To git@github.com:bitfield/cookbook.git
      a063a5b..63bb0c1  master -> master
   ```

3. On your own computer, check out a working copy of the Puppet repo, if you haven't already got one (replace the Git URL with the URL to your own repo):

```
[john@Susie:~/git]$ git clone
  git@github.com:bitfield/cookbook.git
Cloning into 'cookbook'...
remote: Counting objects: 36, done.
remote: Compressing objects: 100% (26/26), done.
remote: Total 36 (delta 1), reused 33 (delta 1)
Receiving objects: 100% (36/36), 5.28 KiB, done.
Resolving deltas: 100% (1/1), done.
```

4. Run the following command, replacing cookbook with the address of your server:

```
[john@Susie:~/git]$ cd cookbook
[john@Susie:~/git/cookbook(master)]$ rake CLIENT=
  cookbook apply
(in /Users/john/git/cookbook)
git push
Everything up-to-date
ssh -A -i ~/git/bitfield/bitfield.pem -l ubuntu cookbook
  pull-updates
Already up-to-date.
Notice: Finished catalog run in 0.18 seconds
Connection to cookbook closed.
```

How it works...

What you'd do manually to update your server is log into it using SSH, and then run pull-updates. The Rakefile simply automates this for you. First, we set up the correct SSH command line:

```
SSH = 'ssh -A -i ~/git/bitfield/bitfield.pem -l ubuntu'
```

The arguments to ssh are as follows:

► -A: Forward your SSH key to the remote server, so that you can use it for further authentication

► -i KEYFILE: Set the SSH private key to use (in this case, it's the Amazon AWS keyfile that I'm using. You may not need this argument if you're already set up for SSH access to the server with your default key.)

► -l ubuntu: Log in as user ubuntu (the standard arrangement on EC2 servers; you may not need this argument if you log into servers using the same username as on your local machine.)

We then define a Rake task named `apply`:

```
desc "Run Puppet on ENV['CLIENT']"
task :apply do

end
```

The `desc` is just a helpful description, which you'll see if you run the command, `rake -T`, which lists available tasks:

```
$ rake -T
(in /Users/john/git/cookbook)
rake apply        # Run puppet on ENV['CLIENT']
```

The code between `task` and `end` will be run when you run `rake apply`. Here's what it does:

```
client = ENV['CLIENT']
```

This captures the value of the `CLIENT` environment variable, which tells the script the address of the remote servers to connect to.

The next line is as follows:

```
sh "git push"
```

`sh` simply runs a command in your local shell, in this case to make sure any changes to the Puppet repo have been pushed to GitHub. If they weren't, they wouldn't be picked up on the remote machine.

```
sh "#{SSH} #{client} pull-updates"
```

This is the line which actually connects to the client, using the `ssh` command line we defined at the start of the script, and the client address. Having logged in, it will then run the `pull-updates` command as the remote user.

Since we already set up the `pull-updates` script to do everything necessary to get the latest changes from GitHub and apply Puppet, that's all we need to do.

There's more...

You can now make and apply Puppet changes to your remote servers without ever explicitly logging into them. Once you've installed Puppet on a machine, checked out a copy of the manifest repo, and run Puppet for the first time, you can then do all the administration for that machine remotely.

If you're as lazy as I am, you're already asking, "Couldn't we use a Rake task to do the initial Puppet install and checkout, as well as just applying changes?"

We certainly can, and we'll see how to do that in the next section.

Bootstrapping Puppet with Rake

To make a newly provisioned machine part of our Puppet infrastructure, we just need to run a few commands on it, so let's make this process even easier by adding a new bootstrap task to the `Rakefile`.

Getting ready...

To get ready for the recipe, do the following:

1. Add the following line to the top of your `Rakefile`:

```
REPO = 'git@github.com:bitfield/cookbook.git'
```

2. Add the following task anywhere in the `Rakefile`:

```
desc "Bootstrap Puppet on ENV['CLIENT'] with
   hostname ENV['HOSTNAME']"
task :bootstrap do
  client = ENV['CLIENT']
  hostname = ENV['HOSTNAME'] || client
  commands = <<BOOTSTRAP
sudo hostname #{hostname} && \
sudo su - c 'echo #{hostname} >/etc/hostname' && \
wget http://apt.puppetlabs.com/puppetlabs-release-precise.deb && \
sudo dpkg -i puppetlabs-release-precise.deb && \
sudo apt-get update && sudo apt-get -y install git
  puppet && \
git clone #{REPO} puppet && \
sudo puppet apply --modulepath=/home/ubuntu/puppet
  /modules /home/ubuntu/puppet/manifests/site.pp
BOOTSTRAP
  sh "#{SSH} #{client} '#{commands}'"
end
```

How to do it...

You'll need a freshly provisioned server (one that you can log in to, but that doesn't have Puppet installed or any other config changes made on it). If you're using EC2, create a new EC2 instance. Get the public instance address from the AWS control panel; it'll be something like:

```
ec2-107-22-22-159.compute-1.amazonaws.com
```

Here are the steps to bootstrap the new server using Rake:

1. Add a node declaration to your `nodes.pp` file for the hostname you'll be using on the new server. For example, if you wanted to call it `cookbook-test`, you could use

```
node 'cookbook-test' {
  include puppet
}
```

2. Run the following command in the Puppet repo on your own machine (substitute the address of the new server as the value of `CLIENT`, and the hostname you want to use as the value of `HOSTNAME`). The command should all be on one line:

```
$ rake CLIENT=ec2-107-22-22-159.compute-1.amazonaws.com
HOSTNAME=cookbook-test bootstrap
```

3. You'll see output something like the following:

```
(in /Users/john/git/cookbook)
ssh -A -i ~/git/bitfield/bitfield.pem -l ubuntu ec2-107-22-22-159.
compute-1.amazonaws.com 'sudo hostname cookbook-test && sudo su -c
'echo cookbook-test >/etc/hostname' && wget http://apt.puppetlabs.
com/puppetlabs-release-precise.deb && sudo dpkg -i puppetlabs-
release-precise.deb && sudo apt-get update && sudo apt-get -y
install git puppet && git clone git@github.com:bitfield/cookbook.
git puppet && sudo puppet apply --modulepath=/home/ubuntu/puppet/
modules /home/ubuntu/puppet/manifests/site.pp'
The authenticity of host 'ec2-107-22-22-159.compute-1.amazonaws.
com (107.22.22.159)' can't be established.
RSA key fingerprint is 23:c5:06:ad:58:f3:8d:e5:75:bd:94:6e:1e:a0:a
3:a4.
Are you sure you want to continue connecting (yes/no)? yes
Warning: Permanently added 'ec2-107-22-22-159.compute-1.amazonaws.
com,107.22.22.159' (RSA) to the list of known hosts.
sudo: unable to resolve host cookbook-test
--2013-03-15 15:53:44--  http://apt.puppetlabs.com/puppetlabs-
release-precise.deb
Resolving apt.puppetlabs.com (apt.puppetlabs.com)...
96.126.116.126, 2600:3c00::f03c:91ff:fe93:711a
Connecting to apt.puppetlabs.com (apt.puppetlabs.
com)|96.126.116.126|:80... connected.
HTTP request sent, awaiting response... 200 OK
Length: 3392 (3.3K) [application/x-debian-package]
Saving to: `puppetlabs-release-precise.deb'
    OK                                                        100%
302M=0s
```

```
2013-03-15 15:53:44 (302 MB/s) - `puppetlabs-release-precise.deb'
saved [3392/3392]
Selecting previously unselected package puppetlabs-release.
(Reading database ... 25370 files and directories currently
installed.)
Unpacking puppetlabs-release (from puppetlabs-release-precise.deb)
...
Setting up puppetlabs-release (1.0-5) ...
Processing triggers for initramfs-tools ...
update-initramfs: Generating /boot/initrd.img-3.2.0-29-virtual
Ign http://us-east-1.ec2.archive.ubuntu.com precise InRelease
[ ... apt output redacted ... ]
Setting up hiera (1.1.2-1puppetlabs1) ...
Setting up puppet-common (3.2.2-1puppetlabs1) ...
Setting up puppet (3.2.2-1puppetlabs1) ...
* Starting puppet agent
puppet not configured to start, please edit /etc/default/puppet to
enable
     ...done.
Processing triggers for libc-bin ...
ldconfig deferred processing now taking place
Cloning into 'puppet'...
Warning: Permanently added 'github.com,207.97.227.239' (RSA) to
the list of known hosts.
Notice: /Stage[main]/Puppet/Cron[run-puppet]/ensure: created
Notice: /Stage[main]/Puppet/File[/usr/local/bin/pull-updates]/
ensure: defined content as '{md5}20cfc6cf2a40155d4055d475a109137d'
Notice: /Stage[main]/Puppet/File[/usr/local/bin/papply]/ensure:
defined content as '{md5}171896840d39664c00909eb8cf47a53c'
Notice: /Stage[main]/Puppet/File[/home/ubuntu/.ssh/id_rsa]/ensure:
defined content as '{md5}db19f750104d3bf4e2603136553c6f3e'
Notice: Finished catalog run in 0.11 seconds
```

How it works...

Here's a line by line breakdown of what the Rake task does. In order to make the machine ready to run Puppet, we need to set its hostname to the name you've chosen:

```
sudo hostname #{hostname}
sudo echo #{hostname} >/etc/hostname
```

Next, we download and install the Puppet Labs repo package, and install Puppet and Git:

```
wget http://apt.puppetlabs.com/puppetlabs-release-precise.deb
sudo dpkg -i puppetlabs-release-precise.deb
sudo apt-get update && sudo apt-get -y install git puppet
```

We need to disable the SSH `StrictHostKeyChecking` option to avoid being prompted when the script clones the Git repo:

```
echo -e \"Host github.com\n\tStrictHostKeyChecking no\n\"
  >> ~/.ssh/config
```

We check out the repo:

```
git clone #{REPO} puppet
```

And finally, run Puppet:

```
sudo puppet apply --modulepath=/home/ubuntu/puppet/modules
  /home/ubuntu/puppet/manifests/site.pp
```

The new machine will now pull and apply Puppet changes automatically, without you ever having to log into it interactively. You can use this Rake task to bring lots of new servers under Puppet control quickly.

Automatic syntax checking with Git hooks

It would be nice if we knew there was a syntax error in the manifest before we even committed it. You can have Puppet check the manifest using the `puppet parser validate` command:

```
ubuntu@cookbook:~/puppet$ puppet parser validate manifests/nodes.pp
Error: Could not parse for environment production: Syntax error at end
of file; expected '}' at /home/ubuntu/puppet/manifests/nodes.pp:3
Error: Try 'puppet help parser validate' for usage
```

This is especially useful because a mistake anywhere in the manifest will stop Puppet from running on any node, even on nodes that don't use that particular part of the manifest. So checking in a bad manifest can cause Puppet to stop applying updates to production for some time, until the problem is discovered, and this could potentially have serious consequences. The best way to avoid this is to automate the syntax check, by using a pre-commit hook in your version control repo.

How to do it...

Follow these steps:

1. In your Puppet repo, create a new `hooks` directory:

    ubuntu@cookbook:~/puppet$ mkdir hooks

2. Create the file `hooks/check_syntax.sh` with the following contents (based on a script by Puppet Labs):

```sh
#!/bin/sh

syntax_errors=0
error_msg=$(mktemp /tmp/error_msg.XXXXXX)

if git rev-parse --quiet --verify HEAD > /dev/null
then
    against=HEAD
else
    # Initial commit: diff against an empty tree object
    against=4b825dc642cb6eb9a060e54bf8d69288fbee4904
fi

# Get list of new/modified manifest and template files
  to check (in git index)
for indexfile in `git diff-index --diff-filter=AM --
  name-only --cached $against | egrep '\.(pp|erb)'`
do
    # Don't check empty files
    if [ `git cat-file -s :0:$indexfile` -gt 0 ]
    then
        case $indexfile in
            *.pp )
                # Check puppet manifest syntax
                git cat-file blob :0:$indexfile |
                  puppet parser validate > $error_msg ;;
            *.erb )
                # Check ERB template syntax
                git cat-file blob :0:$indexfile |
                  erb -x -T - | ruby -c 2> $error_msg >
                    /dev/null ;;
        esac
        if [ "$?" -ne 0 ]
```

```
        then
                echo -n "$indexfile: "
                cat $error_msg
                syntax_errors=`expr $syntax_errors + 1`
        fi
    fi
done

rm -f $error_msg

if [ "$syntax_errors" -ne 0 ]
then
    echo "Error: $syntax_errors syntax errors found,
      aborting commit."
    exit 1
fi
```

3. Set execute permission for the `hook` script with the following command:

    ubuntu@cookbook:~/puppet$ chmod a+x .hooks/check_syntax.sh

4. Add the following task to your Rakefile:

```
desc "Add syntax check hook to your git repo"
task :add_check do
  here = File.dirname(__FILE__)
  sh "ln -s #{here}/hooks/check_syntax.sh
    #{here}/.git/hooks/pre-commit"
  puts "Puppet syntax check hook added"
end
```

5. Run the following command:

    ubuntu@cookbook:~/puppet$ rake add_check

    ln -s /home/ubuntu/puppet/hooks/check_syntax.sh

    /home/ubuntu/puppet/.git/hooks/pre-commit

    Puppet syntax check hook added

How it works...

The `check_syntax.sh` script will prevent you from committing any files with syntax errors:

```
ubuntu@cookbook:~/puppet$ git commit -m "test commit"
Error: Could not parse for environment production: Syntax error at
  '}' at line 3
Error: Try 'puppet help parser validate' for usage
manifests/nodes.pp: Error: 1 syntax errors found, aborting commit.
```

If you add the `hooks` directory to your Git repo, anyone who has a checkout can run the `rake add_check` task and get this syntax checking behavior.

2
Puppet Language and Style

Computer language design is just like a stroll in the park. Jurassic Park, that is.

—Larry Wall

In this chapter we will cover:

- ▶ Using community Puppet style
- ▶ Checking your manifests with puppet-lint
- ▶ Using modules
- ▶ Using standard naming conventions
- ▶ Using inline templates
- ▶ Iterating over multiple items
- ▶ Writing powerful conditional statements
- ▶ Using regular expressions in if statements
- ▶ Using selectors and case statements
- ▶ Using the in operator
- ▶ Using regular expression substitutions

Introduction

In this chapter you'll learn to write elegant Puppet manifests. By elegant in this context I mean readable, efficient, and consistent code that conforms to community usage.

We'll look at how to organize and structure your code into modules following community conventions, so that other people will find it easy to read and maintain your code. I'll also show you some powerful features of the Puppet language which will let you write concise, yet expressive, manifests.

Using community Puppet style

If other people need to read or maintain your manifests, or if you want to share code with the community, it's a good idea to follow the existing style conventions as closely as possible. These govern such aspects of your code as layout, spacing, quoting, alignment, and variable references, and the official Puppet Labs recommendations on style are available at

```
http://docs.puppetlabs.com/guides/style_guide
```

How to do it...

In this section I'll show you a few of the more important examples and how to make sure that your code is style-compliant.

Indentation

Indent your manifests using two spaces (not tabs), as follows:

```
node 'monitoring' inherits 'server' {
  include icinga::server
  include repo::apt
}
```

Quoting

Always quote your resource names, for example:

```
package { 'exim4':
```

Not

```
package { exim4:
```

Use single quotes for all strings, except when:

▸ The string contains variable references (for example, `${name}`)

▸ The string contains character escape sequences (for example, `\n`)

In these cases you should use double quotes. Puppet doesn't process variable references or escape sequences unless they're inside double quotes.

Always quote parameter values that are not reserved words in Puppet. For example, the following values are not reserved words:

```
name => 'Nucky Thompson',
mode => '0700',
owner => 'deploy',
```

But these values are reserved words and therefore not quoted:

```
ensure => installed,
enable => true,
ensure => running,
```

Variables

Always include curly braces ({ }) around variable names when referring to them in strings, for example:

```
source => "puppet:///modules/webserver/${brand}.conf",
```

Otherwise Puppet's parser has to guess which characters should be a part of the variable name and which belong to the surrounding string. Curly braces make it explicit.

Parameters

Always end lines that declare parameters with a comma, even if it is the last parameter:

```
service { 'memcached':
  ensure => running,
  enable => true,
}
```

This is allowed by Puppet, and makes it easier if you want to add parameters later, or re-order the existing parameters.

When declaring a resource with a single parameter, make the declaration all on one line and with no trailing comma:

```
package { 'puppet': ensure => installed }
```

Where there is more than one parameter, give each parameter its own line:

```
package { 'rake':
  ensure   => installed,
  provider => gem,
  require  => Package['rubygems'],
}
```

To make the code easier to read, line up the parameter arrows in line with the longest parameter, as follows:

```
file { "/var/www/${app}/shared/config/rvmrc":
  owner   => 'deploy',
  group   => 'deploy',
  content => template('rails/rvmrc.erb'),
  require => File["/var/www/${app}/shared/config"],
}
```

The arrows should be aligned per resource, but not across the whole file, otherwise it can make it difficult for you to cut and paste code from one file to another.

Symlinks

When declaring `file` resources which are symlinks, use `ensure => link` and set the `target` attribute, as follows:

```
file { '/etc/php5/cli/php.ini':
  ensure => link,
  target => '/etc/php.ini',
}
```

There's more...

When several people are working on a codebase, it's easy for style inconsistencies to creep in. Fortunately, there's a tool available which can automatically check your code for compliance with the style guide: `puppet-lint`. We'll see how to use this in the next section.

Checking your manifests with puppet-lint

The Puppet Labs official style guide outlines a number of style conventions for Puppet code, some of which we've touched on in the preceding section. For example, according to the style guide, manifests:

- ▶ Must use two-space soft tabs
- ▶ Must not use literal tab characters
- ▶ Must not contain trailing white space
- ▶ Should not exceed an 80 character line width
- ▶ Should align parameter arrows (=>) within blocks

Following the style guide will make sure that your Puppet code is easy to read and maintain and, if you're planning to release your code to the public, style compliance is essential. The `puppet-lint` tool will automatically check your code against the style guide. Here's how to use it:

Getting ready

Here's what you need to do to install `puppet-lint`:

1. Run the following command (we'll install `puppet-lint` as a gem, because that version is much more up-to-date than the APT package available in the Ubuntu Precise repo):

```
ubuntu@cookbook:~/puppet$ sudo gem install puppet-lint
   --no-ri --no-rdoc
Successfully installed puppet-lint-0.3.2
1 gem installed
```

How to do it...

Follow these steps to use `puppet-lint`:

1. Choose a Puppet manifest file that you want to check with `puppet-lint`, and run the following command:

```
ubuntu@cookbook:~/puppet$ puppet-lint modules/admin/manifests/ntp.pp
WARNING: indentation of => is not properly aligned on line 9
ERROR: trailing whitespace found on line 13
WARNING: double quoted string containing no variables
   on line 3
```

2. As you can see, `puppet-lint` found a number of problems with the manifest. Correct them, save the file, and rerun `puppet-lint` to check that all is well. If so, you'll see no output:

```
ubuntu@cookbook:~/puppet$ puppet-lint
   modules/admin/manifests/ntp.pp
ubuntu@cookbook:~/puppet$
```

There's more...

You can find out more about `puppet-lint` at the website

```
http://puppet-lint.com/
```

The website lists each of the style checks in detail, and explains what the error messages mean and what to do about them.

Should you follow the Puppet style guide and, by extension, keep your code lint-clean? It's up to you, but here are a couple of things to think about:

▶ It makes sense to use some style conventions, especially when you're working collaboratively on code. Unless you and your colleagues can agree on standards for whitespace, tabs, quoting, alignment, and so on, your code will be messy and difficult to read or maintain.

▶ If you're choosing a set of style conventions to follow, the logical choice would be that issued by Puppet Labs and adopted by the community for use in public modules.

Having said that, it's possible to tell `puppet-lint` to ignore certain checks if you've chosen not to adopt them in your codebase. For example, if you don't want `puppet-lint` to warn you about code lines exceeding 80 characters, you can run `puppet-lint` with the following option:

```
puppet-lint --no-80chars-check
```

Run `puppet-lint --help` to see the complete list of check configuration commands.

See also

▶ The *Automatic syntax checking with Git hooks* recipe in *Chapter 1, Puppet Infrastructure*

▶ The *Testing your manifests with rspec-puppet* recipe in *Chapter 8, External Tools and the Puppet Ecosystem*

Using modules

One of the most important things you can do to make your Puppet manifests clearer and more maintainable is to organize them into modules.

A module is simply a way of grouping related things: for example, a `webserver` module might include everything necessary for a machine to be a web server: Apache configuration files, virtual host templates, and the Puppet code necessary to deploy these.

Separating things into modules makes it easier to re-use and share code; it's also the most logical way to organize your manifests. In this example we'll create a module to manage `memcached`, a memory caching system commonly used with web applications.

How to do it...

Here are the steps to create an example module.

1. Create the following new directories in your Puppet repo:

```
ubuntu@cookbook:~/puppet$ mkdir modules/memcached
```

```
ubuntu@cookbook:~/puppet$ mkdir modules/memcached/manifests
ubuntu@cookbook:~/puppet$ mkdir modules/memcached/files
```

2. Create the file `modules/memcached/manifests/init.pp` with the following contents:

```
# Manage memcached
class memcached {
  package { 'memcached':
    ensure => installed,
  }

  file { '/etc/memcached.conf':
    source  => 'puppet:///modules/memcached/memcached.conf',
    owner   => 'root',
    group   => 'root',
    mode    => '0644',
    require => Package['memcached'],
  }

  service { 'memcached':
    ensure  => running,
    enable  => true,
    require => [Package['memcached'],
               File['/etc/memcached.conf']],
  }
}
```

3. Create the file `modules/memcached/files/memcached.conf` with the following contents:

```
-m 64
-p 11211
-u nobody
-l 127.0.0.1
```

4. Add the following to your `nodes.pp` file:

```
node 'cookbook' {
  include memcached
}
```

5. Run Puppet to test the new configuration:

```
ubuntu@cookbook:~/puppet$ papply
Notice: /Stage[main]/Memcached/Package[memcached]/ensure:
  created
Notice: /Stage[main]/Memcached/File[/etc/memcached.conf]/content:
  content changed '{md5}58c9e04b29e08c2e9b3094794d3ebd0e'
    to '{md5}9429eff3e3354c0be232a020bcf78f75'
Notice: Finished catalog run in 4.54 seconds
```

6. Check whether the new service is running:

```
ubuntu@cookbook:~/puppet$ service memcached status
* memcached is running
```

How it works...

Modules have a specific directory structure. Not all of these directories need to be present, but if they are, this is how they should be organized:

```
modules/
    MODULE_NAME/
        files/
        templates/
        manifests/
```

All manifest files (those containing Puppet code) live in the manifests directory. In our example, the memcached class is defined in the file manifests/init.pp, which will be imported automatically.

Inside the memcached class, we refer to the memcached.conf file:

```
file { '/etc/memcached.conf':
  source => 'puppet:///modules/memcached/memcached.conf',
}
```

As we saw in the section on Puppet's file server and custom mount points, the preceding source parameter tells Puppet to look for the file in

```
MODULEPATH/
    memcached/
        files/
            memcached.conf
```

There's more...

Learn to love modules, because they'll make your Puppet life a lot easier. They're not complicated. However, practice and experience will help you judge when things should be grouped into modules, and how best to arrange your module structure. Here are a few tips which may help you on the way.

Templates

If you need to use a template as a part of the module, place it in the module's templates directory and refer to it as follows:

```
file { '/etc/memcached.conf':
  content => template('memcached/memcached.conf.erb'),
}
```

Puppet will look for the file in:

```
MODULEPATH/
    memcached/
        templates/
            memcached.conf.erb
```

Facts, functions, types, and providers

Modules can also contain custom facts, custom functions, custom types, and providers.
For more information about these, refer to *Chapter 8, External Tools and the Puppet Ecosystem*.

Autogenerating module layout

You can also use the `puppet module generate` command to generate the directory
layout for new modules, rather than doing it by hand. See the *Using public modules* section
in *Chapter 8, External Tools and the Puppet Ecosystem*, for more details.

Third party modules

You can download modules provided by other people and use them in your own manifests just
like the modules you create. For more on this, see the section on using public modules.

Module organization

For more details on how to organize your modules, see the Puppet Labs website:

```
http://docs.puppetlabs.com/puppet/3/reference/modules_fundamentals.
html
```

See also

- The *Creating custom facts* recipe in *Chapter 8, External Tools and the Puppet Ecosystem*
- The *Using public modules* recipe in *Chapter 8, External Tools and the Puppet Ecosystem*
- The *Creating your own resource types* recipe in *Chapter 8, External Tools and the Puppet Ecosystem*
- The *Creating your own providers* recipe in *Chapter 8, External Tools and the Puppet Ecosystem*

Using standard naming conventions

Choosing appropriate and informative names for your modules and classes will be a big help when it comes to maintaining your code. This is even truer if other people need to read and work on your manifests.

How to do it...

Here are some tips on how to name things in your manifests:

1. Name modules after the software or service they manage, for example, `apache` or `haproxy`.

2. Name classes within modules after the function or service they provide to the module, for example, `apache::vhosts` or `rails::dependencies`.

3. If a class within a module disables the service provided by that module, name it `disabled`. For example, a class which disables Apache should be named `apache::disabled`.

4. If a node provides multiple services, have the node definition include one module or class named for each service, for example:

```
node 'server014' inherits 'server' {
  include puppet::server
  include mail::server
  include repo::gem
  include repo::apt
  include zabbix
}
```

5. The module that manages users should be named `user`.

6. Within the `user` module, declare your virtual users within the class `user::virtual` (for more about virtual users and other resources, see the *Using virtual resources* section in *Chapter 5, Users and virtual resources*).

7. Within the `user` module, subclasses for particular groups of users should be named after the group, for example, `user::sysadmins` or `user::contractors`.

8. Where you need to override a class for some specific node or service, inherit that class and prefix the name of the subclass with the node, for example, if your node `cartman` needs a special SSH configuration, and you want to override the `ssh` class, perform the function as follows:

```
class cartman_ssh inherits ssh {
  [ override config here ]
}
```

9. When using Puppet to deploy the config files for different services, name the file after the service, but with a suffix indicating what kind of file it is, for example:

   ❑ Apache init script: `apache.init`

   ❑ Logrotate config snippet for Rails: `rails.logrotate`

   ❑ Nginx vhost file for `mywizzoapp`: `mywizzoapp.vhost.nginx`

   ❑ MySQL config for standalone server: `standalone.mysql`

10. If you need to deploy a different version of a file depending on the operating system release, for example, you can use a naming convention like this one:

    ```
    memcached.lucid.conf
    memcached.precise.conf
    ```

11. You can have Puppet automatically select the appropriate version with:

    ```
    source = > "puppet:///modules/memcached
       /memcached.${::lsbdistrelease}.conf",
    ```

12. If you need to manage, for example, different Ruby versions, name the class after the version it is responsible for, for example, `ruby192` or `ruby186`.

There's more...

The Puppet community maintains a set of best practice guidelines for your Puppet infrastructure which includes some hints on naming conventions:

`http://docs.puppetlabs.com/guides/best_practices.html`

Some people prefer to include multiple classes on a node by using a comma-separated list, rather than separate `include` statements, for example:

```
node 'server014' inherits 'server' {
   include mail::server, repo::gem, repo::apt, zabbix
}
```

This is a matter of style, but I prefer to use separate `include` statements, one to a line, because it makes it easier to copy and move around class inclusions between nodes, without having to tidy up the commas and indentation every time.

I mentioned inheritance in a couple of the preceding examples; if you're not sure what this is, don't worry, I'll explain this in detail in the next chapter.

Using inline templates

Templates are a powerful way of using embedded Ruby to help build config files dynamically and iterate over arrays, for example. But you can embed Ruby in your manifests directly without having to use a separate file by calling the `inline_template` function.

How to do it...

Here's an example of using `inline_template`:

Pass your Ruby code to `inline_template` within the Puppet manifest, as follows:

```
cron { 'chkrootkit':
  command => '/usr/sbin/chkrootkit >
    /var/log/chkrootkit.log 2>&1',
  hour    => inline_template('<%= @hostname.sum % 24 %>'),
  minute  => '00',
}
```

How it works...

Anything inside the string passed to `inline_template` is executed as if it were an ERB template. That is, anything inside `<%=` and `%>` delimiters will be executed as Ruby code, and the rest will be treated as a string.

In this example, we use `inline_template` to compute a different hour for this cron resource (a scheduled job) for each machine, so that the same job does not run at the same time on all machines. For more on this technique, see the *Efficiently distributing cron jobs* section in *Chapter 5*, *Users and Virtual Resources*.

There's more...

In ERB code, whether inside a template file or an `inline_template` string, you can access your Puppet variables directly by name using an @ prefix, if they are in the current scope:

```
<%= @name %>
```

If they are in another scope you can reference them using `scope.lookupvar`, as follows:

```
<%= "The variable from otherclass is " +
  scope.lookupvar('otherclass::variable') %>
```

You should use inline templates sparingly. If you really need to do some complicated logic in your manifest, consider using a custom function instead (see the *Creating custom functions* section in *Chapter 8*, *External tools and the Puppet ecosystem*).

See also

- ▶ The *Using ERB templates* in recipe *Chapter 4, Working with Files and Packages*
- ▶ The *Using array iteration in templates* recipe in *Chapter 4, Working with Files and Packages*

Iterating over multiple items

Arrays are a powerful feature in Puppet; wherever you want to perform the same operation on a list of things, an array may be able to help. You can create an array just by putting its contents in square brackets:

```
$lunch = [ 'franks', 'beans', 'mustard' ]
```

How to do it...

Here's a common example of how arrays are used:

1. Add the following code to your manifest:

```
$packages = [ 'ruby1.8-dev',
              'ruby1.8',
              'ri1.8',
              'rdoc1.8',
              'irb1.8',
              'libreadline-ruby1.8',
              'libruby1.8',
              'libopenssl-ruby' ]

package { $packages: ensure => installed }
```

2. Run Puppet and note that each package should now be installed.

How it works...

Where Puppet encounters an array as the name of a resource, it creates a resource for each element in the array. In the example, a new `package` resource is created for each of the packages in the `$packages` array, with the same parameters (`ensure => installed`). This is a very compact way of instantiating lots of similar resources.

There's more...

Although arrays will take you a long way with Puppet, it's also useful to know about an even more flexible data structure: the hash.

Using hashes

A hash is like an array, but each of the elements can be stored and looked up by name (referred to as the **key**), for example:

```
$interface = {'name' => 'eth0',
              'address' => '192.168.0.1'}
notify { "Interface ${interface['name']} has address
  ${interface['address']}": }


Interface eth0 has address 192.168.0.1
```

Hash values can be anything that you can assign to a variable: strings, function calls, expressions, even other hashes or arrays.

Creating arrays with the split function

You can declare literal arrays using square brackets, as follows:

```
define lunchprint() {
   notify { "Lunch included ${name}": }
}

$lunch = ['egg', 'beans', 'chips']
lunchprint { $lunch: }

Lunch included egg
Lunch included beans
Lunch included chips
```

But Puppet can also create arrays for you from strings, using the `split` function, as follows:

```
$menu = 'egg beans chips'
$items = split($menu, ' ')
lunchprint { $items: }

Lunch included egg
Lunch included beans
Lunch included chips
```

Note that `split` takes two arguments: the first is the string to be split. The second is the character to split on; in this example, a single space. As Puppet works its way through the string, when it encounters a space, it will interpret it as the end of one item and the beginning of the next. So, given the string `egg beans chips`, this will be split into three items.

The character to split on can be any character, or a string:

```
$menu = 'egg and beans and chips'
$items = split($menu, ' and ')
```

It can also be a regular expression, for example, a set of alternatives separated by a | (pipe) character:

```
$lunch = 'egg:beans,chips'
$items = split($lunch, ':|,')
```

Writing powerful conditional statements

Puppet's if statement allows you to change the manifest based on the value of a variable or an expression. With it, you can apply different resources or parameter values depending on certain facts about the node, for example, the operating system, or the memory size. You can also set variables within the manifest which can change the behavior of included classes. For example, nodes in data center A might need to use different DNS servers than nodes in data center B, or you might need to include one set of classes for an Ubuntu system, and a different set for other systems.

How to do it...

Here's an example of a useful conditional statement:

1. Add the following code to your manifest:

```
if $::operatingsystem == 'Ubuntu' {
  notify { 'Running on Ubuntu': }
} else {
  notify { 'Non-Ubuntu system detected. Please upgrade
    to Ubuntu immediately.': }
}
```

How it works...

Puppet treats whatever follows an if keyword as an expression and evaluates it. If the expression evaluates to true, Puppet will execute the code within the curly braces.

Optionally, you can add an else branch, which will be executed if the expression evaluates to false.

There's more...

Here are some more tips on using if statements.

Elsif branches

You can add further tests using the `elsif` keyword, as follows:

```
if $::operatingsystem == 'Ubuntu' {
  notify { 'Running on Ubuntu': }
} elsif $::operatingsystem == 'Debian' {
  notify { 'Close enough...': }
} else {
  notify { 'Non-Ubuntu system detected. Please upgrade to Ubuntu
    immediately.': }
}
```

Comparisons

You can check if two values are equal using the `==` syntax, as in our example:

```
if $::operatingsystem == 'Ubuntu' {
  ...

}
```

Or, you can check if they are *not* equal using `!=`:

```
if $::operatingsystem != 'CentOS' {

}
```

You can also compare numeric values using `<` and `>`:

```
if $::uptime_days > 365 {
  notify { 'Time to upgrade your kernel!': }
}
```

To test if a value is greater (or less) than or equal to another value, use `<=` or `>=`:

```
if $::lsbmajdistrelease <= 12 {

}
```

Combining expressions

You can put together the kind of simple expressions described previously into more complex logical expressions, using `and`, `or`, and `not`:

```
if ($::uptime_days > 365) and ($::operatingsystem == 'Ubuntu') {

}

if ($role == 'webserver') and ( ($datacenter == 'A') or ($datacenter
== 'B') ) {

}
```

See also

▶ *Using the in operator*, in this chapter

▶ *Using selectors and case statements*, in this chapter

Using regular expressions in if statements

Another kind of expression you can test in `if` statements and other conditionals is the regular expression. A regular expression is a powerful way of comparing strings using pattern matching.

How to do it...

This is one example of using a regular expression in a conditional statement:

1. Add the following to your manifest:

```
if $::lsbdistdescription =~ /LTS/ {
  notify { 'Looks like you are using a Long Term Support
    version of Ubuntu.': }
} else {
  notify {'You might want to upgrade to a Long Term Support
    version of Ubuntu...': }
}
```

How it works...

Puppet treats the text supplied between the forward slashes as a regular expression specifying the text to be matched. If the match succeeds, the `if` expression will be true and so the code between the first set of curly braces will be executed.

If you wanted instead to do something if the text does *not* match, use `!~` rather than `=~`:

```
if $::lsbdistdescription !~ /LTS/ {
```

There's more...

Regular expressions are very powerful, but can be difficult to understand and debug. If you find yourself using a regular expression so complex that you can't see at a glance what it does, think about simplifying your design to make it easier. However, one particularly useful feature of regular expressions is the ability to capture patterns.

Capturing patterns

You can not only match text using a regular expression, but also capture the matched text and store it in a variable:

```
$input = 'Puppet is better than manual configuration'
if $input =~ /(.*) is better than (.*)/ {
  notify { "You said '${0}'. Looks like you're comparing ${1}
    to ${2}!": }
}
```

The preceding code produces this output:

You said 'Puppet is better than manual configuration'. Looks

like you're comparing Puppet to manual configuration!

The variable $0 stores the whole matched text (assuming the overall match succeeded). If you put brackets around any part of the regular expression, that creates a group and any matched groups will also be stored in variables. The first matched group will be $1, the second $2, and so on, as in the preceding example.

Regular expression syntax

Puppet's regular expression syntax is the same as Ruby's, so resources that explain Ruby regular expression syntax will also help you with Puppet. You can find a good introduction to Ruby regular expression syntax at this website:

```
http://www.tutorialspoint.com/ruby/ruby_regular_expressions.htm
```

See also

▶   *Using regular expression substitutions*, in this chapter

Using selectors and case statements

Although you could write any conditional statement using if, Puppet provides a couple of extra forms to help you express conditionals more easily: the selector and the case statement.

How to do it...

Here are some examples of selector and case statements:

1.   Add the following code to your manifest:

```
$systemtype = $::operatingsystem ? {
  'Ubuntu' => 'debianlike',
  'Debian' => 'debianlike',
```

```
    'RedHat'  => 'redhatlike',
    'Fedora'  => 'redhatlike',
    'CentOS'  => 'redhatlike',
    default   => 'unknown',
  }

  notify { "You have a ${systemtype} system": }
```

2. Add the following code to your manifest:

```
class debianlike {
  notify { 'Special manifest for Debian-like systems': }
}

class redhatlike {
  notify { 'Special manifest for RedHat-like systems': }
}

case $::operatingsystem {
  'Ubuntu',
  'Debian': {
    include debianlike
  }
  'RedHat',
  'Fedora',
  'CentOS': {
    include redhatlike
  }
  default: {
    notify { "I don't know what kind of system you have!": }
  }
}
```

How it works...

Our example demonstrates both the selector and the `case` statement, so let's see in detail how each of them works.

Selector

In the first example, we used a selector (the `?` operator) to choose a value for the `$systemtype` variable depending on the value of `$::operatingsystem`. This is similar to the ternary operator in C or Ruby, but instead of choosing between two possible values, you can have as many values as you like.

Puppet will compare the value of $::operatingsystem to each of the possible values we have supplied: Ubuntu, Debian, and so on. These values could be regular expressions (for example, for a partial string match, or to use wildcards), but in our case we have just used literal strings. As soon as it finds a match, the selector expression returns whatever value is associated with the matching string. If the value of $::operatingsystem is Fedora, for example, the selector expression will return the string redhatlike and this will be assigned to the variable $systemtype.

Case statement

Unlike selectors, the case statement does not return a value. case statements are handy where you want to execute different code depending on the value of some expression. In our second example, we used the case statement to include either the class debianlike or the class redhatlike, depending on the value of $::operatingsystem.

Again, Puppet compares the value of $::operatingsystem to a list of potential matches. These could be regular expressions or strings, or as in our example, comma-separated lists of strings. When it finds a match, the associated code between curly braces is executed. So, if the value of $::operatingsystem is Ubuntu, then the code include debianlike will be executed.

There's more...

Once you've got the grip with the basic use of selectors and case statements, you may find the following tips useful:

Regular expressions

As with if statements, you can use regular expressions with selectors and case statements, and you can also capture the values of the matched groups and refer to them using $1, $2, and so on:

```
case $::lsbdistdescription {
  /Ubuntu (.+)/: {
    notify { "You have Ubuntu version ${1}": }
  }
  /CentOS (.+)/: {
    notify { "You have CentOS version ${1}": }
  }
  default: {}
}
```

Defaults

Both selectors and case statements let you specify a default value, which is chosen if none of the other options match:

```
$lunch = 'Burger and fries'
$lunchtype =  $lunch ? {
  /fries/ => 'unhealthy',
  /salad/ => 'healthy',
  default => 'unknown',
}

notify { "Your lunch was ${lunchtype}": }
```

Your lunch was unhealthy

Using the in operator

The in operator tests whether one string contains another. Here's an example:

```
if 'spring' in 'springfield'
```

The preceding expression is true if the string spring is a substring of springfield, which it is. The in operator can also test for membership of arrays as follows:

```
if $crewmember in ['Frank', 'Dave', 'HAL' ]
```

When in is used with a hash, it tests whether the string is a key of the hash:

```
$interfaces = { 'lo' => '127.0.0.1',
                'eth0' => '192.168.0.1' }
if 'eth0' in $interfaces {
  notify { "eth0 has address ${interfaces['eth0']}": }
}
```

How to do it...

The following steps will show you how to use the in operator:

1. Add the following code to your manifest:

```
if $::operatingsystem in [ 'Ubuntu', 'Debian' ] {
  notify { 'Debian-type operating system detected': }
} elsif $::operatingsystem in [ 'RedHat', 'Fedora', 'SuSE',
'CentOS' ] {
  notify { 'RedHat-type operating system detected': }
} else {
  notify { 'Some other operating system detected': }
}
```

2. Run Puppet:

```
ubuntu@cookbook:~/puppet$ papply
Notice: Debian-type operating system detected
Notice: /Stage[main]/Admin::Test/Notify[Debian-type operating
system detected]/message: defined 'message' as 'Debian-type
operating system detected'
Notice: Finished catalog run in 0.08 seconds
```

There's more...

The value of an `in` expression is Boolean (true or false) so you can assign it to a variable:

```
$debianlike = $::operatingsystem in [ 'Debian', 'Ubuntu' ]

if $debianlike {
  notify { 'You are in a maze of twisty little packages, all alike': }
}
```

Using regular expression substitutions

Puppet's `regsubst` function provides an easy way to manipulate text, search and replace within strings, or extract patterns from strings. We often need to do this with data obtained from a fact, for example, or from external programs.

In this example, we'll see how to use `regsubst` to extract the first three octets of an IPv4 address (the network part, assuming it's a class C address).

How to do it...

Follow these steps to build the example:

1. Add the following code to your manifest:
   ```
   $class_c = regsubst($::ipaddress, '(.*)\..*', '\1.0')
   notify { "The network part of ${::ipaddress} is
     ${class_c}": }
   ```

2. Run Puppet:

   ```
   ubuntu@cookbook:~/puppet$ papply
   Notice: The network part of 10.96.247.132 is 10.96.247.0
   Notice: /Stage[main]/Admin::Test/Notify[The network part of
   10.96.247.132 is 10.96.247.0]/message: defined 'message' as 'The
   ```

```
network part of 10.96.247.132 is 10.96.247.0'
Notice: Finished catalog run in 0.09 seconds
```

How it works...

regsubst takes at least three parameters: source, pattern, and replacement. In our example, we specified the source string as $::ipaddress, which on this machine is as follows:

```
10.96.247.132
```

We specified the pattern as:

```
(.*)\..*
```

and the replacement as:

```
\1.0
```

The pattern will match the whole IP address, capturing the first three octets in round brackets. The captured text will be available as \1 for use in the replacement string.

The whole of the matched text (in this case the whole string) is replaced with replacement. This is \1 (the captured text from the source string) followed by the string .0, which evaluates to

```
10.96.247.0
```

We could have got the same result in other ways, of course, including:

```
$class_c = regsubst($::ipaddress, '\.\d+$', '.0')
```

There's more

pattern can be any regular expression, using the same (Ruby) syntax as regular expressions in if statements.

See also

▸ The *Importing dynamic information* recipe in *Chapter 3, Writing Better Manifests*
▸ The *Getting information about the environment* recipe in *Chapter 3, Writing Better Manifests*
▸ *Using regular expressions in if statements*, in this chapter

Writing Better Manifests

3

There are only two kinds of programming languages: those people always bitch about and those nobody uses.

—*Bjarne Stroustrup*

In this chapter we will cover:

- ▸ Using arrays of resources
- ▸ Using definitions
- ▸ Using dependencies
- ▸ Using tags
- ▸ Using run stages
- ▸ Using node inheritance
- ▸ Passing parameters to classes
- ▸ Using class inheritance and overriding
- ▸ Writing reusable, cross-platform manifests
- ▸ Getting information about the environment
- ▸ Importing dynamic information
- ▸ Passing arguments to shell commands

Downloading the example code

You can download the example code files for all Packt books you have purchased from your account at http://www.packtpub.com. If you purchased this book elsewhere, you can visit http://www.packtpub.com/support and register to have the files e-mailed directly to you.

Introduction

Your Puppet manifest is the living documentation for your entire infrastructure. Keeping it tidy and well organized is a great way to make it easier to maintain and understand. Puppet gives you a number of tools to do this, including

- Arrays
- Definitions
- Dependencies
- Inheritance
- Class parameters

We'll see how to use all of these and more. As you read through the chapter, try out the examples, and look through your own manifests to see where these features might help you simplify and improve your Puppet code.

Using arrays of resources

Anything you can do to a resource, you can do to an array of resources. Use this idea to refactor your manifests to make them shorter and clearer.

How to do it...

Here are the steps to refactor using arrays of resources:

1. Identify a class in your manifest where you have several instances of the same kind of resource for example, packages:

   ```
   package { 'sudo' : ensure => installed }
   package { 'unzip' : ensure => installed }
   package { 'locate' : ensure => installed }
   package { 'lsof' : ensure => installed }
   package { 'cron' : ensure => installed }
   package { 'rubygems' : ensure => installed }
   ```

2. Group them together and replace them with a single package resource using an array:

   ```
   package { [ 'cron',
               'locate',
               'lsof',
               'rubygems',
               'sudo',
   ```

```
                  'unzip' ]:
     ensure => installed,
}
```

How it works...

Most of Puppet's resource types can accept an array instead of a single name, and will create one instance for each of the elements in the array. All the parameters you provide for the resource (for example, `ensure => installed`) will be assigned to each of the new resource instances.

See also

▶ The *Iterating over multiple items* recipe in *Chapter 2, Puppet Language and Style*

Using definitions

In the previous example, we saw how to reduce redundant code by grouping identical resources into arrays. However, this technique is limited to resources where all the parameters are the same. When you have a set of resources have some parameters in common, you need to use a definition to group them together.

How to do it...

The following steps will show you how to create a definition:

1. Add the following code to your manifest:

   ```
   define tmpfile() {
     file { "/tmp/${name}":
       content => "Hello, world\n",
     }
   }

   tmpfile { ['a', 'b', 'c']: }
   ```

2. Run Puppet:

   ubuntu@cookbook:~/puppet$ papply

   Notice: /Stage[main]/Admin::Test/Admin::Test::Tmpfile[a]/ File[/tmp/a]/ensure: defined content as '{md5} a7966bf58e23583c9a5a4059383ff850'

   Notice: /Stage[main]/Admin::Test/Admin::Test::Tmpfile[b]/

```
File[/tmp/b]/ensure: defined content as '{md5}
a7966bf58e23583c9a5a4059383ff850'
```

```
Notice: /Stage[main]/Admin::Test/Admin::Test::Tmpfile[c]/
File[/tmp/c]/ensure: defined content as '{md5}
a7966bf58e23583c9a5a4059383ff850'
```

```
Notice: Finished catalog run in 0.12 seconds
```

How it works...

You can think of a definition (introduced with the `define` keyword) as a cookie-cutter. It describes a pattern which Puppet can use to create lots of similar resources. Any time you declare a `tmpfile` instance in your manifest, Puppet will insert all the resources contained in the `tmpfile` definition.

In our example, the definition of `tmpfile` contains a single `file` resource, whose content is `Hello, world\n`, and whose path is `/tmp/${name}`. If you declared an instance of `tmpfile` with the name `foo` as follows:

```
tmpfile { 'foo': }
```

Puppet would create a file with the path `/tmp/foo`. In other words, `${name}` in the definition will be replaced by the name of any actual instance that Puppet is asked to create. It's almost as though we created a new kind of resource: `tmpfile`, which has one parameter: its `name`.

Just like with regular resources, we don't have to pass just one name; as in the preceding example, we can provide an array of names and Puppet will create as many resources as required.

There's more...

In the example, we created a definition where the only parameter that varies between instances is the name. But we can add whatever parameters we want, so long as we declare them in the definition, in parentheses after the name, as follows:

```
define tmpfile($greeting) {
  file { "/tmp/${name}":
    content => $greeting,
  }
}
```

And pass values to them when we declare an instance of the resource:

```
tmpfile{ 'foo':
  greeting => "Hello, world\n",
}
```

You can declare multiple parameters as a comma-separated list:

```
define webapp($domain,$path,$platform) {
  ...
}

webapp { 'mywizzoapp':
  domain   => 'mywizzoapp.com',
  path     => '/var/www/apps/mywizzoapp',
  platform => 'Rails',
}
```

You can also declare default values for any parameters which aren't supplied, thus making them optional:

```
define tmpfile($greeting,$mode='0644') {
  ...
}
```

This is a powerful technique for abstracting out everything that's common to certain resources, and keeping it in one place so that you *Don't Repeat Yourself*. In the preceding example, there might be many individual resources contained within webapp: packages, config files, source code checkouts, virtual hosts, and so on. But all of them are the same for every instance of webapp except the parameters we provide. These might be referenced in a template, for example, to set the domain for a virtual host.

See also

▸   *Passing parameters to classes,* in this chapter

Using dependencies

To make sure things happen in the right order, you can specify in Puppet that one resource depends on another; for example, you need to install package X before you can start the service it provides, so you would mark the service as dependent on the package. Puppet will sort out the required order to meet all the dependencies.

In some configuration management systems, resources are applied in the order you write them, in other words, the ordering is implicit. That's not the case with Puppet, where resources are applied in a more or less random (but consistent) order unless you state an explicit order using dependencies. Some people prefer the implicit approach, because you can write the resource definitions in the order that they need to be done, and that's the way they'll be executed.

On the other hand, in many cases the ordering of resources doesn't matter. With an implicit-style system, you can't tell whether resource B is listed after resource A because B depends on A, or because it just happens to have been written in that order. That makes refactoring more difficult, as moving resources around may break some implicit dependency.

Puppet makes you do a little more work by specifying the dependencies up front, but the resulting code is clearer and easier to maintain. We'll see an example of how to do this in the following recipe.

How to do it...

Follow these steps to create an example of resource ordering using dependencies:

1. In your Puppet repo, create the file `modules/admin/manifests/ntp.pp` with the following contents:

```
# Manage NTP
class admin::ntp {
  package { 'ntp':
    ensure => installed,
  }

  service { 'ntp':
    ensure  => running,
    require => Package['ntp'],
  }

  file { '/etc/ntpd.conf':
    source  => 'puppet:///modules/admin/ntp.conf',
    notify  => Service['ntp'],
    require => Package['ntp'],
  }
}
```

2. Create the file `modules/admin/files/ntp.conf` with the following contents:

```
driftfile /var/lib/ntp/ntp.drift

server us.pool.ntp.org prefer
server 0.ubuntu.pool.ntp.org
server 1.ubuntu.pool.ntp.org
server 2.ubuntu.pool.ntp.org
server 3.ubuntu.pool.ntp.org
server ntp.ubuntu.com

restrict -4 default kod notrap nomodify nopeer noquery
```

```
restrict -6 default kod notrap nomodify nopeer noquery
restrict 127.0.0.1
restrict ::1
```

3. Modify your `manifests/nodes.pp` file, as follows:

```
node 'cookbook' {
  include admin::ntp
}
```

4. Run Puppet:

ubuntu@cookbook:~/puppet$ papply

Notice: /Stage[main]/Admin::Ntp/Package[ntp]/ensure: created

Notice: /Stage[main]/Admin::Ntp/File[/etc/ntpd.conf]/content: content changed '{md5}bb59234f5041c60a5b3a869f3e6a38b6' to '{md5}6 5e3b66fbf63d0c6c667179b5d0c5216'

Notice: /Stage[main]/Admin::Ntp/File[/etc/ntpd.conf]/owner: owner changed 'root' to 'ubuntu'

Notice: /Stage[main]/Admin::Ntp/File[/etc/ntpd.conf]/group: group changed 'root' to 'ubuntu'

Notice: /Stage[main]/Admin::Ntp/Service[ntp]: Triggered 'refresh' from 3 events

Notice: Finished catalog run in 11.71 seconds

How it works...

This example demonstrates two kinds of dependency: `require`, and `notify`. In the first case, the `ntp` service requires the `ntp` package to be applied first:

```
service { 'ntp':
  ensure  => running,
  require => Package['ntp'],
}
```

In the second case, the NTP config file is set to `notify` the `ntp` service; in other words, if the file changes, Puppet should restart the `ntp` service to pick up its new configuration.

```
file { '/etc/ntpd.conf':
    source  => 'puppet:///modules/admin/ntp.conf',
    notify  => Service['ntp'],
    require => Package['ntp'],
}
```

This implies that the service depends on the file as well as on the package, and so Puppet will be able to apply all three resources in the correct order:

```
Package['ntp'] -> File['/etc/ntp.conf'] ~> Service['ntp']
```

In fact, this is another way to specify the same dependency chain. Adding the previous line to your manifest will have the same effect as the `require` and `notify` parameters in our example (`->` means `require`, while `~>` means `notify`).

However, I prefer to use `require` and `notify` because the dependencies are defined as part of the resource, so it's easier to see what's going on. For complex chains of dependencies, though, you may want to use the `->` notation instead.

There's more...

You can also specify that a resource depends on a certain class:

```
require => Class['my-apt-repo']
```

You can specify dependencies not just between resources and classes, but between collections, as follows:

```
Yumrepo <| |> -> Package <| provider == yum |>
```

This is a powerful way to express that all `yumrepo` resources should be applied before all package resources whose provider is `yum`.

Getting your dependencies sorted out can be one of the most difficult parts of building a Puppet manifest. It's common to see manifests which require two or three Puppet runs to complete successfully, because the resources aren't being applied in just the right order, for example:

- ▶ Files require their parent directory to exist before they can be applied. For config files, the config directory is often created by the package that provides the software, so the config file should `require` the package.

- ▶ Services require the appropriate package to be installed before the service can be used, so the service should `require` the package.

- ▶ Services controlled by a custom `init` or `upstart` script need the script file to be in place first, so the service should `require` the file.

- ▶ Exec resources that run a script depend on the script file being deployed first, so `exec` should `require` the file.

- ▶ Exec resources that install some important binary (Ruby, for example) must run before anything which uses that binary, so any resources which depend on it should `require` the `exec` resource.

If a resource requires everything in some particular class to be applied before it, a quick way to do this is to have the resource require the whole class (using `require =>` `Class['important_thing']`). If lots of things depend on this class, you might decide it's cleaner to put the class into its own run stage (see the section on *Using run stages*) that comes before anything else.

Once you think you've got a working set of dependencies, test your manifest by re-imaging the machine with a fresh operating system (or use a spare machine) and applying Puppet. The run should complete with no errors and leave you with a working system. If there are any problems with the ordering of resources, add an appropriate dependency and try again.

Using tags

Sometimes one Puppet class needs to know about another or at least, to know whether or not it's present. For example, a class that manages the firewall may need to know whether or not the node is a web server.

Puppet's `tagged` function will tell you whether a named class or resource is present in the catalog for this node. You can also apply arbitrary tags to a node or class and check for the presence of these tags.

How to do it...

To help you find out if you're running on a particular node or class of node, all nodes are automatically tagged with the node name and the names of any parent nodes they inherit from. Here's an example which shows how to use `tagged` to get this information:

1. Add the following code to your `manifests/nodes.pp` file (replacing `cookbook` with your machine's hostname):

```
node 'bitfield_server' {
}

node 'cookbook' inherits 'bitfield_server' {
  if tagged('cookbook') {
    notify { 'this will succeed': }
  }
  if tagged('bitfield_server') {
    notify { 'so will this': }
  }
}
```

2. Run Puppet:

```
ubuntu@cookbook:~/puppet$ papply
Notice: this will succeed
Notice: /Stage[main]//Node[cookbook]/Notify[this will succeed]/
message: defined 'message' as 'this will succeed'
Notice: so will this
Notice: /Stage[main]//Node[cookbook]/Notify[so will this]/message:
defined 'message' as 'so will this'
Notice: Finished catalog run in 0.10 seconds
```

Nodes are also automatically tagged with the names of all the classes they include, and their parent classes. You can use `tagged` to find out what classes are included on the node, as in the following example:

1. Modify your `manifests/nodes.pp` file as follows:

```
node 'cookbook' {
  include admin::ntp

  if tagged('admin::ntp') {
    notify { 'This node is running NTP': }
  }
  if tagged('admin') {
    notify { 'This node includes at least one class from the admin
module': }
  }
}
```

2. Run Puppet:

```
ubuntu@cookbook:~/puppet$ papply
Notice: This node is running NTP
Notice: /Stage[main]//Node[cookbook]/Notify[This node is running
NTP]/message: defined 'message' as 'This node is running NTP'
Notice: This node includes at least one class from the admin
module
Notice: /Stage[main]//Node[cookbook]/Notify[This node includes at
least one class from the admin module]/message: defined 'message'
as 'This node includes at least one class from the admin module'
Notice: Finished catalog run in 0.42 seconds
```

You're not just limited to checking the tags automatically applied by Puppet. You can also add your own. To set an arbitrary tag on a node, use the `tag` function, as in the following example:

1. Modify your `manifests/nodes.pp` file as follows:

```
node 'cookbook' {
```

```
    tag('big-server')
    if tagged('big-server') {
      notify { 'Big server detected. Adding extra workload': }
    }
  }
```

2. Run Puppet:

ubuntu@cookbook:~/puppet$ papply

Notice: Big server detected. Adding extra workload

Notice: /Stage[main]//Node[cookbook]/Notify[Big server detected. Adding extra workload]/message: defined 'message' as 'Big server detected. Adding extra workload'

Notice: Finished catalog run in 0.08 seconds

You can also use tags to determine which parts of the manifest to apply. If you use the `--tags` option on the Puppet command line, Puppet will apply only those classes or resources tagged with the specific tags you include. For example, if you want to update only the `admin::ntp` configuration, but not run any other parts of the manifest, use a command line, as follows:

ubuntu@cookbook:~/puppet$ papply --tags admin::ntp

Notice: /Stage[main]/Admin::Ntp/Service[ntp]/ensure: ensure changed'stopped' to 'running'

Notice: Finished catalog run in 0.70 seconds

There's more...

You can use tags to create a collection of resources, and then make the collection a dependency for some other resource. For example, if some service depends on a config file that is built up from a number of file snippets, as in the following example:

```
class firewall::service {
    service { 'firewall':
        ….
    }

    File <| tag == 'firewall-snippet' |> ~> Service['firewall']
}

class myapp {
    file { '/etc/firewall.d/myapp.conf':
        tag => 'firewall-snippet',
        ….
    }
}
```

Here, we've specified that the `firewall` service should be notified if any file resource tagged `firewall-snippet` is updated. All we need to do to add a firewall config snippet for any particular app or service is to tag it `firewall-snippet`, and Puppet will do the rest.

Although we could add a `notify => Service["firewall"]` to each snippet resource, if our definition of the `firewall` service were ever to change we would have to hunt down and update all the snippets accordingly. The tag lets us encapsulate the logic in one place, making future maintenance and refactoring much easier.

What's the `<| tag == 'firewall-snippet' |>` syntax? It's called a resource collector, and it's a way of specifying a group of resources by searching for some piece of data about them: in this case, the value of a tag. You can find out more about resource collectors and the `<| |>` operator (sometimes known as the **spaceship** operator) on the Puppet Labs website:

`http://docs.puppetlabs.com/puppet/3/reference/lang_collectors.html`

Using run stages

A common requirement is to apply a certain group of resources before other groups (for example, installing a package repository or a custom Ruby version), or after others (for example, deploying an application once its dependencies are installed). Puppet's `run stages` feature allows you to do this.

By default, all resources in your manifest are applied in a single stage named `main`. If you need a resource to be applied before all others, you can assign it to a new run stage that is specified to come before `main`. Similarly, you could define a run stage that comes after `main`. In fact, you can define as many run stages as you need and tell Puppet which order they should be applied in.

In this example, we'll use stages to ensure one class is applied first and another last.

How to do it...

Here are the steps to create an example of using run stages:

1. Create the file `modules/admin/manifests/stages.pp` with the following contents:

```
class admin::stages {
  stage { 'first': before => Stage['main'] }
  stage { 'last': require => Stage['main'] }

  class me_first {
    notify { 'This will be done first': }
```

```
  }

  class me_last {
    notify { 'This will be done last': }
  }

  class { 'me_first':
    stage => 'first',
  }
  class { 'me_last':
    stage => 'last',
  }
}
```

2. Modify your `manifests/nodes.pp` file as follows:

```
node 'cookbook' {
  include admin::stages
}
```

3. Run Puppet:

ubuntu@cookbook:~/puppet$ papply

Notice: This will be done first

Notice: /Stage[first]/Admin::Stages::Me_first/Notify[This will be done first]/message: defined 'message' as 'This will be done first'

Notice: This will be done last

Notice: /Stage[last]/Admin::Stages::Me_last/Notify[This will be done last]/message: defined 'message' as 'This will be done last'

Notice: Finished catalog run in 0.10 seconds

How it works...

Let's examine this code in detail to see what's happening. First, we declare the run stages `first` and `last`, as follows::

```
stage { 'first': before => Stage['main'] }
stage { 'last': require => Stage['main'] }
```

For the `first` stage, we've specified that it should come before `main`. That is, every resource marked as being in stage `first` will be applied before any resource in stage `main` (the default stage).

The `last` stage requires stage `main`, so no resource in `last` can be applied until after every resource in stage `main`.

We then declare some classes which we'll later assign to these run stages:

```
class me_first {
  notify { 'This will be done first': }
}

class me_last {
  notify { 'This will be done last': }
}
```

We can now put it all together, and include these classes on the node, specifying the run stages for each as we do so:

```
class { 'me_first':
  stage => 'first',
}

class { 'me_last':
  stage => 'last',
}
```

Note that in the class declarations for `me_first` and `me_last` we didn't have to specify that they take a `stage` parameter. `stage` is a **metaparameter**, which means it can be applied to any class or resource without having to be explicitly declared.

There's more...

You can define as many run stages as you like, and set up any ordering for them. This can greatly simplify a complicated manifest which otherwise would require lots of explicit dependencies between resources. Beware of accidentally introducing dependency cycles, though; when you assign something to a run stage you're automatically making it dependent on everything in prior stages.

You may like to define your stages in the `site.pp` file instead, so that it's easy to see at the top level of the manifest what stages are available.

Gary Larizza has written a helpful introduction to using run stages, with some real-world examples, on his website:

http://garylarizza.com/blog/2011/03/11/using-run-stages-with-puppet/

A caveat: many people don't like to use run stages, feeling that Puppet already provides sufficient resource ordering control, and that using run stages indiscriminately can make your code very hard to follow (as one of my technical reviewers said, "though useful they tend to be quickly abused"). In my consulting work I often come across tortuously complicated Puppet manifests made almost unmaintainable by the widespread use of run stages. So, think carefully before deciding to solve a problem by using run stages, and use them sparingly.

See also

▶ *Using tags,* in this chapter

▶ The *Drawing dependency graphs* recipe in *Chapter 9, Monitoring, Reporting, and Troubleshooting*

Using node inheritance

Well-organized Puppet manifests are easy to read, and the node declarations (usually in `manifests/nodes.pp`) are the most important part of the manifest. You should be able to tell by looking at a node declaration exactly what the node is for, and ideally also any special configuration it requires.

To make the node declarations as readable as possible, you can use `node inheritance` to remove all duplicated code. For example, some things that might be common to all nodes are:

▶ SSH configuration

▶ NTP

▶ Puppet

▶ Backups

Nodes may also share configuration because they are in the same data center, or located at the same ISP or cloud provider. To avoid repeatedly including the same classes on lots of nodes, you can use **node inheritance** to tidy up your code.

How to do it...

The following steps will show you how to use node inheritance:

1. Modify your `manifests/nodes.pp` file to declare a `base` node, which contains only the classes that all nodes need (these will probably be different for your infrastructure):

```
node 'base' {
    include admin::basics
    include admin::ssh
    include admin::ntp
    include puppet::client
    include backup::client
}
```

2. Have your real nodes inherit from this `base` node:

```
node 'cookbook' inherits 'base' {
  notify { 'I get everything in base': }
}
```

3. If you have special configuration for data center X, declare a `datacenter_x` node that inherits from `base` but adds the required class:

```
node 'datacenter_x' inherits 'base' {
  include admin::datacenter_x
}
```

4. Nodes which need the `datacenter_x` configuration should inherit from this node:

```
node 'cookbook' inherits 'datacenter_x' {
  notify { 'I get everything in base plus datacenter_x': }
}
```

How it works...

When one node inherits from another, it picks up all the configuration that the parent node had. You can then add anything which makes this particular node different.

You can have a node inherit from a node that inherits from another node, and so on. You can't inherit from more than one node at once, though; so you can't have, for example:

```
node 'thiswontwork' inherits datacenter_x, datacenter_y {
    # This won't work
}
```

There's more...

Just as with a normal node definition, you can specify a list of node names which will all inherit the same definition:

```
node 'web' inherits 'base' {
  include webserver
}

node 'web1', 'web2', 'web3' inherits 'web' {}
```

Or a regular expression that will match multiple servers:

```
node /web\d+/ inherits 'web' {}
```

See also

▸ *Using class inheritance and overriding,* in this chapter

▸ The *Importing configuration data with Hiera* recipe in *Chapter 8, External Tools and the Puppet Ecosystem*

Passing parameters to classes

Sometimes it's very useful to parameterize some aspect of a class. For example, you might need to manage different versions of a gem package, and rather than making separate classes for each which differ only in the version number, or using inheritance and overrides, you can pass in the version number as a parameter.

How to do it...

In this example we'll create a definition which accepts parameters:

1. Declare the parameter as a part of the class definition:

```
class eventmachine($version) {
  package { 'eventmachine':
    provider => gem,
    ensure   => $version,
  }
}
```

2. Use the following syntax to include the class on a node:

```
class { 'eventmachine':
  version => '1.0.3',
}
```

How it works...

The class definition

```
class eventmachine($version) {
```

is just like a normal class definition except it specifies that the class takes one parameter: $version. Inside the class, we've defined a package resource:

```
package { 'eventmachine':
  provider => gem,
  ensure   => $version,
}
```

This is a gem package, and we're requesting to install version $version.

When you include the class on a node, instead of the usual `include` syntax

```
include eventmachine
```

there's a `class` statement:

```
class { 'eventmachine':
  version => '1.0.3',
}
```

that has the same effect but also sets a value for the parameter `version`.

There's more...

You can specify multiple parameters for a class

```
class mysql($package, $socket, $port) {
```

and supply them in the same way:

```
class { 'mysql':
    package => 'percona-server-server-5.5',
    socket  => '/var/run/mysqld/mysqld.sock',
    port    => '3306',
}
```

You can also give default values for some of your parameters:

```
class mysql($package, $socket, $port='3306') {
```

or all:

```
class mysql(
  package = percona-server-server-5.5",
  socket  = '/var/run/mysqld/mysqld.sock',
  port    = '3306') {
```

Unlike a definition, only one instance of a parameterized class can exist on a node. So where you need to have several different instances of the resource, use `define` instead.

See also

  ▶ *Using node inheritance*, in this chapter

Using class inheritance and overriding

Just as nodes can inherit from other nodes, the same idea works for classes. You can inherit from any class and add resources to it, or override existing resources with modified versions.

In this section we'll use the `admin::ntp` class we created previously as an example. The NTP servers we set up in the `ntpd.conf` file are US-based, which makes sense if your server is in a US data center. For UK-located servers, we'll create a modified version of `admin::ntp` which uses the official UK NTP servers.

How to do it...

Follow these steps to create the example class:

1. Create the file `modules/admin/manifests/ntp_uk.pp` with the following contents:

```
class admin::ntp_uk inherits admin::ntp {
  File['/etc/ntpd.conf'] {
    source => 'puppet:///modules/admin/ntp_uk.conf',
  }
}
```

2. Create the file `modules/admin/files/ntp_uk.conf` with the following contents:

```
driftfile /var/lib/ntp/ntp.drift

server 0.uk.pool.ntp.org
server 1.uk.pool.ntp.org
server 2.uk.pool.ntp.org
server 3.uk.pool.ntp.org

restrict -4 default kod notrap nomodify nopeer noquery
restrict -6 default kod notrap nomodify nopeer noquery
restrict 127.0.0.1
restrict ::1
```

3. Modify your `manifests/nodes.pp` file as follows:

```
node 'cookbook' {
  include admin::ntp_uk
}
```

4. Run Puppet:

```
Notice: /Stage[main]/Admin::Ntp/File[/etc/ntpd.conf]/content:
content changed '{md5}65e3b66fbf63d0c6c667179b5d0c5216' to '{md5}4
b096d8d8aae71e8745db1415e80d06a'

Notice: /Stage[main]/Admin::Ntp/Service[ntp]: Triggered 'refresh'
from 1 events

Notice: Finished catalog run in 0.57 seconds
```

How it works...

Let's remind ourselves what's in the `admin::ntp` class we're inheriting from:

```
# Manage NTP
class admin::ntp {
  package { 'ntp':
    ensure => installed,
  }

  service { 'ntp':
    ensure  => running,
    require => Package['ntp'],
  }

  file { '/etc/ntpd.conf':
    source  => 'puppet:///modules/admin/ntp.conf',
    notify  => Service['ntp'],
    require => Package['ntp'],
  }
}
```

And here's the beginning of the `admin::ntp_uk` class declaration:

```
class admin::ntp_uk inherits admin::ntp {
```

The `inherits` keyword tells Puppet that we want everything in `admin::ntp` to be included in `admin::ntp_uk`: that is, the `ntp` package, the `ntp` service, and the `ntpd.conf` file.

However, we're going to override the `ntpd.conf` resource as follows:

```
File['/etc/ntpd.conf'] {
  source => 'puppet:///modules/admin/ntp_uk.conf',
}
```

Notice that unlike a normal `file` resource, `File` is capitalized. This tells Puppet that we're not creating a new resource, but referring to one that already exists. We've specified a `source` attribute:

```
source => 'puppet:///modules/admin/ntp_uk.conf',
```

which will override the source of the original file:

```
source  => 'puppet:///modules/admin/ntp.conf',
```

The other attributes of the ntpd.conf file will be inherited unmodified, so the resource Puppet creates will look like the following:

```
file { '/etc/ntpd.conf':
  source  => 'puppet:///modules/admin/ntp_uk.conf',
  notify  => Service['ntp'],
  require => Package['ntp'],
}
```

The result will be exactly the same as if we had copied the whole class definition from admin::ntp but changed the value of source. So we will get identical NTP configuration except for the contents of the ntpd.conf file, which will contain the UK NTP servers.

There's more...

Overriding inherited classes may seem complicated at first. Once you get the idea, though, it's actually quite simple. It's a great way to make your manifests more readable because it removes lots of duplication, and focuses only on the parts which differ. Here are some more ways to use overriding.

Removing inherited attributes

What if you wanted to generate ntpd.conf from a template in your inherited class, or specify a literal content string, instead of using a file source? Well, the obvious approach won't work:

```
File['/etc/ntpd.conf'] {
  content => 'server 0.uk.pool.ntp.org',
}
```

gives

Error: You cannot specify more than one of content, source, target

That's because Puppet adds any attributes you specify to the inherited resource declaration, so you'd end up with this:

```
file { '/etc/ntpd.conf':
  source  => 'puppet:///modules/admin/ntp_uk.conf',
  content => 'server 0.uk.pool.ntp.org',
  notify  => Service['ntp'],
  require => Package['ntp'],
}
```

which isn't allowed. To get what you want, you need to remove the `source` attribute from the inherited resource. To do this, use the `undef` keyword, as follows:

```
File['/etc/ntpd.conf'] {
  source  => undef,
  content => 'server 0.uk.pool.ntp.org',
}
```

Adding extra values using +>

Similarly, instead of replacing a value, you may want to add more values to those defined in the parent class. The **plusignment** operator `+>` will do this:

```
File['/etc/ntpd.conf'] {
  require +> Package['tzdata'],
}
```

The `+>` operator adds a value (or an array of values surrounded by square brackets) to the value defined in the parent class. The `ntpd.conf` file already has a `require` attribute, so ours will be appended to it. The resulting resource will look as follows:

```
file { '/etc/ntpd.conf':
  source  => 'puppet:///modules/admin/ntp.conf',
  notify  => Service['ntp'],
  require => [Package['ntp'], Package['tzdata']],
}
```

Disabling resources

One of the most common uses for inheritance and overrides is to disable services or other resources:

```
class apache::disabled inherits apache {
    Service['apache2'] {
        enable  => false,
        ensure  => stopped,
    }
}
```

Any class which might otherwise conflict with Apache (for example, one that manages Nginx) can easily disable it, as follows:

```
class nginx {
  include apache::disabled
  ...
}
```

- ▶ *Using node inheritance*, in this chapter
- ▶ *Passing parameters to classes*, in this chapter
- ▶ The *Using standard naming conventions* recipe in *Chapter 2, Puppet Language and Style*

Writing reusable, cross-platform manifests

Every system administrator dreams of a unified, homogeneous infrastructure, of identical machines all running the same version of the same OS. As in other areas of life, however, the reality is often messy and doesn't conform to the plan.

You are probably responsible for a bunch of assorted servers of varying age and architecture, running different kernels from different OS distributions, often scattered across different data centers and ISPs.

This situation should strike terror into the hearts of the sysadmins of the SSH in a `for` loop persuasion, because executing the same commands on every server can have different, unpredictable, and even dangerous results.

We should certainly strive to bring older servers up-to-date and get working as far as possible on a single reference platform to make administration simpler, cheaper, and more reliable. But until we get there, Puppet makes coping with heterogeneous environments slightly easier.

How to do it...

Here are some examples of how to make your manifests more portable.

1. If you have servers in different data centers that need slightly different network configuration, for example, use the node inheritance technique to encapsulate the differences:

    ```
    node 'misspiggy' inherits 'datacenter_x' {
      ...
    }
    ```

2. Where you need to apply the same manifest to servers with different OS distributions, the main differences will probably be the names of packages and services, and the location of config files. Try to capture all these differences into a single class, by using selectors to set global variables:

    ```
    $ssh_service = $::operatingsystem? {
      /Ubuntu|Debian/ => 'ssh',
      default         => 'sshd',
    }
    ```

You needn't worry about the differences in any other part of the manifest; when you refer to something, use the variable in confidence that it will point to the right thing in each environment:

```
service { $ssh_service:
  ensure => running,
}
```

3. Often we need to cope with mixed architectures; this can affect the paths to shared libraries, and also may require different versions of packages. Again, try to encapsulate all the required settings in a single architecture class that sets global variables:

```
$libdir = $::architecture ? {
  amd64   => '/usr/lib64',
  default => '/usr/lib',
}
```

Then you can use these wherever an architecture-dependent value is required, in your manifests or even in templates:

```
; php.ini
[PHP]
; Directory in which the loadable extensions (modules) reside.
extension_dir = <%= @libdir %>/php/modules
```

How it works...

The advantage of this approach (which could be called top-down) is that you only need to make your choices once. The alternative, bottom-up approach would be, to have a selector or `case` statement everywhere a setting is used:

```
service { $::operatingsystem? {
  /Ubuntu|Debian/ => 'ssh',
  default         => 'sshd' }:
  ensure => running,
}
```

This not only results in lots of duplication, but makes the code harder to read. And when a new operating system is added to the mix, you'll need to make changes throughout the whole manifest, instead of just in one place.

There's more...

If you are writing a module for public distribution (for example, on Puppet Forge), you can make it much more valuable by making it as cross-platform as possible. As far as you can, test it on lots of different distributions, platforms, and architectures, and add the appropriate variables so it works everywhere.

If you use a public module and adapt it to your own environment, consider updating the public version with your changes if you think they might be helpful to other people.

Even if you are not thinking of publishing a module, bear in mind that it may be in production use for a long time and may have to adapt to many changes in the environment. If it's designed to cope with this from the start, it'll make life easier for you or whoever ends up maintaining your code.

> *Always code as if the guy who ends up maintaining your code will be a violent psychopath who knows where you live.*

> *—Dave Carhart*

See also

- *Using node inheritance*, in this chapter
- *Using class inheritance and overriding*, in this chapter
- The *Using public modules* recipe in *Chapter 8, External Tools and the Puppet Ecosystem*
- The *Importing configuration data with Hiera* recipe in *Chapter 8, External Tools and the Puppet Ecosystem*

Getting information about the environment

Often in a Puppet manifest, you need to know some local information about the machine you're on. **Facter** is the tool that accompanies Puppet to provide a standard way of getting information (facts) from the environment about things such as

- Operating system
- Memory size
- Architecture
- Processor count

To see a complete list of the facts available on your system, run:

ubuntu@cookbook:~/puppet$ sudo facter
```
architecture => amd64
augeasversion => 0.10.0
domain => compute-1.internal
ec2_ami_id => ami-137bcf7a
ec2_ami_launch_index => 0
...
```

While it can be handy to get this information from the command line, the real power of Facter lies in being able to access these facts in your Puppet manifests.

How to do it...

Here's an example of using Facter facts in a manifest.

1. Reference a Facter fact in your manifest like any other variable. Facts are global variables in Puppet, so should be prefixed with a double colon (::), as in the following code snippet:

```
notify { "This is $::operatingsystem version
$::operatingsystemrelease, on $::architecture architecture, kernel
version $::kernelversion": }
```

2. When Puppet runs, it will fill in the appropriate values for the current node:

```
ubuntu@cookbook:~/puppet$ papply

Notice: This is Ubuntu version 12.04, on amd64 architecture,
kernel version 3.2.0
```

How it works...

Facter provides an abstraction layer for Puppet, and a standard way for manifests to get information about their environment. When you refer to a fact in a manifest, Puppet will query Facter to get the current value, and insert it into the manifest.

There's more...

You can also use facts in ERB templates. For example, you might want to insert the node's hostname into a file, or change a config setting for an application based on the memory size of the node. When you use fact names in templates, remember that they don't need a dollar sign, because this is Ruby, not Puppet:

```
$KLogPath <%= case @kernelversion when '2.6.31' then '/var/run/
rsyslog/kmsg' else '/proc/kmsg' end %>
```

See also

▸ The *Creating custom Facter facts* recipe in *Chapter 8, External Tools and the Puppet Ecosystem*

Importing dynamic information

Even though some system administrators like to wall themselves off from the rest of the office using piles of old printers, we all need to exchange information with other departments from time to time. For example, you may want to insert data into your Puppet manifests which is derived from some outside source. The `generate` function is ideal for this.

Getting ready

Follow these steps to prepare for running the example.

1. Create the script `/usr/local/bin/message.rb` with the following contents:

   ```
   #!/usr/bin/env ruby

   puts "Hi, I'm Ruby! Will you play with me?"
   ```

2. Make the script executable:

   ubuntu@cookbook:~/puppet$ sudo chmod a+x /usr/local/bin/message.rb

How to do it...

This example calls the external script we created previously and gets its output.

1. Add the following to your manifest:

   ```
   $message = generate('/usr/local/bin/message.rb')
   notify { $message: }
   ```

2. Run Puppet:

   ubuntu@cookbook:~/puppet$ papply
   Notice: Hi, I'm Ruby! Will you play with me?

How it works...

The `generate` function runs the specified script or program and returns the result, in this case, a cheerful message from Ruby.

This isn't terribly useful as it stands, but you get the idea. Anything a script can do, print, fetch, or calculate, for example, the results of a database query can be brought into your manifest using `generate`. You can also, of course, run standard UNIX utilities such as `cat` and `grep`.

There's more...

If you need to pass arguments to the executable called by `generate`, add them as extra arguments to the function call:

```
$message = generate('/bin/cat', '/etc/motd')
```

Puppet will try to protect you from malicious shell calls by restricting the characters you can use in a call to `generate`, so shell pipes and redirection aren't allowed, for example. The simplest and safest thing to do is to put all your logic into a script and then call that script.

See also

▶ The *Creating custom Facter facts* recipe in *Chapter 8, External Tools and the Puppet Ecosystem*

▶ The *Importing configuration data with Hiera* recipe in *Chapter 8, External Tools and the Puppet Ecosystem*

Passing arguments to shell commands

If you want to insert values into a command line (to be run by an `exec` resource, for example), they often need to be quoted, especially if they contain spaces. The `shellquote` function will take any number of arguments, including arrays, and quote each of the arguments and return them all as a space-separated string that you can pass to commands.

In this example, we would like to set up an `exec` resource which will rename a file, but both the source and the target name contain spaces, so they need to be correctly quoted in the command line.

How to do it...

Here's an example of using the `shellquote` function.

1. Add the following to your manifest:
```
$source = 'Hello Jerry'
```

```
$target = 'Hello... Newman'
$argstring = shellquote($source, $target)
$command = "/bin/mv ${argstring}"
notify { $command: }
```

2. Run Puppet:

ubuntu@cookbook:~/puppet$ papply

No0tice: /bin/mv "Hello Jerry" "Hello... Newman"

How it works...

First we define the $source and $target variables, which are the two filenames we want to use in the command line.

```
$source = 'Hello Jerry'
$target = 'Hello... Newman'
```

Then we call shellquote to concatenate these variables into a quoted, space-separated string.

```
$argstring = shellquote($source, $target)
```

Then we put together the final command line:

```
$command = "/bin/mv ${argstring}"
```

The result is:

/bin/mv "Hello Jerry" "Hello... Newman"

This command line can now be run with an exec resource. What would happen if we didn't use shellquote?

```
$source = 'Hello Jerry'
$target = 'Hello... Newman'
$command = "/bin/mv ${source} ${target}"
notify { $command: }
```

Notice: /bin/mv Hello Jerry Hello... Newman

This won't work because mv expects space-separated arguments, so will interpret this as a request to move three files Hello, Jerry, and Hello... into a directory named Newman, which probably isn't what we want.

4
Working with Files and Packages

A writer has the duty to be good, not lousy; true, not false; lively, not dull; accurate, not full of error.

—E.B. White

In this chapter we will cover:

- ▸ Making quick edits to config files
- ▸ Using Augeas to automatically edit config files
- ▸ Building config files using snippets
- ▸ Using ERB templates
- ▸ Using array iteration in templates
- ▸ Using GnuPG to encrypt secrets
- ▸ Installing packages from a third-party repository
- ▸ Building packages automatically from source
- ▸ Comparing package versions

Introduction

In this chapter we'll see how to make small edits to files, how to make larger changes in a structured way using the Augeas tool, how to construct files from concatenated snippets, and how to generate files from templates. We'll also learn how to install packages from additional repositories, and how to manage those repositories. In addition, we'll see how to store and decrypt secret data with Puppet.

Making quick edits to config files

When you need to have Puppet change a particular setting in a config file, it's common to simply deploy the whole file with Puppet. This isn't always possible, though; especially if it's a file which several different parts of your Puppet manifest may need to modify.

What would be useful is a simple recipe to add a line to a config file if it's not already present, for example, adding a module name to `/etc/modules` to tell the kernel to load that module at boot. You can use an `exec` resource to do jobs like this.

How to do it...

This example shows how to use `exec` to append a line to a text file:

1. Add the following code to your `manifests/site.pp` file:

```
define append_if_no_such_line($file,$line) {
  exec { "/bin/echo '${line}' >> '${file}'":
    unless => "/bin/grep -Fx '${line}' '${file}'",
  }
}
```

2. Modify your `manifests/nodes.pp` file as follows:

```
node 'cookbook' {
  append_if_no_such_line { 'enable-ip-conntrack':
    file => '/etc/modules',
    line => 'ip_conntrack',
  }
}
```

3. Run Puppet:

```
ubuntu@cookbook:~/puppet$ papply
Notice: /Stage[main]//Node[cookbook]/Append_if_no_such_
line[enable-ip-conntrack]/Exec[/bin/echo 'ip_conntrack' >> '/etc/
modules']/returns: executed successfully
Notice: Finished catalog run in 0.60 seconds
```

How it works...

First of all, Puppet will run the command specified in the `unless` parameter, to check whether or not the line is already present:

```
/bin/grep -Fx 'ip_conntrack' '/etc/modules'
```

The first time you run Puppet, this command will fail (because /etc/modules doesn't contain this line), and so Puppet will run:

```
/bin/echo 'ip_conntrack' >> '/etc/modules'
```

On future runs, the grep command will succeed because the line is already present, and so Puppet will not run the echo command again.

You can use the append_if_no_such_line definition anywhere in your manifest when you need to add a single line to a config file.

There's more...

You can use similar definitions to perform other minor operations on text files. For example, this will enable you to search and replace within a file:

```
define replace_matching_line($file,$match,$replace) {
  exec { "/usr/bin/ruby -i -p -e 'sub(%r{$match}, \"$replace\")'
${file}":
    onlyif => "/bin/grep -E '${match}' ${file}",
  }
}

replace_matching_line { 'disable-ip-conntrack':
  file    => '/etc/modules',
  match   => '^ip_conntrack',
  replace => '#ip_conntrack',
}
```

Using Augeas to automatically edit config files

Sometimes it seems like every application has its own subtly different config file format, and writing regular expressions to parse and modify all of them can be a tiresome business.

Thankfully, Augeas is here to help. Augeas is a system that aims to simplify working with different config file formats by presenting them all as a simple tree of values. Puppet's Augeas support allows you to create augeas resources that can make the required config changes intelligently and automatically.

How to do it...

Follow these steps to create an example `augeas` resource:

1. Modify your `manifests/nodes.pp` file as follows:

```
node 'cookbook' {
  augeas { 'enable-ip-forwarding':
    context => '/files/etc/sysctl.conf',
    changes => ['set net.ipv4.ip_forward 1'],
  }
}
```

2. Run Puppet:

ubuntu@cookbook:~/puppet$ papply

Notice: /Stage[main]//Node[cookbook]/Augeas[enable-ip-forwarding]/ returns: executed successfully

Notice: Finished catalog run in 0.55 seconds

3. Check that the setting has been correctly applied:

ubuntu@cookbook:~/puppet$ sudo sysctl -p |grep forward

net.ipv4.ip_forward = 1

How it works...

We declare an `augeas` resource named `enable-ip-forwarding`:

```
augeas { 'enable-ip-forwarding':
```

We specify that we want to make changes in the context of the file `/etc/sysctl.conf`:

```
context => '/files/etc/sysctl.conf',
```

The `changes` parameter specifies the changes we want to make. Its value is an array, because we can supply several changes at once. In this example, there is only change, so the value is an array of one element:

```
changes => ['set net.ipv4.ip_forward 1'],
```

In general Augeas changes take the form

```
set <parameter> <value>
```

Augeas uses a set of translation files called **lenses** to enable it to write these settings in the appropriate format for the given config file. In this case, the setting will be translated into a line like this in `/etc/sysctl.conf`:

```
net.ipv4.ip_forward=1
```

There's more...

I've chosen `/etc/sysctl.conf` as the example because it can contain a wide variety of kernel settings and you may want to change these settings for all sorts of different purposes and in different Puppet classes. You might want to enable IP forwarding, as in the example, for a router class, but you might also want to tune the value of `net.core.somaxconn` for a load-balancer class.

This means that simply Puppetizing the `/etc/sysctl.conf` file and distributing it as a text file won't work, because you might have several different and conflicting versions, depending on the setting you want to modify. Augeas is the right solution here because you can define `augeas` resources in different places which modify the same file, and they won't conflict.

For more about using Puppet and Augeas, see the page on the Puppet Labs website:

`http://projects.puppetlabs.com/projects/1/wiki/Puppet_Augeas`

Building config files using snippets

Sometimes you can't deploy a whole config file in one piece, yet making line-by-line edits isn't enough. Often, you need to build up a config file from various bits of configuration managed by different classes. For example, you might have two or three services which require `rsync` modules to be configured, so you can't distribute a single `rsyncd.conf` file. In this situation, you can use a snippet approach: write several separate snippets or fragments which are then concatenated into a single file.

How to do it...

Here's an example of building a config file using the snippet pattern:

1. Create the file `modules/admin/manifests/rsyncdconf.pp` with the following contents:

```
class admin::rsyncdconf {
  file { '/etc/rsyncd.d':
    ensure => directory,
  }

  exec { 'update-rsyncd.conf':
    command    => '/bin/cat /etc/rsyncd.d/*.conf > /etc/rsyncd.
conf',
    refreshonly => true,
  }
}
```

2. Create the file `modules/admin/files/myapp.rsync` with the following contents:

```
[myapp]
    uid = myappuser
    gid = myappuser
    path = /opt/myapp/shared/data
    comment = Data for myapp
    list = no
    read only = no
    auth users = myappuser
```

3. Modify your `nodes.pp` file as follows:

```
node 'cookbook' {
    include admin::rsyncdconf

    file { '/etc/rsyncd.d/myapp.conf':
        ensure  => present,
        source  => 'puppet:///modules/admin/myapp.rsync',
        require => File['/etc/rsyncd.d'],
        notify  => Exec['update-rsyncd.conf'],
    }
}
```

4. Run Puppet:

```
ubuntu@cookbook:~/puppet$ papply
```

Notice: /Stage[main]//Node[cookbook]/File[/etc/rsyncd.d/myapp.conf]/ensure: defined content as '{md5} d85e5aa28aca2faf3e32b98e96b405e4'

Notice: /Stage[main]/Admin::Rsyncdconf/Exec[update-rsyncd.conf]: Triggered 'refresh' from 1 events

Notice: Finished catalog run in 0.31 seconds

5. Check that the `rsyncd.conf` file has been assembled correctly:

```
ubuntu@cookbook:~/puppet$ sudo cat /etc/rsyncd.conf
[myapp]
    uid = myappuser
    gid = myappuser
    path = /opt/myapp/shared/data
    comment = Data for myapp
    list = no
    read only = no
    auth users = myappuser
```

How it works...

The `admin::rsyncdconf` class creates a directory for the `rsync` config snippets to be placed into:

```
file { '/etc/rsyncd.d':
  ensure => directory,
}
```

It doesn't matter what the directory is called, since it's just for our use. `rsync` itself only reads the single file `/etc/rsynd.conf`, so we will write our snippets into the `/etc/rsyncd.d` directory and then concatenate them all into the main file.

When you create a config snippet, all you need to do is have it `require` this directory:

```
require => File['/etc/rsyncd.d'],
```

and `notify` the `exec` that updates the main config file:

```
notify   => Exec['update-rsyncd.conf'],
```

This `exec` will then be run every time one of these snippets is updated:

```
exec { 'update-rsyncd.conf':
  command     => '/bin/cat /etc/rsyncd.d/*.conf > /etc/rsyncd.conf',
  refreshonly => true,
}
```

which will concatenate all the snippets in `/etc/rsyncd.d` into `rsyncd.conf`.

Note that the `refreshonly` parameter means that the `exec` command will only be run when it's triggered by a `notify` from another resource, in this case, the `myapp.conf` snippet.

The reason this is useful is that you can have many different snippet resources spread throughout different classes and modules, all of which will eventually be combined into a single `rsyncd.conf` file, but you can keep the code to do this combining in one place.

There's more...

This is a useful pattern whenever you have a service such as `rsync` that has a single config file which may contain distinct snippets. In effect, it gives you the same functionality as Apache's `conf.d` or PHP's `php-ini.d` directories.

See also

- The *Using tags* recipe in *Chapter 3, Writing Better Manifests*

Using ERB templates

While you can deploy config files easily with Puppet as simple text files, templates are much more powerful. A template file can do calculations, execute Ruby code, or reference the values of variables from your Puppet manifests. Anywhere you might deploy a text file using Puppet, you can use a template instead.

In the simplest case, a template can just be a static text file. More usefully, you can insert variables into it using the **ERB** (**embedded Ruby**) syntax. For example:

```
<%= @name %>, this is a very large drink.
```

If the template is used in a context where the variable $name contains Zaphod Beeblebrox, the template will evaluate to:

```
Zaphod Beeblebrox, this is a very large drink.
```

This simple technique is very useful for generating lots of files which only differ in the values of one or two variables, for example, virtual hosts, and for inserting values into a script such as database names and passwords.

How to do it...

In this example, we'll use an ERB template to insert a password into a backup script:

1. Create the file `modules/admin/templates/backup-mysql.sh.erb` with the following contents:

   ```
   #!/bin/sh
   /usr/bin/mysqldump -uroot -p<%= @mysql_password %> --all-databases
   | /bin/gzip > /backup/mysql/all-databases.sql.gz
   ```

2. Modify your `manifests/nodes.pp` file as follows:

   ```
   node 'cookbook' {
     $mysql_password = 'secret'
     file { '/usr/local/bin/backup-mysql':
       content => template('admin/backup-mysql.sh.erb'),
       mode    => '0755',
     }
   }
   ```

3. Run Puppet:

```
ubuntu@cookbook:~/puppet$ papply
Notice: /Stage[main]//Node[cookbook]/File[/usr/local/bin/backup-
mysql]/ensure: defined content as '{md5}5853b6d4dd72420e341fa7ecb8
91ad43'
Notice: Finished catalog run in 0.09 seconds
```

4. Check that Puppet has correctly inserted the password into the template:

```
ubuntu@cookbook:~/puppet$ cat /usr/local/bin/backup-mysql
#!/bin/sh
/usr/bin/mysqldump -uroot -psecret --all-databases | /bin/gzip > /
backup/mysql/all-databases.sql.gz
```

How it works...

Wherever a variable is referenced in the template, for example

```
<%= @mysql_password %>
```

Puppet will replace it with the corresponding value

```
secret
```

There's more...

In the example, we only used one variable in the template, but you can have as many as you like. These can also be facts:

```
ServerName <%= @fqdn %>
```

or Ruby expressions:

```
MAILTO=<%= @emails.join(',') %>
```

or any Ruby code you want:

```
ServerAdmin <%= @sitedomain == 'coldcomfort.com' ? 'seth@coldcomfort.
com' : 'flora@poste.com' %>
```

See also

▸ *Using GnuPG to encrypt secrets*, in this chapter

Using array iteration in templates

In the previous example we saw that you can use Ruby to interpolate different values in templates depending on the result of an expression. But you're not limited to getting one value at a time. You can put lots of them in a Puppet array and then have the template generate some content for each element of the array, using a loop.

How to do it...

Follow these steps to build an example of iterating over arrays:

1. Modify your `manifests/nodes.pp` file as follows:

   ```
   node 'cookbook' {
     $ipaddresses = ['192.168.0.1',
                     '158.43.128.1',
                     '10.0.75.207' ]

     file { '/tmp/addresslist.txt':
       content => template('admin/addresslist.erb')
     }
   }
   ```

2. Create the file `modules/admin/templates/addresslist.erb` with the following contents:

   ```
   <% @ipaddresses.each do |ip| -%>
   IP address <%= ip %> is present.
   <% end -%>
   ```

3. Run Puppet:

   ```
   ubuntu@cookbook:~/puppet$ papply
   Notice: /Stage[main]//Node[cookbook]/File[/tmp/addresslist.txt]/
   ensure: defined content as '{md5}7ad1264ebdae101bb5ea0afef474b3ed'
   Notice: Finished catalog run in 0.08 seconds
   ```

4. Check the contents of the generated file:

   ```
   ubuntu@cookbook:~/puppet$ cat /tmp/addresslist.txt
   IP address 192.168.0.1 is present.
   IP address 158.43.128.1 is present.
   IP address 10.0.75.207 is present.
   ```

How it works...

In the first line of the template, we reference the array `ipaddresses`, and call its `each` method:

```
<% @ipaddresses.each do |ip| -%>
```

In Ruby, this creates a loop which will execute once for each element of the array. Each time round the loop, the variable `ip` will be set to the value of the current element.

In our example, the `ipaddresses` array contains three elements, so the following line will be executed three times, once for each element:

```
IP address <%= ip %> is present.
```

This will result in three output lines:

```
IP address 192.168.0.1 is present.
IP address 158.43.128.1 is present.
IP address 10.0.75.207 is present.
```

The final line ends the loop:

```
<% end -%>
```

Note that the first and last lines end with `-%>`, instead of just `%>` as we saw before. The effect of the `-` is to suppress the newline that would otherwise be generated on each pass through the loop, giving us unwanted blank lines in the file.

There's more...

Templates can also iterate over hashes, or arrays of hashes:

```
$interfaces = [ {name => 'eth0', ip => '192.168.0.1'},
                {name => 'eth1', ip => '158.43.128.1'},
                {name => 'eth2', ip => '10.0.75.207'} ]

<% @interfaces.each do |interface| -%>
Interface <%= interface['name'] %> has the address <%= interface['ip'] %>.
<% end -%>

Interface eth0 has the address 192.168.0.1.
Interface eth1 has the address 158.43.128.1.
Interface eth2 has the address 10.0.75.207.
```

See also

▶ *Using ERB templates*, in this chapter

Using GnuPG to encrypt secrets

We often need Puppet to have access to secret information, such as passwords or crypto keys, for it to configure systems properly. But how do you avoid putting such secrets directly into your Puppet code, where they're visible to anyone who has read access to your repository?

It's a common requirement for third-party developers and contractors to be able to make changes via Puppet, but they definitely shouldn't see any confidential information. Similarly, if you're using a distributed Puppet setup like that described in *Chapter 1, Puppet Infrastructure*, every machine has a copy of the whole repo, including secrets for other machines that it doesn't need and shouldn't have. How can we prevent this?

One answer is to encrypt the secrets using the GnuPG tool, so that any secret information in the Puppet repo is undecipherable (for all practical purposes) without the appropriate key. Then we distribute the key securely to the people or machines who need it.

Getting ready

First you'll need an encryption key, so follow these steps to generate one. If you already have a GnuPG key that you'd like to use, go on to the next section:

1. Run the following command. Answer the prompts as shown, except to substitute your name and e-mail address for mine. When prompted for a passphrase, just hit **Enter**:

```
ubuntu@cookbook:~/puppet$ gpg --gen-key
gpg (GnuPG) 1.4.11; Copyright (C) 2010 Free Software Foundation,
Inc.
This is free software: you are free to change and redistribute it.
There is NO WARRANTY, to the extent permitted by law.


Please select what kind of key you want:
    (1) RSA and RSA (default)
    (2) DSA and Elgamal
    (3) DSA (sign only)
    (4) RSA (sign only)
Your selection? 1
RSA keys may be between 1024 and 4096 bits long.
What keysize do you want? (2048) 2048
Requested keysize is 2048 bits
Please specify how long the key should be valid.
        0 = key does not expire
```

```
       <n>  = key expires in n days
       <n>w = key expires in n weeks
       <n>m = key expires in n months
       <n>y = key expires in n years
Key is valid for? (0) 0
Key does not expire at all
Is this correct? (y/N) y


You need a user ID to identify your key; the software constructs
the user ID
from the Real Name, Comment and Email Address in this form:
     "Heinrich Heine (Der Dichter) <heinrichh@duesseldorf.de>"


Real name: John Arundel
Email address: john@bitfieldconsulting.com
Comment:
You selected this USER-ID:
     "John Arundel <john@bitfieldconsulting.com>"


Change (N)ame, (C)omment, (E)mail or (O)kay/(Q)uit? o
You need a Passphrase to protect your secret key.
Enter passphrase:

You don't want a passphrase—this is probably a *bad* idea!
I will do it anyway.  You can change your passphrase at any time,
using this program with the option "--edit-key".


..+++++.+++++.........++++++++++
gpg: key 46055037 marked as ultimately trusted
public and secret key created and signed.


gpg: checking the trustdb
gpg: 3 marginal(s) needed, 1 complete(s) needed, PGP trust model
gpg: depth: 0  valid:   1  signed:   0  trust: 0-, 0q, 0n, 0m, 0f,
1u
pub   2048R/46055037 2013-05-06
      Key fingerprint = 8C7C CCF5 C9C9 8F1F 8756  3818 E084 73F2
4605 5037
uid                  John Arundel <john@bitfieldconsulting.com>
sub   2048R/D5B0735B 2013-05-06
```

2. You may see a message like this if your system is not configured with a source of randomness:

```
We need to generate a lot of random bytes. It is a good idea to
perform some other action (type on the keyboard, move the mouse,
utilize the disks) during the prime generation; this gives the
random number generator a better chance to gain enough entropy.
```

```
Not enough random bytes available.  Please do some other work
to give the OS a chance to collect more entropy! (Need 274 more
bytes)
```

3. In this case, run the following command:

```
ubuntu@cookbook:~/puppet$ sudo apt-get install haveged
```

This will install and start the HAVEGE daemon, which helps the system generate random digits required for your key.

How to do it...

With your encryption key installed on the `ubuntu` user's keyring (the key generation process described in the previous section will do this for you), you're ready to set up Puppet to decrypt secrets:

1. Create the following directory:

```
ubuntu@cookbook:~/puppet$ mkdir -p modules/admin/lib/puppet/
parser/functions
```

2. Create the file `modules/admin/lib/puppet/parser/functions/secret.rb` with the following contents:

```
module Puppet::Parser::Functions
  newfunction(:secret, :type => :rvalue) do |args|
    `gpg --no-tty -d #{args[0]}`
  end
end
```

3. Create the file `/home/ubuntu/secret_message` with the following contents:

```
The money is buried under the old oak.
```

4. Encrypt this file with the following command (use the e-mail address you supplied when creating the GnuPG key):

```
ubuntu@cookbook:~/puppet$ gpg -e -r john@bitfieldconsulting.com/
home/ubuntu/secret_message
```

5. Move the resulting encrypted file into your Puppet repo:

```
ubuntu@cookbook:~/puppet$ mv /home/ubuntu/secret_message.gpg
modules/admin/files/
```

6. Remove the original (plaintext) file:

```
ubuntu@cookbook:~/puppet$ rm /home/ubuntu/secret_message
```

7. Modify your `nodes.pp` file as follows:

```
node 'cookbook' {
    $message = secret('/home/ubuntu/puppet/modules/admin/files/
secret_message.gpg')
    notify { "The secret message is: ${message}": }
}
```

8. Run Puppet:

```
ubuntu@cookbook:~/puppet$ papply
```

```
gpg: encrypted with 2048-bit RSA key, ID D5B0735B, created 2013-
05-06
        "John Arundel <john@bitfieldconsulting.com>"
Notice: The secret message is: The money is buried under the old
oak.
```

How it works...

First, we've created a custom function to allow Puppet to decrypt the secret files using GnuPG:

```
module Puppet::Parser::Functions
  newfunction(:secret, :type => :rvalue) do |args|
    `gpg --no-tty -d #{args[0]}`
  end
end
```

The preceding code creates a function named `secret` that takes a file path as argument, and returns the decrypted text. It doesn't manage encryption keys, so you need to ensure that the `ubuntu` user has the necessary key installed. You can check this with:

```
ubuntu@cookbook:~/puppet$ gpg --list-secret-keys

/home/ubuntu/.gnupg/secring.gpg
-----------------------------
sec   2048R/46055037 2013-05-06
uid                  John Arundel <john@bitfieldconsulting.com>
ssb   2048R/D5B0735B 2013-05-06
```

Having set up the `secret` function and the required key, we now encrypt a message to this key:

```
ubuntu@cookbook:~/puppet$ gpg -e -r john@bitfieldconsulting.com /home/
ubuntu/secret_message
```

This creates an encrypted file which can only be read by someone with access to the secret key (or Puppet running on a machine which has the secret key).

We then call the `secret` function to decrypt this file and get the contents:

```
$message = secret('/home/ubuntu/puppet/modules/admin/files/secret_
message.gpg')
```

There's more...

You should use the `secret` function, or something like it, to protect any confidential data in your Puppet repo: passwords, AWS credentials, license keys, even other secret keys such as SSL host keys.

You may decide to use a single key which you push to machines as they're built, perhaps as part of a bootstrap process like that described in the *Bootstrapping Puppet with Rake* recipe in *Chapter 1, Puppet Infrastructure*. For even greater security, you might like to create a new key for each machine, or group of machines, and encrypt a given secret only for the machines that need it.

For example, your web servers might need a certain secret that you don't want to be accessible on any other machine. You could create a key for web servers, and encrypt the data only for this key.

If you want to use encrypted data with Hiera, there is a GnuPG backend for Hiera available:

```
http://www.craigdunn.org/2011/10/secret-variables-in-puppet-with-
hiera-and-gpg/
```

See also

- ▶ The *Importing configuration data with Hiera* recipe in *Chapter 8, External Tools and the Puppet Ecosystem*
- ▶ The *Storing secret data with hiera-gpg recipe* in *Chapter 8, External Tools and the Puppet Ecosystem*

Installing packages from a third-party repository

Most often you will want to install packages from the main distribution repo, so a simple `package` resource will do:

```
package { 'exim4': ensure => installed }
```

Sometimes, though, you need a package which is only found in a third-party repository (an Ubuntu PPA, for example). Or it might be that you need a more recent version of a package than that provided by the distribution, which is available from a third party.

On a manually-administered machine, you would normally do this by adding the repo source configuration to `/etc/apt/sources.list.d` (and, if necessary, a GPG key for the repo) before installing the package. We can automate this process easily with Puppet.

How to do it...

In this example we'll use the popular Percona APT repo (Percona is a MySQL consulting firm who maintain and release their own specialized version of MySQL).

1. Create the file `modules/admin/manifests/percona_repo.pp` with the following contents:

```
# Install Percona APT repo
class admin::percona_repo {
  exec { 'add-percona-apt-key':
    unless  => '/usr/bin/apt-key list |grep percona',
    command => '/usr/bin/gpg --keyserver  hkp://keys.gnupg.net
--recv-keys 1C4CBDCDCD2EFD2A && /usr/bin/gpg -a --export CD2EFD2A
| apt-key add -',
    notify  => Exec['percona-apt-update'],
  }

  exec { 'percona-apt-update':
    command     => '/usr/bin/apt-get update',
    require     => [File['/etc/apt/sources.list.d/percona.list'],
File['/etc/apt/preferences.d/00percona.pref']],
    refreshonly => true,
  }

  file { '/etc/apt/sources.list.d/percona.list':
    content => 'deb http://repo.percona.com/apt precise main',
    notify  => Exec['percona-apt-update'],
  }
```

```
file { '/etc/apt/preferences.d/00percona.pref':
   content => "Package: *\nPin: release o=Percona Development
Team\nPin-Priority: 1001",
   notify  => Exec['percona-apt-update'],
  }
}
```

2. Modify your `manifests/nodes.pp` file as follows:

```
node 'cookbook' {
   include admin::percona_repo

   package { 'percona-server-server-5.5':
     ensure  => installed,
     require => Class['admin::percona_repo'],
   }
}
```

3. Run Puppet:

ubuntu@cookbook:~/puppet$ papply

Notice: /Stage[main]/Admin::Percona_repo/Exec[add-percona-apt-key]/returns: executed successfully

Notice: /Stage[main]/Admin::Percona_repo/File[/etc/apt/sources.list.d/percona.list]/ensure: defined content as '{md5} b8d479374497255804ffbf0a7bcdf6c2'

Notice: /Stage[main]/Admin::Percona_repo/Exec[percona-apt-update]: Triggered 'refresh' from 2 events

Notice: /Stage[main]//Node[cookbook]/Package[percona-server-server-5.5]/ensure: ensure changed 'purged' to 'present'

Notice: Finished catalog run in 55.16 seconds

How it works...

In order to install any Percona package, we need first to have the repository configuration installed on the machine. This is why the `percona-server-server-5.5` package (Percona's version of the standard MySQL server) requires the `admin::percona_repo` class:

```
package { 'percona-server-server-5.5':
  ensure  => installed,
  require => Class['admin::percona_repo'],
}
```

So, what does the `admin::percona_repo` class do?

- ▸ Installs the Percona APT key with which the packages are signed
- ▸ Configures the Percona repo URL as a file in `/etc/apt/sources.list.d`
- ▸ Runs `apt-get update` to retrieve the repo metadata
- ▸ Adds an APT pin configuration in `/etc/apt/preferences.d`

First of all, we install the APT key:

```
exec { 'add-percona-apt-key':
  unless  => '/usr/bin/apt-key list |grep percona',
  command => '/usr/bin/gpg --keyserver  hkp://keys.gnupg.net --recv-
keys 1C4CBDCDCD2EFD2A && /usr/bin/gpg -a --export CD2EFD2A | apt-key
add -',
  notify  => Exec['percona-apt-update'],
}
```

The `unless` parameter checks the output of `apt-key list` to make sure that the Percona key is not already installed, in which case we needn't do anything. Assuming it isn't, the `command` runs:

/usr/bin/gpg --keyserver hkp://keys.gnupg.net --recv-keys 1C4CBDCDCD2EFD2A && /usr/bin/gpg -a --export CD2EFD2A | apt-key add -

This command retrieves the key from the GnuPG keyserver, exports it in the ASCII format, and pipes this into the `apt-key add` command, which adds it to the system keyring. You can use a similar pattern for most third-party repos which require an APT signing key.

Having installed the key, we add the repo configuration:

```
file { '/etc/apt/sources.list.d/percona.list':
  content => 'deb http://repo.percona.com/apt precise main',
  notify  => Exec['percona-apt-update'],
}
```

and then run `apt-get update` to update the system APT cache with the metadata from the new repo:

```
exec { 'percona-apt-update':
  command    => '/usr/bin/apt-get update',
  require    => [File['/etc/apt/sources.list.d/percona.list'],
File['/etc/apt/preferences.d/00percona.pref']],
  refreshonly => true,
}
```

Finally, we configure the APT pin priority for the repo:

```
file { '/etc/apt/preferences.d/00percona.pref':
  content => "Package: *\nPin: release o=Percona Development Team\
nPin-Priority: 1001",
  notify  => Exec['percona-apt-update'],
}
```

This ensures that packages installed from the Percona repo will never be superseded by packages from somewhere else (the main Ubuntu distro, for example). Otherwise you could end up with broken dependencies and be unable to install the Percona packages automatically.

There's more...

The APT package framework is specific to the Debian and Ubuntu systems, which as we've said is our reference platform for the book. If you're on a Red Hat or CentOS-based system, you can use the `yumrepo` resources to manage RPM repositories directly:

http://docs.puppetlabs.com/references/latest/type.html#yumrepo

See also

▸   The *Distributing directory trees* recipe in *Chapter 5, Users and Virtual Resources*

Building packages automatically from source

Packages aren't always available, or convenient to create, for the software you need to manage with Puppet. A source install (downloading the program source files and compiling them on the target machine) is sometimes the only way to get what you need.

If you have to build a program from source, Puppet can help with this process. The general procedure is to automate the following steps:

1.   Download the source tarball
2.   Unpack the tarball
3.   Configure and build the program
4.   Install the program

How to do it...

In this example we'll build the popular load testing tool Httperf (there's no need to do this for production, as there's a distro package available in Ubuntu, but it's a pretty straightforward example of a source install):

1. Modify your `manifests/nodes.pp file` as follows:

```
node 'cookbook' {
  exec { 'install-httperf':
    cwd      => '/root',
    command => '/usr/bin/wget https://httperf.googlecode.com/
files/httperf-0.9.0.tar.gz && /bin/tar xvzf httperf-0.9.0.tar.gz
&& cd httperf-0.9.0 && ./configure && make all && make install',
    creates => '/usr/local/bin/httperf',
    timeout => 0,
  }
}
```

2. Run Puppet (it may take a while):

ubuntu@cookbook:~/puppet$ papply

Notice: /Stage[main]//Node[cookbook]/Exec[install-httperf]/ returns: executed successfully

Notice: Finished catalog run in 147.51 seconds

How it works...

First, we check whether Httperf has already been installed, by looking for the `httperf` executable with `creates`:

```
creates    => '/usr/local/sbin/httperf',
```

Assuming this isn't present, we execute the installation command, which is in five separate stages, delimited by the `&&` operators. This means that should any subcommand fail, the whole command will stop and fail. It's a useful construct for making sure each subcommand has succeeded before going on to the next.

The first stage downloads the source tarball:

```
/usr/bin/wget https://httperf.googlecode.com/files/httperf-0.9.0.tar.
gz
```

The second stage unpacks it:

```
/bin/tar xvzf httperf-0.9.0.tar.gz
```

The third stage changes working directory to the source tree:

```
cd httperf-0.9.0
```

The fourth stage runs the `configure` script (this is usually where you will need to specify any options or customizations):

```
./configure
```

The final stage builds and installs the software:

```
make all && make install
```

Because the compilation process may take a while, we set a zero `timeout` parameter (Puppet times out `exec` commands after 5 minutes by default):

```
timeout => 0,
```

There's more...

If you have to build quite a few packages from source, it may be worth converting the preceding recipe into a definition, so that you can use more or less the same code to build each package.

For maximum control and flexibility, you can build packages yourself and distribute them to machines from a local APT repository. This can also be a cache server for the main distribution repo (Ubuntu, for example), which may speed up package operations significantly and reduce bandwidth costs, especially if you're managing a large number of machines.

See also

▸ The *Using definitions* recipe in *Chapter 3, Writing Better Manifests*

Comparing package versions

Package version numbers are odd things. They look like decimal numbers, but they're not: a version number is often in the form `2.6.4`, for example. If you need to compare one version number with another, you can't do a straightforward string comparison: `2.6.4` would be interpreted as greater than `2.6.12`. And a numeric comparison won't work because they're not valid numbers.

Puppet's `versioncmp` function comes to the rescue. If you pass two things that look like version numbers, it will compare them and return a value indicating which is the greater:

```
versioncmp( A, B )
```

returns:

- 0 if A and B are equal
- Greater than 1 if A is higher than B
- Less than 0 if A is less than B

How to do it...

Here's an example using the `versioncmp` function:

1. Modify your `manifests/nodes.pp` file as follows:

```
node 'cookbook' {
  $app_version = '1.2.2'
  $min_version = '1.2.10'

  if versioncmp($app_version, $min_version) >= 0 {
    notify { 'Version OK': }
  } else {
    notify { 'Upgrade needed': }
  }
}
```

2. Run Puppet:

    ubuntu@cookbook:~/puppet$ papply

    Notice: Upgrade needed

3. Now change the value of `$app_version`:

    ```
    $app_version = '1.2.14'
    ```

4. Run Puppet again:

    ubuntu@cookbook:~/puppet$ papply

    Notice: Version OK

How it works...

We've specified that the minimum acceptable version (`$min_version`) is `1.2.10`. So in the first example, we want to compare it with `$app_version` of `1.2.2`. A simple alphabetic comparison of these two strings (in Ruby, for example) would give the wrong result, but `versioncmp` correctly determines that `1.2.2` is less than `1.2.10` and alerts us that we need to upgrade.

In the second example, `$app_version` is now `1.2.14` which `versioncmp` correctly recognizes as greater than `$min_version` and so we get the message **Version OK**.

5
Users and Virtual Resources

There are no big problems, there are just a lot of little problems.

—Henry Ford

In this chapter we will cover:

- ▶ Using virtual resources
- ▶ Managing users with virtual resources
- ▶ Managing users' SSH access
- ▶ Managing users' customization files
- ▶ Efficiently distributing cron jobs
- ▶ Using schedules to limit when resources can be applied
- ▶ Using host resources
- ▶ Using multiple file sources
- ▶ Distributing directory trees
- ▶ Cleaning up old files
- ▶ Auditing resources
- ▶ Temporarily disabling resources

Introduction

Users can be a real pain. I don't mean the people, though doubtless that's sometimes true. But keeping UNIX user accounts and file permissions in sync across a network of machines, some of them running different operating systems, can be very challenging without some kind of centralized configuration management.

So a new developer joins the organization and needs an account on every machine, along with `sudo` privileges and group memberships, and needs her SSH key authorized for a bunch of different accounts? The sysadmin who has to take care of this manually will be at the job all day. The sysadmin who uses Puppet will be done in minutes, and heading out for an early lunch.

In this chapter we'll look at some handy patterns and techniques for managing users and their associated resources. Users are also one of the most common applications for virtual resources, so we'll find out all about those. We'll also see how to schedule resources in Puppet, how to spread cron jobs around the clock for efficiency, how to handle `/etc/hosts` entries, and how to have Puppet collect audit data so you know when someone's messing with your machines.

Using virtual resources

Virtual resources in Puppet might seem complicated and confusing, but in fact they're very simple. They're exactly like regular resources, but they don't actually take effect until they're realized (in the sense of "made real"). Whereas a regular resource can only be declared once per node (so two classes can't declare the same resource, for example), a virtual resource can be realized as many times as you like.

This comes in handy when you need to move applications and services around between machines. If two applications that use the same resource end up sharing a machine, they would cause a conflict unless you make the resource virtual.

To clarify this, let's look at a typical situation where virtual resources might come in useful.

You are responsible for two popular web applications, FaceSquare and Flipr. Both are web apps running on Apache, so they both require the Apache package to be installed. The definition for FaceSquare might look something like the following:

```
class app::facesquare {
  package { 'apache2-mpm-worker': ensure => installed }
  ...
}
```

The definition for Flipr might look like this:

```
class app::flipr {
  package { 'apache2-mpm-worker': ensure => installed }
  ...
}
```

All is well until you need to consolidate both apps onto a single server:

```
node 'bigbox' {
  include app::facesquare
  include app::flipr
}
```

Now Puppet will complain because you tried to define two resources with the same name: `apache2-mpm-worker`.

Error: Duplicate declaration: Package[apache2-mpm-worker] is already declared in file /home/ubuntu/puppet/modules/app/manifests/facesquare.pp at line 2; cannot redeclare on node cookbook.compute-1.internal

Error: Duplicate declaration: Package[apache2-mpm-worker] is already declared in file /home/ubuntu/puppet/modules/app/manifests/facesquare.pp at line 2; cannot redeclare on node cookbook.compute-1.internal

You could remove the duplicate package definition from one of the classes, but then it would fail if you tried to include the app class on another server that didn't already have Apache.

You can get round this problem by putting the Apache package in its own class and then using `include apache` everywhere it's needed; Puppet doesn't mind you including the same class multiple times. But this has the disadvantage that every potentially conflicting resource must have its own class.

Virtual resources to the rescue. A virtual resource is just like a normal resource, except that it starts with an @ character:

```
@package { 'apache2-mpm-worker': ensure => installed }
```

You can think of it as being like an **FYI** resource: Puppet, I'm just giving you a description of this resource, and I don't actually want you to do anything with it yet. Puppet will read and remember virtual resource definitions, but won't actually create the resource until you say so.

To create the resource, use the `realize` function:

```
realize(Package['apache2-mpm-worker'])
```

You can call `realize` as many times as you want on the resource and it won't result in a conflict. So virtual resources are the way to go when several different classes all require the same resource and they may need to co-exist on the same node.

How to do it...

Here's how to build the example using virtual resources:

1. Run the following command:

   ```
   ubuntu@cookbook:~/puppet$ mkdir -p modules/app/manifests
   ```

2. Create the file `modules/app/manifests/facesquare.pp` with the following contents:

   ```
   class app::facesquare {
     include admin::virtual
     realize(Package['apache2-mpm-worker'])
   }
   ```

3. Create the file `modules/app/manifests/flipr.pp` with the following contents:

   ```
   class app::flipr {
     include admin::virtual
     realize(Package['apache2-mpm-worker'])
   }
   ```

4. Create the file `modules/admin/manifests/virtual.pp` with the following contents:

   ```
   class admin::virtual {
     @package { 'apache2-mpm-worker': ensure => installed }
   }
   ```

5. Modify your `manifests/nodes.pp` file as follows:

   ```
   node 'cookbook' {
     include app::facesquare
     include app::flipr
   }
   ```

6. Run Puppet:

   ```
   ubuntu@cookbook:~/puppet$ papply
   Notice: /Stage[main]/Admin::Virtual/Package[apache2-mpm-worker]/
   ensure: ensure changed 'purged' to 'present'
   Notice: Finished catalog run in 7.86 seconds
   ```

How it works...

You define the package as a virtual resource in one place, the `admin::virtual` class. All nodes can include this class and you can put all your virtual packages in it. None of them will actually be installed on a node until you call `realize`.

```
class admin::virtual {
  @package { 'apache2-mpm-worker': ensure => installed }
}
```

Every class that needs the Apache package can call `realize` on this virtual resource:

```
class app::flipr {
  include admin::virtual
  realize(Package['apache2-mpm-worker'])
}
```

Puppet knows, because you made the resource virtual, that you intended multiple references to the same package, and didn't just accidentally create two resources with the same name. So it does the right thing.

There's more...

To realize virtual resources you can also use the collection syntax:

```
Package <| title = "apache2-mpm-worker" |>
```

The advantage of this syntax is that you're not restricted to the resource name; you could also use a tag, for example:

```
Package <| tag = "security" |>
```

Or you can just specify all instances of the resource type, by leaving the query section blank:

```
Package <| |>
```

Managing users with virtual resources

Users are a great example of a resource which may need to be realized by multiple classes. Consider the following situation. To simplify administration of a large number of machines, you have defined classes for two kinds of users: `developers` and `sysadmins`. All machines need to include `sysadmins`, but only some machines need `developer` access.

```
node 'server' {
  include user::sysadmins
}

node 'webserver' inherits 'server' {
  include user::developers
}
```

But some users may be members of both groups. If each group simply declares its members as regular `user` resources, this will lead to a conflict when a node includes both `developers` and `sysadmins`, as in the `webserver` example.

To avoid this conflict, a common pattern is to make all users virtual resources, defined in a single class `user::virtual` that every machine includes, and then realizing the users where they are needed. This way, there will be no conflict if a user is a member of multiple groups.

How to do it...

Follow these steps to create a `user::virtual` class:

1. Run the following command:

   ```
   ubuntu@cookbook:~/puppet$ mkdir -p modules/user/manifests
   ```

2. Create the file `modules/user/manifests/virtual.pp` with the following contents:

   ```
   class user::virtual {
     @user { 'nirmala': ensure => present }
     @user { 'sarah': ensure => present }
     @user { 'jeff': ensure => present }
     @user { 'ayomide': ensure => present }
   }
   ```

3. Create the file `modules/user/manifests/developers.pp` with the following contents:

   ```
   class user::developers {
     realize(User['nirmala'])
     realize(User['jeff'])
   }
   ```

4. Create the file `modules/user/manifests/sysadmins.pp` with the following contents:

   ```
   class user::sysadmins {
     realize(User['nirmala'])
     realize(User['sarah'])
   }
   ```

5. Modify your `nodes.pp` file as follows:

   ```
   node 'cookbook' {
     include user::virtual
     include user::sysadmins
     include user::developers
   }
   ```

6. Run Puppet:

```
ubuntu@cookbook:~/puppet$ papply
Notice: /Stage[main]/User::Virtual/User[nirmala]/ensure: created
Notice: /Stage[main]/User::Virtual/User[jeff]/ensure: created
Notice: /Stage[main]/User::Virtual/User[sarah]/ensure: created
Notice: Finished catalog run in 1.02 seconds
```

How it works...

When we include the `user::virtual` class, all the users are declared as virtual resources (because we included the @ symbol):

```
@user { 'nirmala': ensure => present }
@user { 'sarah': ensure => present }
@user { 'jeff': ensure => present }
@user { 'ayomide': ensure => present }
```

That is to say, the resources exist in Puppet's catalog; they can be referred to by and linked with other resources, and they are in every respect identical to regular resources, except that Puppet doesn't actually create the corresponding users on the machine.

In order for that to happen, we need to call `realize` on the virtual resources. When we include the `user::sysadmins` class, we get the following code:

```
realize(User['nirmala'])
realize(User['sarah'])
```

Calling `realize` on a virtual resource tells Puppet, "OK, go ahead and create the user now. This is what it does, as we can see from the run output:

```
Notice: /Stage[main]/User::Virtual/User[nirmala]/ensure: created
```

But Nirmala is in both the `developers` and the `sysadmins` class! Won't that mean we end up calling `realize` twice on the same resource?

```
realize(User['nirmala'])
...
realize(User['nirmala'])
```

Yes, it does, and that's fine. You're explicitly allowed to realize resources multiple times, and there will be no conflict. So long as some class, somewhere, calls `realize` on Nirmala's account, it will be created. If not, it won't.

Notice that the `ayomide` user wasn't created in our example. Although we declared it as a virtual resource in `user::virtual` along with the others, no class we include actually realizes `ayomide`, so it remains a virtual resource and Puppet doesn't create it on the machine.

There's more...

When you use this pattern to manage your own users, every node should include the `user::virtual` class, as a part of your basic housekeeping configuration. This class will declare all users (as virtual) in your organization or site. This should also include any users who exist only to run applications or services (such as `Apache`, `www-data`, or `deploy`, for example). Then you can realize them as needed on individual nodes or in specific classes.

For production use, you'll probably also want to specify a UID and GID for each user or group, so that these numeric identifiers are synchronized across your network. You can do this using the `uid` and `gid` parameters for the `user` resource. If you don't specify a user's UID, for example, you'll just get whatever is the next ID number available on a given machine, so the same user on different machines will have a different UID. This can lead to permission problems when using shared storage, or moving files around between machines.

See also

 ▸ *Using virtual resources*, in this chapter
 ▸ *Managing users' customization files*, in this chapter

Managing users' SSH access

A sensible approach to access control for servers is to use named user accounts with passphrase-protected SSH keys, rather than having users share an account with a widely known password. Puppet makes this easy to manage thanks to the built-in `ssh_authorized_key` type.

To combine this with virtual users, as described in the previous section, you can create `define` which includes both the `user` and `ssh_authorized_key`. This will also come in useful for adding customization files and other per-user resources.

How to do it...

Follow these steps to extend your virtual users class to include SSH access:

1. Modify your `modules/user/manifests/virtual.pp` file as follows (if you haven't created this yet, work through the *Managing users with virtual resources* section first):

```
class user::virtual {
  define ssh_user($key) {
    user { $name:
      ensure     => present,
      managehome => true,
```

```
    }

    file { "/home/${name}/.ssh":
      ensure => directory,
      mode   => '0700',
      owner  => $name,
    }

    ssh_authorized_key { "${name}_key":
      key     => $key,
      type    => 'ssh-rsa',
      user    => $name,
      require => File["/home/${name}/.ssh"],
    }
  }

  @ssh_user { 'aliza':
    key => 'AAAAB3NzaC1yc2EAAAABIwAAAIEA3ATqENg+GWACa
2BzeqTdGnJhNoBer8x6pfWkzNzeM8Zx7/2Tf2pl7kHdbsiTXEUawq
zXZQtZzt/j3Oya+PZjcRpWNRzprSmd2UxEEPTqDw9LqY5S2B8og/
NyzWaIYPsKoatcgC7VgYHplcTbzEhGu8BsoEVBGYu3IRy5RkAcZik=',
  }
}
```

2. Modify your `modules/user/manifests/sysadmins.pp` file as follows:

```
class user::sysadmins {
  search User::Virtual

  realize(Ssh_user['aliza'])
}
```

3. Modify your `manifests/nodes.pp` file as follows:

```
node 'cookbook' {
  include user::virtual
  include user::sysadmins
}
```

4. Run Puppet:

ubuntu@cookbook:~/puppet$ papply

**Notice: /Stage[main]/User::Virtual/User::Virtual::Ssh_user[aliza]/
User[aliza]/ensure: created**

**Notice: /Stage[main]/User::Virtual/User::Virtual::Ssh_user[aliza]/
File[/home/aliza/.ssh]/ensure: created**

**Notice: /Stage[main]/User::Virtual/User::Virtual::Ssh_user[aliza]/
Ssh_authorized_key[aliza_key]/ensure: created**

Notice: Finished catalog run in 0.29 seconds

How it works...

For each user in our `user::virtual` class, we need to create:

▶ The user account itself

▶ The user's home directory and `.ssh` directory

▶ The user's `.ssh/authorized_keys` file

We could declare separate resources to implement all of these for each user, but it's much easier to create a definition instead which wraps them into a single resource:

```
define ssh_user($key) {
  user { $name:
    ensure      => present,
    managehome => true,
  }

  file { "/home/${name}/.ssh":
    ensure => directory,
    mode   => '0700',
    owner  => $name,
  }

  ssh_authorized_key { "${name}_key":
    key     => $key,
    type    => 'ssh-rsa',
    user    => $name,
    require => File["/home/${name}/.ssh"],
  }
}
```

You can see that the user account is implemented by the `user` resource. The user's home directory is created by the user's `managehome` parameter, which if `true` causes Puppet to create the directory `/home/${name}`.

Finally, the `authorized_keys` file will be created by the `ssh_authorized_key` resource. All we need to pass in is the value for `key`. Here's where we do that while declaring the `aliza` user (as virtual, thanks to the `@` prefix):

```
@ssh_user { 'aliza':
  key => 'AAAAB3NzaC1yc2EAAAABIwAAAIEA3ATqENg+GWACa2
BzeqTdGnJhNoBer8x6pfWkzNzeM8Zx7/2Tf2pl7kHdbsiTXEUawq
zXZQtZzt/j3Oya+PZjcRpWNRzprSmd2UxEEPTqDw9LqY5S2B8og/
NyzWaIYPsKoatcgC7VgYHplcTbzEhGu8BsoEVBGYu3IRy5RkAcZik=',
}
```

Now, everything's set. We just need to call `realize` on `aliza` for all these resources to take effect:

```
realize(Ssh_user['aliza'])
```

Notice that this time the virtual resource we're realizing is not simply the `user` resource, as before, but the `ssh_user` definition we created, which includes the user and the related resources needed to set up SSH access:

```
Notice: /Stage[main]/User::Virtual/User::Virtual::Ssh_user[aliza]/
User[aliza]/ensure: created

Notice: /Stage[main]/User::Virtual/User::Virtual::Ssh_user[aliza]/File[/
home/aliza/.ssh]/ensure: created

Notice: /Stage[main]/User::Virtual/User::Virtual::Ssh_user[aliza]/Ssh_
authorized_key[aliza_key]/ensure: created
```

> What's the search `User::Virtual` syntax? As you know, we normally refer to definitions and classes using their full namespace path, in this case, we would need to refer to `Ssh_user` as `User::Virtual::Ssh_user` (module `User`, class `Virtual`, definition `Ssh_user`).
>
> To save ourselves a lot of typing, we can tell Puppet to search the `User::Virtual` namespace for names we mention thereafter. That's what the `search` keyword does. You can use this wherever you would otherwise have to specify an unwieldy namespace path for a resource.

There's more...

Of course you can add whatever resources you like to the `ssh_user` definition, to have Puppet automatically create them for new users. We'll see an example of this in the next section, *Managing users' customization files*.

Managing users' customization files

Users, like cats, often feel the need to mark their territory. Unlike most cats, though, users tend to customize their shell environments, terminal colors, aliases, and so forth. This is usually achieved by a number of **dotfiles** in their home directory, for example, `.bash_profile` or `.emacs`.

You can use Puppet to synchronize and update each user's dotfiles across a number of machines by extending the virtual user setup we've developed throughout this chapter.

How to do it...

Here's what you need to do:

1. Modify the `modules/user/manifests/virtual.pp` file as follows:

```
class user::virtual {
  define user_dotfile($user) {
    $source = regsubst($name, "^/home/${user}/.(.*)$", "puppet:///
modules/user/${user}-\\1")
    file { $name:
      source => $source,
      owner  => $user,
      group  => $user,
    }
  }

  define ssh_user($key,$dotfile='') {
    user { $name:
      ensure     => present,
      managehome => true,
      shell      => '/bin/bash',
    }

    file { "/home/${name}/.ssh":
      ensure => directory,
      mode   => '0700',
      owner  => $name,
    }

    ssh_authorized_key { "${name}_key":
      key     => $key,
      type    => 'ssh-rsa',
      user    => $name,
      require => File["/home/${name}/.ssh"],
    }

    if $dotfile {
      $filepath = regsubst($dotfile,'^(.*)$',"/home/${name}/.\\0",
'G')
      user_dotfile { $filepath:
        user => $name,
      }
    }
  }
```

```
    }

  @ssh_user { 'jamil':
    key    => 'xyz',
    dotfile => ['bashrc','vimrc'],
  }

  @ssh_user { 'scarlet':
    key    => 'abc',
    dotfile => ['rvmrc','emacs'],
  }
}
```

2. Modify the file `modules/user/manifests/sysadmins.pp` as follows:

```
class user::sysadmins {
  search User::Virtual

  realize(Ssh_user['jamil'])
  realize(Ssh_user['scarlet'])
}
```

3. Run the following command:

ubuntu@cookbook:~/puppet$ mkdir -p modules/user/files

4. Create the file `modules/user/files/jamil-bashrc` with the following contents:

```
echo Hello, world.
```

5. Create the file `modules/user/files/jamil-vimrc` with the following contents:

```
syn on
```

6. Create the file `modules/user/files/scarlet-rvmrc` with the following contents:

```
rvm use 1.9.3
```

7. Create the file `modules/user/files/scarlet-emacs` with the following contents:

```
(setq inhibit-startup-screen t)
```

8. Make sure your `manifests/nodes.pp` file reads as follows:

```
node 'cookbook' {
  include user::virtual
  include user::sysadmins
}
```

9. Run Puppet:

```
ubuntu@cookbook:~/puppet$ papply
Notice: /Stage[main]/User::Virtual/User::Virtual::Ssh_
user[scarlet]/User[scarlet]/ensure: created
Notice: /Stage[main]/User::Virtual/User::Virtual::Ssh_
user[scarlet]/File[/home/scarlet/.ssh]/ensure: created
Notice: /Stage[main]/User::Virtual/User::Virtual::Ssh_
user[scarlet]/User::Virtual::User_dotfile[/home/scarlet/.rvmrc]/
File[/home/scarlet/.rvmrc]/ensure: defined content as '{md5}393765
cc540ad44696266bec1ae38b5a'
Notice: /Stage[main]/User::Virtual/User::Virtual::Ssh_
user[scarlet]/User::Virtual::User_dotfile[/home/scarlet/.emacs]/
File[/home/scarlet/.emacs]/ensure: defined content as '{md5}
fadb5fcf67fae2377c8d4e6e92344e0c'
Notice: /Stage[main]/User::Virtual/User::Virtual::Ssh_
user[scarlet]/Ssh_authorized_key[scarlet_key]/ensure: created
Notice: /Stage[main]/User::Virtual/User::Virtual::Ssh_user[jamil]/
User[jamil]/ensure: created
Notice: /Stage[main]/User::Virtual/User::Virtual::Ssh_user[jamil]/
File[/home/jamil/.ssh]/ensure: created
Notice: /Stage[main]/User::Virtual/User::Virtual::Ssh_user[jamil]/
Ssh_authorized_key[jamil_key]/ensure: created
Notice: /Stage[main]/User::Virtual/User::Virtual::Ssh_user[jamil]/
User::Virtual::User_dotfile[/home/jamil/.bashrc]/File[/home/
jamil/.bashrc]/content: content changed '{md5}8da3d6b1fdbdfe97c6be
8adadce98172' to '{md5}300f56a869ff41ce0ca7a36cd64df1a3'
Notice: /Stage[main]/User::Virtual/User::Virtual::Ssh_user[jamil]/
User::Virtual::User_dotfile[/home/jamil/.bashrc]/File[/home/
jamil/.bashrc]/mode: mode changed '0644' to '0664'
Notice: /Stage[main]/User::Virtual/User::Virtual::Ssh_
user[jamil]/User::Virtual::User_dotfile[/home/jamil/.vimrc]/
File[/home/jamil/.vimrc]/ensure: defined content as '{md5}
cb1778d0e1588852145eaece9a86c239'
Notice: Finished catalog run in 0.87 seconds
```

How it works...

We've added a new user_dotfile definition:

```
define user_dotfile($user) {
  $source = regsubst($name, "^/home/${user}/.(.*)$", "puppet:///
modules/user/${user}-\\1")
  file { $name:
```

```
      source => $source,
      owner  => $user,
      group  => $user,
    }
  }
```

This takes a full path to a user's dotfile as the `$name` parameter, and the appropriate username as `$user`. For example, we might call this definition as follows:

```
user_dotfile { '/home/john/.muttrc':
  user => 'john',
}
```

This will look for a file named `modules/user/files/john-muttrc` and deploy it to the node as `/home/john/.muttrc`. Here's how that works.

```
$source = regsubst($name, "^/home/${user}/.(.*)$", "puppet:///modules/
user/${user}-\\1")
```

This nasty-looking `regsubst` call takes the dotfile path (`/home/john/.muttrc` in our example) and transforms it into the source parameter Puppet needs to find the file (`modules/user/files/john-muttrc`). For more information about `regsubst`, see the *Using regular expression substitutions* section in *Chapter 2, Puppet Language and Style*.

So, how do we specify dotfiles for individual users?

```
@ssh_user { 'jamil':
  key     => 'xyz',
  dotfile => ['bashrc','vimrc'],
}
```

We've passed in an array of strings to the `dotfile` parameter of our `ssh_user` definition. Here's where that gets expanded into resource declarations:

```
if $dotfile {
  $filepath = regsubst($dotfile,'^(.*)$',"/home/${name}/.\\0", 'G')
  user_dotfile { $filepath:
    user => $name,
  }
}
```

So, if a value is passed in for `dotfile`, we first of all transform it into the full path for dotfile (`bashrc` becomes `/home/jamil/.bashrc`) using `regsubst`. Then we declare an instance of `user_dotfile`:

```
user_dotfile { '/home/jamil/.bashrc':
  user => 'jamil',
}
```

Why do we need these strange `regsubst` calls? Couldn't we just pass in the name of the dotfile and the name of the user? The answer is complicated, but has to do with the way Puppet handles arrays of resources. Each resource title must be unique, so the name of the dotfile resource must include at least the username and the filename. We might try to interpolate these in a string, as follows:

```
user_dotfile { "${name}-${dotfile}": }
```

But this fails when `$dotfile` is an array. When you reference an array variable in a string context, Puppet simply concatenates all the array elements together, and we'd end up with:

```
user_dotfile { 'jamil-bashrcvimrc': }
```

which clearly isn't what we want. We wanted Puppet to declare two resources, one for Jamil's `.bashrc` and one for his `.vimrc`. To do that, we have to go via this slightly weird route, to transform the string before referring to it in a resource context.

If this doesn't make much sense to you, don't worry; it really doesn't matter. The important thing is that a trick like this lets us declare multiple `user_dotfile` resources from an array of names, which otherwise we wouldn't be able to do. The way Puppet handles arrays may change in the future to make this unnecessary, but for now we need this workaround.

See also

▶ *Managing users with virtual resources*, in this chapter

Efficiently distributing cron jobs

When you have many servers executing the same cron job, it's usually a good idea not to run them all at the same time. If the jobs all access a common server (for example, when running backups), it may put too much load on that server, and even if they don't, all the servers will be busy at the same time, which may affect their capacity to provide other services.

As usual, Puppet can help; this time using the `inline_template` function to calculate a unique time for each job.

How to do it...

Here's how to have Puppet schedule the same job at a different time for each machine:

1. Modify your `manifests/nodes.pp` file as follows:

```
node 'cookbook' {
  cron { 'run-backup':
    ensure  => present,
    command => '/usr/local/bin/backup',
    hour    => inline_template('<%= @hostname.sum % 24 %>'),
    minute  => '00',
  }
}
```

2. Run Puppet:

```
ubuntu@cookbook:~/puppet$ papply
```

Notice: /Stage[main]//Node[cookbook]/Cron[run-backup]/ensure: created

Notice: Finished catalog run in 0.24 seconds

3. Check the cron tab to see how the job has been configured:

```
ubuntu@cookbook:~/puppet$ sudo crontab -l
```

 # HEADER: This file was autogenerated at Mon May 20 17:14:51 +0000 2013 by puppet.

 # HEADER: While it can still be managed manually, it is definitely not recommended.

 # HEADER: Note particularly that the comments starting with 'Puppet Name' should

 # HEADER: not be deleted, as doing so could cause duplicate cron jobs.

 # Puppet Name: run-backup

0 15 * * * /usr/local/bin/backup

How it works...

We want to choose a random hour for each cron job; that is, not genuinely random (or it would change every time Puppet runs), but simply different for each host (or as widely distributed across the day as possible).

We can do this by using Ruby's `sum` method which computes a numerical value from a string which is unique to the machine (in this case, the machine's hostname). The value will be the same each time, so although the value looks random, it will not change when Puppet runs again.

sum will generate a large integer (in the case of the string cookbook, the sum is 855), and we want values for hour between 0 and 23, so we use Ruby's % (modulo) operator to restrict the result to this range. We should get a reasonably good (though not statistically uniform) distribution of values, depending on your hostnames.

If all your machines have the same name (it does happen) don't expect this trick to work! In this case, you can use some other string which is unique to the machine, such as ipaddress.

There's more...

If you have several cron jobs per machine and you want to run them a certain number of hours apart, add this number to the hostname.sum resource before taking the modulus. Let's say we want to run the dump_database job at some arbitrary time and the run_backup job an hour later.

```
cron { 'dump-database':
  ensure  => present,
  command => '/usr/local/bin/dump_database',
  hour    => inline_template('<%= @hostname.sum % 24 %>'),
  minute  => '00',
}

cron { 'run-backup':
  ensure  => present,
  command => '/usr/local/bin/backup',
  hour    => inline_template('<%= ( @hostname.sum + 1) % 24 %>'),
  minute  => '00',
}
```

The two jobs will end up with different hour values for each machine Puppet runs on, but run_backup will always be one hour after dump_database.

See also

▶ The *Running Puppet from cron* recipe in *Chapter 1, Puppet Infrastructure*

Using schedules to limit when resources can be applied

So far, we've looked at what Puppet can do, and the order that it does things in, but not when it does them. One way to control this is to use the `schedule` metaparameter (a parameter you can apply to any type of resource).

When you need to limit the number of times a resource is applied within a specified period, `schedule` can help. For example:

```
exec { "/usr/bin/apt-get update":
    schedule => daily,
}
```

The most important thing to understand about `schedule` is that it can only stop a resource being applied. It doesn't guarantee that the resource will be applied with a certain frequency. For example, the `exec` resource shown above has `schedule => daily`, but this just represents an upper limit on the number of times the `exec` resource can run per day. It won't be applied more than once a day. If you don't run Puppet at all, the resource won't be applied at all.

That being so, `schedule` is best used to *restrict* resources from running when they shouldn't, or don't need to; for example, you might want to make sure that `apt-get update` isn't run more than once an hour. There are some built-in schedules available for you to use:

- ▶ `hourly`
- ▶ `daily`
- ▶ `weekly`
- ▶ `monthly`
- ▶ `never`

However, you can modify these and create your own custom schedules, using `schedule` resources. We'll see how to do this in the following example. Let's say we want to make sure that an `exec` resource representing a maintenance job won't run during office hours, when it might interfere with production.

How to do it...

In this example, we'll create a custom `schedule` and assign this to the resource:

1. Modify your manifests/nodes.pp file as follows:

```
node 'cookbook' {
  schedule { 'outside-office-hours':
    period => daily,
    range  => ['17:00-23:59','00:00-09:00'],
    repeat => 1,
  }

  exec { '/bin/echo Doing some maintenance':
    schedule => 'outside-office-hours',
  }
}
```

2. Run Puppet. What you'll see will depend on the time of day. If it's currently outside the office hours period you've defined, Puppet will apply the resource:

    `ubuntu@cookbook:~/puppet$ papply`

    `Notice: /Stage[main]//Node[cookbook]/Exec[/bin/echo Doing some maintenance]/returns: executed successfully`

    `Notice: Finished catalog run in 0.36 seconds`

3. If the time is within the office hours period, Puppet will do nothing:

    `ubuntu@cookbook:~/puppet$ papply`

    `Notice: Finished catalog run in 0.11 seconds`

How it works...

A schedule consists of three bits of information:

-   The `period` (`hourly`, `daily`, `weekly`, or `monthly`)
-   The `range` (defaults to the whole period, but can be a smaller part of it)
-   The `repeat` count (how often the resource is allowed to be applied within the range)

Our custom schedule named `outside-office-hours` supplies these three parameters:

```
schedule { 'outside-office-hours':
  period => daily,
  range  => ['17:00-23:59','00:00-09:00'],
  repeat => 1,
}
```

The `period` is `daily`, and the `range` is defined as an array of two time intervals:

```
17:00-23:59
00:00-09:00
```

The schedule named `outside-office-hours` is now available for us to use with any resource, just as though it were built into Puppet like the `daily` or `hourly` schedules. In our example, we assign this schedule to the `exec` resource using the `schedule` metaparameter:

```
exec { '/bin/echo Doing some maintenance':
  schedule => 'outside-office-hours',
}
```

Without this `schedule` parameter, the resource would be applied every time Puppet runs. With it, Puppet will check the following to decide whether or not to apply the resource:

- ▸ Whether the time is in the permitted range
- ▸ Whether the resource has already been run the maximum permitted number of times in this period

For example, let's consider what happens if Puppet runs at 4 p.m., 5 p.m., and 6 p.m. on a given day:

- ▸ 4 p.m.: It's outside the permitted time range, so Puppet will do nothing
- ▸ 5 p.m.: It's inside the permitted time range, and the resource hasn't been run yet in this period, so Puppet will apply the resource
- ▸ 6 p.m.: It's inside the permitted time range, but the resource has already been run the maximum number of times in this period, so Puppet will do nothing.

And so on until the next day.

There's more...

The `repeat` parameter governs how many times the resource will be applied given the other constraints of the schedule. For example, to apply a resource no more than six times an hour, use a schedule as follows:

```
period => hourly,
repeat => 6,
```

Remember that this won't guarantee that the job is run six times an hour. It just sets an upper limit; no matter how often Puppet runs or anything else happens, the job won't be run if it has already run six times this hour. If Puppet only runs once a day, the job will just be run once. So `schedule` is best used for making sure things don't happen at certain times (or don't exceed a given frequency).

Using host resources

It's not always practical or convenient to use DNS to map your machine names to IP addresses, especially in cloud infrastructures where those addresses may be changing all the time. However, if you use entries in the /etc/hosts file instead, you then have the problem of how to distribute these entries to all machines and keep them up to date.

Here's a better way to do it; Puppet's host resource type controls a single /etc/hosts entry, and you can use this to map a hostname to an IP address easily across your whole network. For example, if all your machines need to know the address of the main database server, you can manage it with a host resource.

How to do it...

Follow these steps to create an example host resource:

1. Modify your manifests/nodes.pp file as follows:

```
node 'cookbook' {
  host { 'bitfieldconsulting.com':
    ensure => present,
    ip     => '109.74.195.241',
    target => '/etc/hosts',
  }
}
```

2. Run Puppet:

```
ubuntu@cookbook:~/puppet$ papply
Notice: /Stage[main]//Node[cookbook]/Host[bitfieldconsulting.com]/
ensure: created
Notice: Finished catalog run in 0.21 seconds
```

How it works...

Puppet will check the target file (usually /etc/hosts) to see if the host entry already exists, and if not, add it. If an entry for that hostname already exists with a different address, Puppet will change the address to match the manifest.

There's more...

Organizing your host resources into classes can be helpful. For example, you could put the host resources for all your DB servers into one class called admin::dbhosts which is included by all web servers.

Where machines may need to be defined in multiple classes (for example, a database server might also be a repository server), virtual resources can solve this problem. For example, you could define all your hosts as virtual in a single class:

```
class admin::allhosts {
  @host { 'db1.bitfieldconsulting.com':
    ...
  }
}
```

and then realize the hosts you need in the various classes:

```
class admin::dbhosts {
  realize(Host['db1.bitfieldconsulting.com'])
}

class admin::repohosts {
  realize(Host['db1.bitfieldconsulting.com'])
}
```

Using multiple file sources

A neat feature of Puppet's `file` resource is that you can specify multiple values for the `source` parameter. Puppet will search them in order. If the first source isn't found, it moves on to the next, and so on. You can use this to specify a default substitute if the particular file isn't present, or even a series of increasingly generic substitutes.

How to do it...

This example demonstrates using multiple file sources:

1. Modify your `manifests/nodes.pp` file as follows:

    ```
    node 'cookbook' {
      file { '/tmp/greeting':
        source => [ 'puppet:///modules/admin/hello.txt',
                    'puppet:///modules/admin/generic.txt'],
      }
    }
    ```

2. Create the file `modules/admin/files/hello.txt` with the following contents:

    ```
    Hello, world.
    ```

3. Create the file `modules/admin/files/generic.txt` with the following contents:

    ```
    All-purpose greeting, sentient beings.
    ```

4. Run Puppet:

    ```
    ubuntu@cookbook:~/puppet$ papply
    ```

    ```
    Notice: /Stage[main]//Node[cookbook]/File[/tmp/greeting]/ensure:
    defined content as '{md5}54098b367d2e87b078671fad4afb9dbb'
    ```

    ```
    Notice: Finished catalog run in 0.15 seconds
    ```

5. Check the contents of the `/tmp/greeting` file:

    ```
    ubuntu@cookbook:~/puppet$ cat /tmp/greeting
    ```

    ```
    Hello, world.
    ```

6. Now remove the `hello.txt` file from Puppet:

    ```
    ubuntu@cookbook:~/puppet$ rm modules/admin/files/hello.txt
    ```

7. Rerun Puppet:

    ```
    ubuntu@cookbook:~/puppet$ papply
    ```

    ```
    Notice: /Stage[main]//Node[cookbook]/File[/tmp/greeting]/content:
    content changed '{md5}54098b367d2e87b078671fad4afb9dbb' to '{md5}6
    b0734a22d9796e299bac1eba6ceed0f'
    ```

    ```
    Notice: Finished catalog run in 0.11 seconds
    ```

8. Check the contents of `/tmp/greeting` again:

    ```
    ubuntu@cookbook:~/puppet$ cat /tmp/greeting
    ```

    ```
    All-purpose greeting, sentient beings.
    ```

How it works...

On the first Puppet run, it searches for available file sources in the order given:

```
source => [ 'puppet:///modules/admin/hello.txt',
            'puppet:///modules/admin/generic.txt'],
```

The file `hello.txt` is first in the list, and is present, so Puppet uses that as the source for `/tmp/greeting`:

```
Hello, world.
```

On the second Puppet run, `hello.txt` is missing, so Puppet goes on to look for the next file, `generic.txt`. This is present, so it becomes the source for `/tmp/greeting`:

```
All-purpose greeting, sentient beings.
```

There's more...

You can use this trick anywhere you have a `file` resource. For example, some nodes might need machine-specific configuration, but not others, so you could do something like:

```
file { '/etc/stuff.cfg':
  source => [ "puppet:///modules/admin/${::hostname}.cfg",
              'puppet:///modules/admin/generic.cfg' ],
}
```

Then you put the default configuration in `generic.cfg`. If machine `cartman` needs a special config, just put it in the file `cartman.cfg`. This will be used in preference to the generic file because it is listed first in the array of sources.

See also

▶ The *Passing parameters to classes* recipe in *Chapter 3, Writing Better Manifests*

Distributing directory trees

Puppet's `file` resource has another trick. It can deploy not just a single file, but a whole directory; in fact, a whole tree of files, directories, subdirectories, and so on, all with just one parameter, `recurse`.

How to do it...

Here's how to use the `recurse` parameter with `file` resources:

1. Create a suitable directory tree in the Puppet repo:

   ubuntu@cookbook:~/puppet$ mkdir -p modules/admin/files/tree/a/b/c/ d/e/f

2. Modify your `manifests/nodes.pp` file as follows:

```
node 'cookbook' {
  file { '/tmp/tree':
    source  => 'puppet:///modules/admin/tree',
    recurse => true,
  }
}
```

3. Run Puppet:

```
ubuntu@cookbook:~/puppet$ papply
Notice: /Stage[main]//Node[cookbook]/File[/tmp/tree]/ensure:
created
Notice: /File[/tmp/tree/a]/ensure: created
Notice: /File[/tmp/tree/a/b]/ensure: created
Notice: /File[/tmp/tree/a/b/c]/ensure: created
Notice: /File[/tmp/tree/a/b/c/d]/ensure: created
Notice: /File[/tmp/tree/a/b/c/d/e]/ensure: created
Notice: /File[/tmp/tree/a/b/c/d/e/f]/ensure: created
Notice: Finished catalog run in 0.15 seconds
```

How it works...

If a `file` resource has the `recurse` parameter set on it, and it is a directory, Puppet will deploy not only the directory itself, but all its contents (including subdirectories and their contents). This is a great way to put a whole tree of files onto a node, or to quickly create a large number of paths using a single resource.

There's more...

Sometimes you want to deploy files to an existing directory, but remove any files which aren't managed by Puppet. For example, in Ubuntu's `/etc/apt/sources.list.d` directory, you might want to make sure there are no files present which don't come from Puppet.

The `purge` parameter will do this for you. Define the directory as a resource in Puppet:

```
file { '/etc/apt/sources.list.d':
  purge   => true,
  recurse => true,
}
```

The combination of `recurse` and `purge` will remove all files and subdirectories in `/etc/apt/sources.list.d` that are not deployed by Puppet. You can then deploy your own files to that location using a separate resource:

```
file { '/etc/apt/sources.list.d/bitfield.list':
  content => "deb http://packages.bitfieldconsulting.com/ precise
main\n",
}
```

If there are subdirectories which contain files you don't want to purge, just define the subdirectory as a Puppet resource, and it will be left alone:

```
file { '/etc/exim4/conf.d/acl':
  ensure => directory,
}
```

> Be aware that, at least in current implementations of Puppet, recursive file copies can be quite slow and place a heavy memory load on the server. If the data doesn't change very often, it might be better to deploy and unpack a `tar.gz` file instead.

Cleaning up old files

Puppet's `tidy` resource will help you clean up old or out-of-date files, reducing disk usage. For example, if you have Puppet reporting enabled as described in the section on generating reports, you might want to regularly delete old report files.

How to do it...

Let's get started:

1. Modify your `manifests/nodes.pp` file as follows:

```
node 'cookbook' {
  tidy { '/var/lib/puppet/reports':
    age     => '1w',
    recurse => true,
  }
}
```

2. Run Puppet:

```
Notice: /Stage[main]//Node[cookbook]/Tidy[/var/lib/puppet/
reports]: Tidying File[/var/lib/puppet/reports/cookbook.compute-1.
internal/201303151215.yaml]

Notice: /Stage[main]//Node[cookbook]/Tidy[/var/lib/puppet/
reports]: Tidying File[/var/lib/puppet/reports/cookbook.compute-1.
internal/201305151327.yaml]

Notice: /Stage[main]//Node[cookbook]/Tidy[/var/lib/puppet/
reports]: Tidying File[/var/lib/puppet/reports/cookbook.compute-1.
internal/201304121116.yaml]
```

```
Notice: /Stage[main]//Node[cookbook]/Tidy[/var/lib/puppet/
reports]: Tidying File[/var/lib/puppet/reports/cookbook.compute-1.
internal/201304081612.yaml]

Notice: /Stage[main]//Node[cookbook]/Tidy[/var/lib/puppet/
reports]: Tidying File[/var/lib/puppet/reports/cookbook.compute-1.
internal/201305161117.yaml]

...

Notice: /File[/var/lib/puppet/reports/cookbook.compute-1.
internal/201303151215.yaml]/ensure: removed

Notice: /File[/var/lib/puppet/reports/cookbook.compute-1.
internal/201305151327.yaml]/ensure: removed

Notice: /File[/var/lib/puppet/reports/cookbook.compute-1.
internal/201304121116.yaml]/ensure: removed

Notice: /File[/var/lib/puppet/reports/cookbook.compute-1.
internal/201304081612.yaml]/ensure: removed

Notice: /File[/var/lib/puppet/reports/cookbook.compute-1.
internal/201305161117.yaml]/ensure: removed

Notice: Finished catalog run in 1.47 seconds
```

How it works...

Puppet searches the specified path for any files matching the age parameter; in this case, 1w (one week). It also searches subdirectories (recurse => true).

Any files matching your criteria will be deleted.

There's more...

You can specify file ages in seconds, minutes, hours, days, or weeks by using a single character to specify the time unit, as follows:

- ► 60s
- ► 180m
- ► 24h
- ► 30d
- ► 4w

You can specify that files greater than a given size should be removed, as follows:

```
size => '100m',
```

removes files of 100 megabytes and over. For kilobytes, use k, and for bytes, use b.

 Note that if you specify both age and size parameters, they are treated as independent criteria. For example, if you specify:

```
age  => "1d",
size => "512k",
```

Puppet will remove all files which are *either* at least one day old, *or* at least 512 KB in size.

Auditing resources

Dry run mode, using the --noop switch, is a simple way to audit any changes to a machine under Puppet's control. However, Puppet also has a dedicated audit feature, which can report changes to resources or specific attributes.

How to do it...

Here's an example showing Puppet's auditing capabilities:

1. Modify your manifests/nodes.pp file as follows:

   ```
   node 'cookbook' {
     file { '/etc/passwd':
       audit => [ owner, mode ],
     }
   }
   ```

2. Run Puppet:

   ubuntu@cookbook:~/puppet$ papply

   Notice: /Stage[main]//Node[cookbook]/File[/etc/passwd]/owner: audit change: newly-recorded value 0

   Notice: /Stage[main]//Node[cookbook]/File[/etc/passwd]/mode: audit change: newly-recorded value 644

   Notice: Finished catalog run in 0.27 seconds

How it works...

The `audit` metaparameter tells Puppet that you want to record and monitor certain things about the resource. The value can be a list of the parameters which you want to audit.

In this case, when Puppet runs, it will now record the owner and mode of the `/etc/passwd` file. On future runs, Puppet will spot if either of these have changed. For example, if you run:

```
ubuntu@cookbook:~/puppet$ sudo chmod 666 /etc/passwd
```

Puppet will pick up this change and log it on the next run:

```
Notice: /Stage[main]//Node[cookbook]/File[/etc/passwd]/mode: audit
change: previously recorded value 0644 has been changed to 0666
```

There's more...

This feature is very useful for auditing large networks for any changes to machines, either malicious or accidental. It's also very handy for keeping an eye on things which aren't managed by Puppet, for example, application code on production servers. You can read more about Puppet's auditing capability here:

```
http://puppetlabs.com/blog/all-about-auditing-with-puppet/
```

If you just want to audit everything about a resource, use `all`:

```
file { '/etc/passwd':
  audit => all,
}
```

See also

▸ The *Doing a dry run* recipe in *Chapter 9, Monitoring, Reporting, and Troubleshooting*

Temporarily disabling resources

Sometimes you want to disable a resource for the time being, so that it doesn't interfere with other work. For example, you might want to tweak a configuration file on the server until you have the exact settings you want, before checking it into Puppet. You don't want Puppet to overwrite it with an old version in the meantime, so you can set the `noop` metaparameter on the resource:

```
noop => true,
```

How to do it...

This example shows you how to use the `noop` metaparameter.

1. Modify your `manifests/nodes.pp` file as follows:

```
node 'cookbook' {
  file { '/tmp/test.cfg':
    content => "Hello, world!\n",
    noop    => true,
  }
}
```

2. Run Puppet:

ubuntu@cookbook:~/puppet$ papply

Notice: /Stage[main]//Node[cookbook]/File[/tmp/test.cfg]/ensure: current_value absent, should be file (noop)

Notice: Node[cookbook]: Would have triggered 'refresh' from 1 events

Notice: Class[Main]: Would have triggered 'refresh' from 1 events

Notice: Stage[main]: Would have triggered 'refresh' from 1 events

Notice: Finished catalog run in 0.24 seconds

3. Now remove the `noop` parameter:

```
node 'cookbook' {
  file { '/tmp/test.cfg':
    content => "Hello, world!\n",
  }
}
```

4. Run Puppet again:

ubuntu@cookbook:~/puppet$ papply

Notice: /Stage[main]//Node[cookbook]/File[/tmp/test.cfg]/ensure: defined content as '{md5}746308829575e17c3331bbcb00c0898b'

Notice: Finished catalog run in 0.24 seconds

How it works...

The first time we ran Puppet, the `noop` metaparameter was set to `true`, so for this particular resource it's as if you had run Puppet with the `--noop` flag. Puppet noted that the resource would have been applied, but otherwise did nothing.

In the second case, with `noop` removed, the resource is applied as normal.

6
Applications

The best software in the world only sucks. The worst software is significantly worse than that.

—Luke Kanies

In this chapter we will cover:

- ► Managing Apache servers
- ► Creating Apache virtual hosts
- ► Creating Nginx virtual hosts
- ► Managing MySQL
- ► Managing Ruby

Introduction

Without applications, a server is just a very expensive space heater. In this chapter, I'll present some recipes for managing some specific software with Puppet: MySQL, Apache, Nginx, and Ruby. I hope the recipes will be useful to you in themselves. However, the patterns and techniques they use are applicable to almost any software, so you can adapt them to your own purposes without much difficulty.

One point to watch (if you're not using Ubuntu 12) is that package names will often be different from one Linux distribution to the next (`mysqld` instead of `mysql-server`, for example). So check with your distribution to find out the correct name for a given package. The name of the service and the location of the config files for a package may also vary depending on the packager's preferences. The logic of the Puppet manifests, however, shouldn't be affected by these local differences. If you need to make your manifest portable across distributions, you could use a mechanism like Hiera to abstract out these variations (see the recipe *Importing configuration data with Hiera* in *Chapter 8, External Tools and the Puppet Ecosystem*).

Managing Apache servers

Apache is the world's favorite web server, so it's highly likely that part of your Puppetly duties will include installing and managing Apache.

How to do it...

Here's some working code to get you started:

1. Run the following command:

    ```
    ubuntu@cookbook:~/puppet$ mkdir -p modules/apache/manifests
    ```

2. Create the file `modules/apache/manifests/init.pp` with the following contents:

    ```
    # Manage Apache
    class apache {
      package { 'apache2-mpm-prefork': ensure => installed }

      service { 'apache2':
        ensure => running,
        enable => true,
        require => Package['apache2-mpm-prefork'],
      }
    }
    ```

3. Modify your `manifests/nodes.pp` file as follows:

    ```
    node 'cookbook' {
      include apache
    }
    ```

4. Apache and Nginx both want to listen on the same port, so make sure Nginx is stopped if it happens to be installed:

    ```
    ubuntu@cookbook:~/puppet$ sudo service nginx stop
    Stopping nginx: nginx.
    ```

5. Run Puppet:

    ```
    ubuntu@cookbook:~/puppet$ papply
    Notice: /Stage[main]/Apache/Package[apache2-mpm-prefork]/ensure:
    ensure changed 'purged' to 'present'
    Notice: Finished catalog run in 7.12 seconds
    ```

There's more...

In the next section, we'll look at how to create virtual host definitions for Apache. However, you may find that you need special configuration options for the Apache server as a whole. You could set these up by deploying apache2.conf with Puppet, but it's neater to put a config snippet into /etc/apache2/conf.d. For example, you could create an apache::snippet class as follows (in modules/apache/manifests/snippet.pp):

```
# Deploy an Apache config snippet
define apache::snippet() {
  include apache

  file { "/etc/apache2/conf.d/${name}":
    source  => "puppet:///modules/apache/${name}",
    require => Package['apache2-mpm-prefork'],
    notify  => Service['apache2'],
  }
}
```

and include this on a node:

```
apache::snippet { 'site-specific.conf': }
```

Creating Apache virtual hosts

Apache virtual hosts are an ideal place to use Puppet templates, because they generally consist of boilerplate code with just a few different bits of information for each site.

How to do it...

Here's a recipe to manage a simple virtual host:

1. Create the file modules/apache/manifests/vhost.pp with the following contents:

```
# Manage an Apache virtual host
define apache::vhost($domain='UNSET',$root='UNSET') {
  include apache

  if $domain == 'UNSET' {
    $vhost_domain = $name
  } else {
    $vhost_domain = $domain
  }
```

```
    if $root == 'UNSET' {
      $vhost_root = "/var/www/${name}"
    } else {
      $vhost_root = $root
    }

    file { "/etc/apache2/sites-available/${vhost_domain}.conf":
      content => template('apache/vhost.erb'),
      require => Package['apache2-mpm-prefork'],
      notify  => Exec["enable-${vhost_domain}-vhost"],
    }

    exec { "enable-${vhost_domain}-vhost":
      command     => "/usr/sbin/a2ensite
        ${vhost_domain}.conf",
      require     => File["/etc/apache2/sites-available/${vhost_
domain}.conf"],
      refreshonly => true,
      notify      => Service['apache2'],
    }
}
```

2. Run this command:

   ubuntu@cookbook:~/puppet$ mkdir modules/apache/templates

3. Create the file modules/apache/templates/vhost.erb with the following contents:

```
<VirtualHost *:80>
  ServerName <%= @vhost_domain %>
  DocumentRoot <%= @vhost_root %>
  ErrorLog /var/log/apache2/<%= @vhost_domain %>-error_log
  CustomLog /var/log/apache2/<%= @vhost_domain %>-access_log
    common

  <Directory <%= @vhost_root %>>
    Allow from all
    Options +Includes +Indexes +FollowSymLinks
    AllowOverride all
  </Directory>
</VirtualHost>
```

4. Modify your `manifests/nodes.pp` file as follows::

```
node 'cookbook' {
  apache::vhost { 'cat-pictures.com': }
}
```

5. Run Puppet:

```
ubuntu@cookbook:~/puppet$ papply
```

```
Notice: /Stage[main]//Node[cookbook]/Apache::Vhost[cat-pictures.
com]/File[/etc/apache2/sites-available/cat-pictures.com.conf]/
ensure: defined content as
  '{md5}2d4a3b043f5f487bfbd753a5cb6fa962'
```

```
Notice: /Stage[main]//Node[cookbook]/Apache::Vhost[cat-pictures.
com]/Exec[enable-cat-pictures.com-vhost]: Triggered
  'refresh' from 1 events
```

```
Notice: /Stage[main]/Apache/Service[apache2]: Triggered
  'refresh' from 1 events
```

```
Notice: Finished catalog run in 1.81 seconds
```

6. Run this command to check that Puppet has correctly created the virtual host file:

```
ubuntu@cookbook:~/puppet$ cat /etc/apache2/sites-enabled/cat-
pictures.com.conf
```

```
<VirtualHost *:80>

  ServerName cat-pictures.com

  DocumentRoot /var/www/cat-pictures.com

  ErrorLog /var/log/apache2/cat-pictures.com-error_log

  CustomLog /var/log/apache2/cat-pictures.com-access_log
    common


  <Directory /var/www/cat-pictures.com>

    Allow from all

    Options +Includes +Indexes +FollowSymLinks

    AllowOverride all

  </Directory>

</VirtualHost>
```

How it works...

We need to do two things to create and enable a virtual host:

1. Create the virtual host file in `/etc/apache2/sites-available`
2. Enable the virtual host using the `a2ensite` command

For the first step, we need to know two pieces of information: the domain name of the site, and the directory where the site files will be located. We've designed our `apache::vhost` definition so both of these values can be passed in as arguments:

```
define apache::vhost($domain='UNSET',$root='UNSET')
```

In both cases, we've specified a default value of `UNSET`, so that you can leave these parameters unspecified. If the domain argument isn't specified, we default to the name of the `apache::vhost` resource (`cat-pictures.com` in our example):

```
if $domain == 'UNSET' {
  $vhost_domain = $name
} else {
  $vhost_domain = $domain
}
```

If the `root` argument isn't specified, we default to `/var/www/${name}`, where again `$name` is the name of the `apache::vhost` resource:

```
if $root == 'UNSET' {
  $vhost_root = "/var/www/${name}"
} else {
  $vhost_root = $root
}
```

Next, we create the virtual host file based on a template:

```
file { "/etc/apache2/sites-available/${vhost_domain}.conf":
  content => template('apache/vhost.erb'),
  require => Package['apache2-mpm-prefork'],
  notify  => Exec["enable-${vhost_domain}-vhost"],
}
```

Here's the template:

```
<VirtualHost *:80>
  ServerName <%= @vhost_domain %>
  DocumentRoot <%= @vhost_root %>
  ErrorLog /var/log/apache2/<%= @vhost_domain %>-error_log
  CustomLog /var/log/apache2/<%= @vhost_domain %>-access_log common
```

```
  <Directory <%= @vhost_root %>>
    Allow from all
    Options +Includes +Indexes +FollowSymLinks
    AllowOverride all
  </Directory>
</VirtualHost>
```

You can see that the only pieces of information which need to be inserted into the template are the `vhost_domain` parameter and the `vhost_root` parameter.

Finally, we call the `a2ensite` command to tell Apache this site should be enabled:

```
exec { "enable-${vhost_domain}-vhost":
  command      => "/usr/sbin/a2ensite ${vhost_domain}.conf",
  require      => [ File["/etc/apache2/sites-available/${vhost_domain}.
conf"], Package['apache2-mpm-prefork']
],
  refreshonly => true,
  notify       => Service['apache2'],
}
```

Here the value of `exec` is `refreshonly`, so it will only be triggered when the `${vhost_domain}.conf` file is created or changed. It also notifies the `apache2` service, to pick up the new configuration.

There's more...

This simple definition is enough to get you to start running websites with Apache, but there's a lot more you can do with it.

Custom domains and docroots

As we've seen, the `vhost_domain` parameter will default to the resource's name (`cat-pictures.com` in the example). If you want the virtual host's domain to be something different, pass in the `domain` parameter:

```
apache::vhost { 'networkr':
  domain => 'networkr.com',
}

apache::vhost { 'networkr_staging':
  domain => 'staging.networkr.com',
}
```

Similarly, if you need to specify a different `DocumentRoot` parameter for the virtual host than the default (`/var/www/${name}`), just pass in the `root` parameter:

```
apache::vhost { 'communitysafety.org':
  root => '/var/apps/commsafe',
}
```

Modifying all sites

The beauty of the template system is that if you want to make a slight change to the configuration for all sites (for example, adding a `ServerAdmin` e-mail address) you can do it once in the template file, and Puppet will update all the virtual hosts it manages.

In the example, we only used two variables in the template, but you can have as many as you like. These can be local variables, as in the example, or they can be facts:

```
ServerName <%= @fqdn %>
```

Ruby expressions:

```
ServerAdmin<%= @emails["admin"] %>
```

or arbitrary Ruby code:

```
ServerAdmin <%= vhost_domain == 'coldcomfort.com' ?
  'seth@coldcomfort.com' : 'flora@poste.com' %>
```

See also

The *Using array iteration in templates* recipe in *Chapter 4, Working with Files and Packages*

Creating Nginx virtual hosts

Nginx is a fast, lightweight web server that is preferred over Apache in many contexts, especially where high performance is important. The specifics of managing virtual hosts with Nginx are a little different, but the principles are the same.

How to do it...

In this recipe we'll see how to use Puppet to create and enable Nginx virtual hosts.

1. Run the following commands:

```
ubuntu@cookbook:~/puppet$ mkdir -p modules/nginx/manifests

ubuntu@cookbook:~/puppet$ mkdir -p modules/nginx/templates
```

2. Create the file `modules/nginx/manifests/init.pp` with the following contents:

```
# Manage Nginx
class nginx {
  package { 'nginx': ensure => installed }

  service { 'nginx':
    ensure => running,
    enable => true,
  }

  exec { 'reload nginx':
    command     => '/usr/sbin/service nginx reload',
    require     => Package['nginx'],
    refreshonly => true,
  }
}
```

3. Create the file `modules/nginx/manifests/vhost.pp` with the following contents:

```
# Manage an Nginx virtual host
define nginx::vhost($domain='UNSET',$root='UNSET') {
  include nginx

  if $domain == 'UNSET' {
    $vhost_domain = $name
  } else {
    $vhost_domain = $domain
  }

  if $root == 'UNSET' {
    $vhost_root = "/var/www/${name}"
  } else {
    $vhost_root = $root
  }

  file { "/etc/nginx/sites-available/${vhost_domain}.conf":
    content => template('nginx/vhost.erb'),
    require => Package['nginx'],
  }

  file { "/etc/nginx/sites-enabled/${vhost_domain}.conf":
    ensure  => link,
    target  => "/etc/nginx/sites-available/${vhost_domain}.conf",
    require => File["/etc/nginx/sites-available/${vhost_domain}.
conf"],
    notify  => Exec['reload nginx'],
  }
}
```

4. Create the file `modules/nginx/templates/vhost.erb` with the following contents:

```
server {
  listen 80;
  server_name <%= @vhost_domain %>;

  access_log /var/log/nginx/<%= @vhost_domain %>-access_log;
  root <%= @vhost_root %>;
}
```

5. Modify your `manifests/nodes.pp` file as follows:

```
node 'cookbook' {
  nginx::vhost { 'cat-pictures.com': }
}
```

6. Run Puppet:

```
ubuntu@cookbook:~/puppet$ papply

Notice: /Stage[main]/Nginx/Package[nginx]/ensure: ensure changed
'purged' to 'present'

Notice: /Stage[main]/Nginx/Service[nginx]/ensure: ensure changed
'stopped' to 'running'

Notice: /Stage[main]//Node[cookbook]/Nginx::Vhost[cat-pictures.
com]/File[/etc/nginx/sites-available/cat-pictures.com.conf]/
ensure: defined content as '{md5}2f6b68e6e5e9b707fe20f0d8d70c5fda'

Notice: /Stage[main]//Node[cookbook]/Nginx::Vhost[cat-pictures.
com]/File[/etc/nginx/sites-enabled/cat-pictures.com.conf]/ensure:
created

Notice: /Stage[main]/Nginx/Exec[reload nginx]: Triggered 'refresh'
from 1 events

Notice: Finished catalog run in 6.81 seconds
```

How it works...

Just as in the recipe for Apache virtual hosts, the `nginx::vhost` definition creates a virtual host file based on an ERB template, into which we insert the virtual host domain and the document root:

```
server {
  listen 80;
  server_name <%= @vhost_domain %>;

  access_log /var/log/nginx/<%= @vhost_domain %>-access_log;
  root <%= @vhost_root %>;
}
```

There's no Nginx equivalent of Apache's `a2ensite` command to actually enable the site, so we use Puppet to create a symlink to the virtual host file in `/etc/nginx/sites-enabled`:

```
file { "/etc/nginx/sites-enabled/${vhost_domain}.conf":
  ensure  => link,
  target  => "/etc/nginx/sites-available/${vhost_domain}.conf",
  require => File["/etc/nginx/sites-available/${vhost_domain}.conf"],
  notify  => Exec['reload nginx'],
}
```

Creating the `sites-enabled` symlink also triggers the `reload nginx` resource, so the web server will pick up the new configuration.

There's more...

Unlike Apache, Nginx doesn't support dynamic modules (yet). This means if you want to add support for some special feature which isn't included by default, you need to recompile Nginx yourself. You could build Nginx with the options you need and create a package using FPM or a similar tool:

`http://www.ducea.com/2011/08/31/build-your-own-packages-easily-with-fpm/`

However, some Puppet administrators skip this step and simply pull down and build the Nginx source on the target server. To do this, use an `exec` with a similar pattern to that in the recipe on *Building packages automatically from source* in *Chapter 4, Working With Files and Packages*. In an agile development environment, which often means one where the management changes its mind about the product every few days, this kind of approach can be quicker and cheaper than continuous repackaging.

Managing MySQL

MySQL is a very widely used database server, and it's fairly certain you'll need to install and configure a MySQL server at some point. This recipe will show you how to do that, as well as how to automatically create databases and users for apps.

How to do it...

Follow these steps to create the example:

1. Run the following commands:

    ```
    ubuntu@cookbook:~/puppet$ mkdir -p modules/mysql/manifests

    ubuntu@cookbook:~/puppet$ mkdir -p modules/mysql/files
    ```

2. Create the file `modules/mysql/manifests/server.pp` with the following contents:

```
# Manage MySQL server
class mysql::server {
  $password = 'sekrit'
  $version  = 'mysql-server'

  package { $version: ensure => installed }

  service { 'mysql':
    ensure  => running,
    enable  => true,
    require => Package[$version],
  }

  file { '/etc/mysql/my.cnf':
    source  => 'puppet:///modules/mysql/my.cnf',
    owner   => 'mysql',
    group   => 'mysql',
    notify  => Service['mysql'],
    require => Package[$version],
  }

  exec { 'set-mysql-password':
    unless  => "/usr/bin/mysqladmin -uroot -p${password}
      status",
    command => "/usr/bin/mysqladmin -uroot password
      ${password}",
    require => Service['mysql'],
  }
}
```

3. Create the file `modules/mysql/files/my.cnf` with the following contents:

```
[client]
port            = 3306
socket          = /var/run/mysqld/mysqld.sock

[mysqld_safe]
socket          = /var/run/mysqld/mysqld.sock
nice            = 0

[mysqld]
user            = mysql
pid-file        = /var/run/mysqld/mysqld.pid
socket          = /var/run/mysqld/mysqld.sock
port            = 3306
basedir         = /usr
datadir         = /var/lib/mysql
tmpdir          = /tmp
```

```
lc-messages-dir = /usr/share/mysql
skip-external-locking
bind-address            = 127.0.0.1
key_buffer              = 16M
max_allowed_packet      = 16M
thread_stack            = 192K
thread_cache_size       = 8
myisam-recover          = BACKUP
query_cache_limit       = 1M
query_cache_size        = 16M
log_error = /var/log/mysql/error.log
expire_logs_days        = 10
max_binlog_size         = 100M

[mysqldump]
quick
quote-names
max_allowed_packet      = 16M

[mysql]
[isamchk]
key_buffer              = 16M

!includedir /etc/mysql/conf.d/
```

4. Modify your `manifests/nodes.pp` file as follows:

```
node 'cookbook' {
  include mysql::server
}
```

5. Run Puppet:

```
ubuntu@cookbook:~/puppet$ papply
```

Notice: /Stage[main]/Mysql::Server/Package[mysql-server]/ensure:
ensure changed 'purged' to 'present'

Notice: /Stage[main]/Mysql::Server/File[/etc/mysql/my.cnf]/owner:
owner changed 'root' to 'mysql'

Notice: /Stage[main]/Mysql::Server/File[/etc/mysql/my.cnf]/group:
group changed 'root' to 'mysql'

Notice: /Stage[main]/Mysql::Server/File[/etc/mysql/my.cnf]/mode:
mode
changed '0644' to '0664'

Notice: /Stage[main]/Mysql::Server/Service[mysql]: Triggered
'refresh' from 3 events

Notice: /Stage[main]/Mysql::Server/Exec[set-mysql-password]/
returns: executed successfully

Notice: Finished catalog run in 28.01 seconds

How it works...

First of all we define the MySQL `root` user password, which we'll need for any future admin operations such as creating databases:

```
$password = 'sekrit'
```

If you're concerned about putting secret data such as passwords in your Puppet manifests, see the recipe on *Using GnuPG to encrypt secrets* in *Chapter 4, Working with Files and Packages* for a better solution.

We also define a variable representing the name of the MySQL package to install:

```
$version = 'mysql-server'
```

This is because we need to refer to this package in a few places, and we might need to change the name in future, so it's a good practice to make it a variable that we can find and alter easily.

Next we install the package and start the service:

```
package { $version: ensure => installed }

service { 'mysql':
  ensure  => running,
  enable  => true,
  require => Package[$version],
}
```

We deploy the main MySQL config file, `my.cnf`:

```
file { '/etc/mysql/my.cnf':
  source  => 'puppet:///modules/mysql/my.cnf',
  owner   => 'mysql',
  group   => 'mysql',
  notify  => Service['mysql'],
  require => Package[$version],
}
```

In fact, the file we're using is a copy of the default Ubuntu MySQL `my.cnf`. You'll almost certainly want to modify this, however, and so we'd like to have Puppet to control the file.

Finally, we set the MySQL root user password:

```
exec { 'set-mysql-password':
  unless  => "/usr/bin/mysqladmin -uroot -p${password} status",
  command => "/usr/bin/mysqladmin -uroot password ${password}",
  require => Service['mysql'],
}
```

This `exec` first of all tests whether the desired password is already set. If so, this command will succeed, and we can skip the `exec` resource:

```
/usr/bin/mysqladmin -uroot -p${password} status
```

Assuming this fails, it means the root password hasn't been set, so we set it with this command:

```
/usr/bin/mysqladmin -uroot password ${password}
```

MySQL is now ready to use.

There's more...

Many applications require a MySQL database to be present, usually together with a MySQL user with appropriate permissions on the database. We can automate this setup process with Puppet very easily, as we'll see in the following examples.

Creating MySQL databases

Here's a definition for `mysql::db` which will create a database and user, and issue appropriate grants for the user. This is done with an `exec` resource in a way very similar to the part of `mysql::server` which sets the `root` password. You may want to modify the SQL `grant` statements to suit your application.

1. Create the file `modules/mysql/manifests/db.pp` with the following contents:

    ```
    # Create a MySQL database/user
    define mysql::db($user,$password) {
      include mysql::server

      exec { "create-${name}-db":
        unless  => "/usr/bin/mysql -u${user} -p${password} ${name}",
        command => "/usr/bin/mysql -uroot -p${mysql::server::password}
    -e \"create database ${name}; grant all on ${name}.* to
    ${user}@'localhost' identified by '${password}'; grant all on
    ${name}.* to ${user}@'%' identified by '${password}'; flush
    privileges;\"",
        require => Service['mysql'],
      }
    }
    ```

2. Modify your `manifests/nodes.pp` file as follows:

    ```
    node 'cookbook' {
      mysql::db { 'myapp':
        user     => 'myapp_user',
        password => 'xyzzy',
      }
    }
    ```

3. Run Puppet:

```
ubuntu@cookbook:~/puppet$ papply
Notice: /Stage[main]//Node[cookbook]/Mysql::Db[myapp]/Exec[create-
myapp-db]/returns: executed successfully
Notice: Finished catalog run in 0.76 seconds
```

4. Check that the database has been created with the correct user and permissions by running the following command:

```
ubuntu@cookbook:~/puppet$ mysql -umyapp_user -pxyzzy myapp
Welcome to the MySQL monitor.  Commands end with ; or \g.
Your MySQL connection id is 74
Server version: 5.5.31-0ubuntu0.12.04.1 (Ubuntu)

Copyright (c) 2000, 2013, Oracle and/or its affiliates. All rights
reserved.

Oracle is a registered trademark of Oracle Corporation and/or its
affiliates. Other names may be trademarks of their respective
owners.

Type 'help;' or '\h' for help. Type '\c' to clear the current
input statement.

mysql>
```

If you need several databases with the same user and permissions, you can pass in an array to `mysql::db`:

```
mysql::db { ['db1','db2','db3']:
  user     => 'myapp_user',
  password => 'xyzzy',
}
```

Managing Ruby

Ruby is a popular language for web apps, and it's a common sysadmin challenge to manage the different Ruby versions required for different applications. Managing Ruby with Puppet adds a little extra fun as Puppet itself requires a certain version of Ruby.

The most common ways to manage Ruby on servers are:

▶ Use the distro package (for example stock Ruby 1.8.7 from Ubuntu Precise)

▶ Source install a custom version of Ruby

- ▸ Package your own build of Ruby
- ▸ Use RVM to manage Ruby versions
- ▸ Use rbenv to manage Ruby versions

In many cases the distro package will be fine, which makes things easy. However, if you need a different version of Ruby from the distro package, you have a choice to make about how to manage it. If you install a custom Ruby from source, or package your own, you'll either have to replace the system Ruby, or figure out how to have both versions co-exist without interfering with one another.

RVM and rbenv are specifically designed to handle different versions of Ruby on a machine, and also to manage different sets of Ruby gems. Although they do more or less the same job, I've found rbenv slightly easier to use in real-life applications.

How to do it...

In this section, I'll show you an example Puppet recipe for managing Ruby using rbenv:

1. Run the following commands:

   ```
   ubuntu@cookbook:~/puppet$ mkdir -p modules/ruby/manifests
   ubuntu@cookbook:~/puppet$ mkdir -p modules/ruby/files
   ```

2. Create the file modules/ruby/manifests/build.pp with the following contents:

   ```
   # Install ruby-build
   class ruby::build {
     $rb_deps = ['libruby',
                 'libreadline-dev',
                 'libpcre3-dev',
                 'libcurl4-openssl-dev',
                 'zlib1g-dev',
                 'curl',
                 'git-core',
                 'libssl-dev',
                 'build-essential']

     package { $rb_deps:
       ensure => installed,
     }

     exec { 'clone-ruby-build':
       cwd     => '/root',
       command => '/usr/bin/git clone
         git://github.com/sstephenson/ruby-build.git',
       creates => '/root/ruby-build',
       require => [Package['git-core'],Package[$rb_deps]],
     }
   ```

```
    exec { 'install-ruby-build':
      cwd     => '/root/ruby-build',
      command => '/root/ruby-build/install.sh',
      require => Exec['clone-ruby-build'],
      creates => '/usr/local/bin/ruby-build',
    }
}
```

3. Create the file `modules/ruby/manifests/rbenv.pp` with the following contents:

```
# Install rbenv
class ruby::rbenv {
  include ruby::build

  exec { 'install-rbenv':
    cwd     => '/home/ubuntu',
    user    => 'ubuntu',
    command => '/usr/bin/git clone git://github.com/sstephenson/
rbenv.git .rbenv',
    creates => '/home/ubuntu/.rbenv/bin/rbenv',
    require => [Package['git-core'],Exec['install-ruby-build']],
  }

  file { '/home/ubuntu/.bashrc':
    source => 'puppet:///modules/ruby/rbenv-bashrc',
  }
}
```

4. Create the file `modules/ruby/files/rbenv-bashrc` with the following contents:

```
if [ -x /home/ubuntu/.rbenv/bin/rbenv ]; then
  export PATH="$HOME/.rbenv/bin:$PATH"
  eval "$(rbenv init -)"
fi
```

5. Create the file `modules/ruby/manifests/version.pp` with the following contents:

```
# Manage Ruby via rbenv
define ruby::version() {
  include ruby::rbenv

  $version = $name
  exec { "install-ruby-${version}":
    command    => "/bin/su - ubuntu -c
      '/home/ubuntu/.rbenv/bin/rbenv install ${version}'",
    creates    => "/home/ubuntu/.rbenv/versions/${version}",
    require    => [Exec['install-rbenv'],
                   File['/home/ubuntu/.rbenv/version'],
                   Package['curl']],
```

```
      timeout    => 0,
   }

   file { '/home/ubuntu/.rbenv/version':
     content => $version,
     require => Exec['install-rbenv'],
   }
 }
```

6. Modify your `manifests/nodes.pp` file as follows:

```
node 'cookbook' {
  ruby::version { '2.0.0-p195': }
}
```

7. Run Puppet:

```
ubuntu@cookbook:~/puppet$ papply

Notice: /Stage[main]/Ruby::Build/Package[libcurl4-openssl-dev]/
ensure: ensure changed 'purged' to 'present'

Notice: /Stage[main]/Ruby::Build/Package[libreadline-dev]/ensure:
ensure changed 'purged' to 'present'

Notice: /Stage[main]/Ruby::Build/Package[libpcre3-dev]/ensure:
ensure changed 'purged' to 'present'

Notice: /Stage[main]/Ruby::Rbenv/File[/home/ubuntu/.bashrc]/
ensure:
defined content as '{md5}4f194691794978332a5e2f5ad9d99643'

Notice: /Stage[main]/Ruby::Build/Exec[install-ruby-build]/returns:
executed successfully

Notice: /Stage[main]/Ruby::Rbenv/Exec[install-rbenv]/returns:
executed successfully

Notice: /Stage[main]//Node[cookbook]/Ruby::Version[2.0.0-p195]/
File[/home/ubuntu/.rbenv/version]/ensure: defined
content as '{md5}fc7e8eb66252a8ed142322b31570add2'
```

How it works...

This is a slightly more complicated recipe than usual, as there are several interacting components. Let's take it step-by-step and look at the details of what's happening.

ruby-build

First of all we need to install `ruby-build`, which is a tool that `rbenv` uses to build different versions of Ruby. We do this in the `ruby::build` class:

```
# Install ruby-build
class ruby::build {
```

There are some packages that `ruby-build` requires to do its work:

```
$rb_deps = ['libruby',
            'libreadline-dev',
            'libpcre3-dev',
            'libcurl4-openssl-dev',
            'zlib1g-dev',
            'curl',
            'git-core',
            'libssl-dev',
            'build-essential']

package { $rb_deps:
  ensure => installed,
}
```

 If you have any conflicts with these packages because you've also defined them elsewhere in your manifest, make them virtual as shown in the *Using virtual resources* recipe in *Chapter 5*, Users and Virtual Resources.

Now we can use Git to clone the `ruby-build` repository onto our machine:

```
exec { 'clone-ruby-build':
  cwd     => '/root',
  command => '/usr/bin/git clone
    git://github.com/sstephenson/ruby-build.git',
  creates => '/root/ruby-build',
  require => [Package['git-core'],Package[$rb_deps]],
}
```

With the `ruby-build` repo in place, all we have to do is run the `install.sh` script to create a `ruby-build` binary in /usr/local/bin.

```
exec { 'install-ruby-build':
  cwd     => '/root/ruby-build',
  command => '/root/ruby-build/install.sh',
  require => Exec['clone-ruby-build'],
  creates => '/usr/local/bin/ruby-build',
}
```

rbenv

So far, so easy. Next we want to install `rbenv` itself, using the `ruby::rbenv` class:

```
# Install rbenv
class ruby::rbenv {
```

We know that `rbenv` will require `ruby-build`:

```
include ruby::build
```

To install `rbenv`, we can `git clone` it directly into the `ubuntu` user's `.rbenv` directory:

```
exec { 'install-rbenv':
  cwd      => '/home/ubuntu',
  user     => 'ubuntu',
  command  => '/usr/bin/git clone git://github.com/sstephenson/rbenv.
git .rbenv',
  creates  => '/home/ubuntu/.rbenv/bin/rbenv',
  require  => [Package['git-core'],Exec['install-ruby-build']],
}
```

This will provide some shim binaries for executables such as `ruby` and `irb`, which will make sure that the `ubuntu` user gets whatever version of Ruby is configured in `rbenv`. To put these in the user's PATH, we use a little `.bashrc` file:

```
file { '/home/ubuntu/.bashrc':
  source => 'puppet:///modules/ruby/rbenv-bashrc',
}
```

This simply checks that `rbenv` exists and adds it to the PATH variable, then runs `rbenv init` to set up the `rbenv` environment:

```
if [ -x /home/ubuntu/.rbenv/bin/rbenv ]; then
  export PATH="$HOME/.rbenv/bin:$PATH"
  eval "$(rbenv init -)"
fi
```

We now have `rbenv` fully installed and configured, with `ruby-build` ready to build a specific version of Ruby. To do that, we've created the `ruby::version` class:

```
# Manage Ruby via rbenv
define ruby::version() {
```

We know we'll need `rbenv` for this:

```
include ruby::rbenv
```

The `namevar` parameter of this class will be the Ruby version we want (`2.0.0-p195` in our example), so we store this in `$version`:

```
$version = $name
```

To install the required Ruby, we call `rbenv install $version`:

```
exec { "install-ruby-${version}":
  command   => "/bin/su - ubuntu -c '/home/ubuntu/.rbenv/bin/rbenv
install ${version}'",
  creates   => "/home/ubuntu/.rbenv/versions/${version}",
  require   => [Exec['install-rbenv'],
               File['/home/ubuntu/.rbenv/version'],
               Package['curl']],
  timeout   => 0,
}
```

Note that we set a `timeout` of `0`, which disables the default `exec` timeout of 300 seconds: compiling Ruby can take a long time!

We also set this version as the default Ruby for `ubuntu`, using the `.rbenv/version` file, which simply contains the name of the version we want (from the `$version` variable):

```
file { '/home/ubuntu/.rbenv/version':
  content => $version,
  require => Exec['install-rbenv'],
}
```

Finally, we want to declare an instance of `ruby::version` to get the specific Ruby version required, in the `manifests/nodes.pp` file:

```
node 'cookbook' {
  ruby::version { '2.0.0-p195': }
}
```

There's more...

If you want to use `rbenv` to manage Ruby versions for a different user (`www-data` or `deploy`, for example), simply change `ubuntu` to the username you want. For extra credit, make the user a parameter so that you can manage `rbenv` with any user.

For more about `rbenv`, visit the website:

```
https://github.com/sstephenson/rbenv
```

7
Servers and Cloud Infrastructure

Rest is not idleness, and to lie sometimes on the grass under trees on a summer's day, listening to the murmur of the water, or watching the clouds float across the sky, is by no means a waste of time.

—John Lubbock

In this chapter we will cover:

- ▶ Building high-availability services using Heartbeat
- ▶ Managing NFS servers and file shares
- ▶ Using HAProxy to load-balance multiple web servers
- ▶ Managing firewalls with iptables
- ▶ Managing EC2 instances
- ▶ Managing virtual machines with Vagrant

Introduction

As powerful as Puppet is for managing the configuration of a single server, it's even more useful when controlling networks of many machines. In this chapter we'll explore ways of using Puppet to help you create high-availability clusters, share files across your network, set up automated firewalls, use load-balancing to get more out of the machines you have, and create new virtual machines on the cloud and on the desktop.

Building high-availability services using Heartbeat

High-availability services are those that can survive the failure of an individual machine or network connection. The primary technique for high availability is redundancy, otherwise known as throwing hardware at the problem. Although the eventual failure of an individual server is certain, the simultaneous failure of two servers is unlikely enough that this provides a good level of redundancy for most applications.

One of the simplest ways to build a redundant pair of servers is to have them share an IP address using Heartbeat. Heartbeat is a daemon which runs on both machines and exchanges regular messages—heartbeats—between the two. One server is the primary, and normally has the resource: in this case, an IP address (known as a **virtual IP**, or **VIP**). If the secondary server fails to detect a heartbeat from the primary, it can take over the address, ensuring continuity of service.

In this recipe, we'll set up two machines in this configuration using Puppet, and I'll explain how to use it to provide a high-availability service.

Getting ready...

You'll need two machines, of course, and an extra IP address to use as the VIP. You can usually request this from your ISP, if necessary. In this example, I'll be using machines named cookbook and cookbook2, with cookbook being the primary. I'll assume you have a way of putting your Puppet config on both machines, perhaps the Git-based setup described in *Chapter 1, Puppet Infrastructure*.

How to do it...

Follow these steps to build the example:

1. Run the following commands:

   ```
   ubuntu@cookbook:~/puppet$ mkdir -p modules/heartbeat/manifests
   ubuntu@cookbook:~/puppet$ mkdir -p modules/heartbeat/templates
   ```

2. Create the file `modules/heartbeat/manifests/init.pp` with the following contents:

   ```
   # Manage Heartbeat
   class heartbeat {
     package { 'heartbeat':
   ```

```
      ensure => installed,
   }

   service { 'heartbeat':
     ensure  => running,
     enable  => true,
     require => Package['heartbeat'],
   }

   exec { 'reload-heartbeat':
     command     => '/usr/sbin/service heartbeat reload',
     refreshonly => true,
   }

   file { '/etc/ha.d/authkeys':
     content => "auth 1\n1 sha1 TopSecret",
     mode    => '0600',
     require => Package['heartbeat'],
     notify  => Exec['reload-heartbeat'],
   }
}
```

3. Create the file `modules/heartbeat/manifests/vip.pp` with the
    following contents:

```
# Manage a specific VIP with Heartbeat
class
  heartbeat::vip($node1,$node2,$ip1,$ip2,$vip,$interface='eth0:1')
{
  include heartbeat

  file { '/etc/ha.d/haresources':
    content => "${node1} IPaddr::${vip}/${interface}\n",
    notify  => Exec['reload-heartbeat'],
    require => Package['heartbeat'],
  }

  file { '/etc/ha.d/ha.cf':
    content => template('heartbeat/vip.ha.cf.erb'),
    notify  => Exec['reload-heartbeat'],
    require => Package['heartbeat'],
  }
}
```

4. Create the file `modules/heartbeat/templates/vip.ha.cf.erb` with the following contents:

```
use_logd yes
udpport 694
autojoin none
ucast eth0 <%= @ip1 %>
ucast eth0 <%= @ip2 %>
keepalive 1
deadtime 10
warntime 5
auto_failback off
node <%= @node1 %>
node <%= @node2 %>
```

5. Modify your `manifests/nodes.pp` file as follows. Replace the `ip1` and `ip2` addresses with the primary IP addresses of your two nodes, `vip` with the virtual IP address you'll be using, and `node1` and `node2` with the hostnames of the two nodes. (Heartbeat uses the fully-qualified domain name of a node to determine if it's a member of the cluster, so the values for `node1` and `node2` should match what's given by `facter fqdn` on each machine.)

```
node 'cookbook' {
  class { 'heartbeat::vip':
    ip1   => '10.96.247.132',
    ip2   => '10.96.247.133',
    node1 => 'cookbook',
    node2 => 'cookbook2',
    vip   => '10.96.247.134/24',
  }
}

node 'cookbook2' {
  class { 'heartbeat::vip':
    ip1   => '10.96.247.132',
    ip2   => '10.96.247.133',
    node1 => 'cookbook',
    node2 => 'cookbook2',
    vip   => '10.96.247.134/24',
  }
}
```

6. Run Puppet on each of the two servers:

```
ubuntu@cookbook:~/puppet$ papply
```

```
Notice: /Stage[main]/Heartbeat/Package[heartbeat]/ensure: ensure
changed 'purged' to 'present'
```

```
Notice: /Stage[main]/Heartbeat/File[/etc/ha.d/authkeys]/ensure:
defined content as '{md5}3e37bd1ccf7a47cc8ebb117de7d76db1'
```

```
Notice: /Stage[main]/Heartbeat::Vip/File[/etc/ha.d/haresources]/
ensure: defined content as '{md5}5771d43731bbcc3b911ee784ede9c858'

Notice: /Stage[main]/Heartbeat::Vip/File[/etc/ha.d/ha.cf]/ensure:
defined content as '{md5}b5198da86c034c4925bb4a42effef60d'

Notice: /Stage[main]/Heartbeat/Exec[reload-heartbeat]: Triggered
'refresh' from 3 events

Notice: Finished catalog run in 41.14 seconds
```

How it works...

We need to install Heartbeat first of all, using class `heartbeat`:

```
# Manage Heartbeat
class heartbeat {
  package { 'heartbeat':
    ensure => installed,
  }
  ...
}
```

Next, we use class `heartbeat::vip` to manage a specific virtual IP:

```
# Manage a specific VIP with Heartbeat
class
  heartbeat::vip($node1,$node2,$ip1,$ip2,$vip,$interface='eth0:1') {
  include heartbeat
```

As you can see, the class includes an `interface` argument; by default, the VIP will be configured on `eth0:1`, but if you need to use a different interface you can pass it in using this parameter.

Each pair of servers that we configure with a virtual IP will use class `heartbeat::vip` with the same parameters. These will be used to build the `haresources` file:

```
file { '/etc/ha.d/haresources':
  content => "${node1} IPaddr::${vip}/${interface}\n",
  notify  => Exec['reload-heartbeat'],
  require => Package['heartbeat'],
}
```

This tells Heartbeat about the resource it should manage (that's a Heartbeat resource, such as an IP address or a service, not a Puppet resource). The resulting `haresources` file might look as follows:

```
cookbook IPaddr::10.96.247.134/24/eth0:1
```

The file is interpreted by Heartbeat as follows:

- `cookbook`: This is the name of the primary node, which should be the default owner of the resource
- `IPaddr`: This is the type of resource to manage, in this case an IP address
- `10.96.247.134/24`: This is the value for the IP address
- `eth0:1`: This is the virtual interface to configure with the managed IP address

We will also build the `ha.cf` file that tells Heartbeat how to communicate between cluster nodes:

```
file { '/etc/ha.d/ha.cf':
  content => template('heartbeat/vip.ha.cf.erb'),
  notify  => Exec['reload-heartbeat'],
  require => Package['heartbeat'],
}
```

To do this, we use the template file:

```
autojoin none
ucast eth0 <%= @ip1 %>
ucast eth0 <%= @ip2 %>
keepalive 1
deadtime 10
warntime 5
udpport 694
auto_failback off
node <%= @node1 %>
node <%= @node2 %>
use_logd yes
```

The interesting values here are the IP addresses of the two nodes (`ip1` and `ip2`), and the names of the two nodes (`node1` and `node2`).

Finally, we create an instance of `heartbeat::vip` on both machines and pass it an identical set of parameters as follows:

```
class { 'heartbeat::vip':
  ip1   => '10.96.247.132',
  ip2   => '10.96.247.133',
  node1 => 'cookbook',
  node2 => 'cookbook2',
  vip   => '10.96.247.134/24',
}
```

There's more...

With Heartbeat set up as described in the example, the virtual IP address will be configured on `cookbook` by default. If something happens to interfere with this (for example, if you halt or reboot `cookbook`, or stop the `heartbeat` service, or the machine loses network connectivity) `cookbook2` will immediately take over the virtual IP.

The `auto_failback` setting in `ha.cf` governs what happens next. If `auto_failback` is set to `on`, when `cookbook` becomes available once more, it will automatically take over the IP address. Without `auto_failback`, the IP will stay where it is until you manually fail it over again (by stopping `heartbeart` on `cookbook2`, for example).

One common use for a Heartbeat-managed virtual IP is to provide a highly-available website or service. To do this, set the DNS name for the service (for example, `cat-pictures.com`) to point to the virtual IP. Requests for the service will be routed to whichever of the two servers currently has the virtual IP. If this server should go down, requests will go to the other, with no visible interruption in service to users.

You can also use Heartbeat to manage other resources, such as daemons (HAProxy for load balancing, for example) or shared storage (for example, DRBD). You can find out more about advanced uses of Heartbeat at the Linux-HA User's Guide website:

`http://www.linux-ha.org/doc/users-guide/users-guide.html`

Managing NFS servers and file shares

NFS (the **Network File System**) is a protocol for mounting a shared directory from a remote server. For example, a pool of web servers might all mount the same NFS share to serve static assets such as images and stylesheets. Although NFS is rather old technology, it's still widely used, so you will very likely come across it.

How to do it...

Here's a recipe that will show you how to create an NFS server using Puppet and set up shared directories:

1. Run the following command:

   ubuntu@cookbook:~/puppet$ mkdir -p modules/nfs/manifests

2. Create the file `modules/nfs/manifests/init.pp` with the following contents:

   ```
   # Manage NFS server
   class nfs {
     package { 'nfs-kernel-server': ensure => installed }
   ```

```
service { 'nfs-kernel-server':
  ensure      => running,
  enable      => true,
  hasrestart => true,
  require     => Package['nfs-kernel-server'],
}

file { '/etc/exports.d':
  ensure => directory,
}

exec { 'update-etc-exports':
  command     => '/bin/cat /etc/exports.d/*
>/etc/exports',
  notify      => Service['nfs-kernel-server'],
  refreshonly => true,
}
}
```

3. Create the file `modules/nfs/manifests/share.pp` with the following contents:

```
# Export a specific file share via NFS
define nfs::share($path,$allowed,$options='') {
  include nfs

  file { $path:
    ensure => directory,
  }

  file { "/etc/exports.d/${name}":
    content => "${path} ${allowed}(${options})\n",
    notify  => Exec['update-etc-exports'],
  }
}
```

4. Modify your `manifests/nodes.pp` file as follows. Replace the value of `allowed` with an IP address range suitable for your network.

```
node 'cookbook' {
  nfs::share { 'data':
    path    => '/data',
    allowed => '10.96.247.132/31',
```

```
      options => 'rw,sync,no_root_squash',
  }

  nfs::share { 'data2':
    path    => '/data2',
    allowed => '10.96.247.132/31',
    options => 'rw,sync,no_root_squash',
  }
}
```

5. Run Puppet:

ubuntu@cookbook:~/puppet$ papply

Notice: /Stage[main]/Nfs/Package[nfs-kernel-server]/ensure: ensure changed 'purged' to 'present'

Notice: /Stage[main]/Nfs/File[/etc/exports.d]/ensure: created

Notice: /Stage[main]//Node[cookbook]/Nfs::Share[data2]/File[/data2]/ensure: created

Notice: /Stage[main]//Node[cookbook]/Nfs::Share[data]/File[/data]/ensure: created

Notice: /Stage[main]//Node[cookbook]/Nfs::Share[data]/File[/etc/exports.d/data]/ensure: defined content as '{md5}b5444caad49afe8c467682598266880d'

Notice: /Stage[main]//Node[cookbook]/Nfs::Share[data2]/File[/etc/exports.d/data2]/ensure: defined content as '{md5}87a48401732e1923fb54b190aa649961'

Notice: /Stage[main]/Nfs/Exec[update-etc-exports]: Triggered 'refresh' from 2 events

Notice: /Stage[main]/Nfs/Service[nfs-kernel-server]: Triggered 'refresh' from 1 events

Notice: Finished catalog run in 15.23 seconds

6. Test the export settings by mounting one of the shares from another server:

ubuntu@cookbook2:~/puppet$ sudo mkdir /mnt/data

ubuntu@cookbook2:~/puppet$ sudo mount cookbook:/data /mnt/data

How it works...

The `nfs` class installs and starts the `nfs-kernel-server` service, which listens for network connections to the file share. The `nfs::share` definition makes a specific directory available via NFS, so that you can declare any number of these on a given server, as shown in the following code snippet:

```
nfs::share { 'data':
  path    => '/data',
  allowed => '10.96.247.132/31',
  options => 'rw,sync,no_root_squash',
}
```

The `name` of the resource is whatever label you want to give it: `data`, in this case. The label will be used when you mount the share from another machine.

The `path` specifies the directory to share. The `allowed` parameter can be a CIDR address range (as it is here), a single IP address, a hostname, or a whitespace-separated list of addresses and hostnames. Only the specified hosts will be allowed to mount the share.

The `options` parameter specifies the options to NFS (as they appear in the `/etc/exports` file; see `man exports` for precise details).

When you declare an `nfs::share` resource, this creates a file snippet in `/etc/exports.d`, which then triggers `Exec['update-etc-exports']` to concatenate all the snippets into `/etc/exports` and restart the NFS service to pick up the changes. You might remember this snippet pattern from the *Building config files using snippets* recipe in *Chapter 4, Working with Files and Packages*.

Using HAProxy to load-balance multiple web servers

Once upon a time a load balancer was a big box that sat in a rack and cost eighty thousand dollars. Although you can still buy those, for most organizations a software load balancer solution using commodity Linux servers is a better value proposition.

HAProxy is the software load balancer of choice for most people: fast, powerful, and highly configurable.

How to do it...

In this recipe, I'll show you how to build an HAProxy server to load-balance web requests across two existing backend servers.

1. Run the following commands:

```
ubuntu@cookbook:~/puppet$ mkdir -p modules/haproxy/manifests
ubuntu@cookbook:~/puppet$ mkdir -p modules/haproxy/files
```

2. Create the file modules/haproxy/manifests/init.pp with the following contents:

```
# Manage HAProxy
class haproxy {
  package { 'haproxy': ensure => installed }

  file { '/etc/default/haproxy':
    content => "ENABLED=1\n",
    require => Package['haproxy'],
  }

  service { 'haproxy':
    ensure  => running,
    enable  => true,
    require => Package['haproxy'],
  }

  file { '/etc/haproxy/haproxy.cfg':
    source  => 'puppet:///modules/haproxy/haproxy.cfg',
    require => Package['haproxy'],
    notify  => Service['haproxy'],
  }
}
```

3. Create the file modules/haproxy/files/haproxy.cfg with the following contents. In the myapp section, replace the IP address in each server line with the IP address of your backend server, and the :8000 port number with the port number where your server is listening.

```
global
        daemon
        user haproxy
        group haproxy
        pidfile /var/run/haproxy.pid

defaults
        log     global
        stats   enable
        mode    http
```

```
                option  httplog
                option  dontlognull
                option  dontlog-normal
                retries 3
                option  redispatch
                contimeout 4000
                clitimeout 60000
                srvtimeout 30000


        listen  stats :8080
                mode http
                stats uri /
                stats auth haproxy:topsecret


        listen  myapp 0.0.0.0:80
                balance leastconn
                server myapp1 10.0.2.30:8000    check maxconn 100
                server myapp2 10.0.2.40:8000    check maxconn 100
```

4. Modify your `manifests/nodes.pp` file as follows:

```
node 'cookbook' {
  include haproxy
}
```

5. Before you apply the manifest, make sure another process is not already listening on port 80 (HAProxy will not be able to start if it can't acquire this port).

```
ubuntu@cookbook:~/puppet$ sudo netstat -an |grep LISTEN |grep 80
```

6. Run Puppet:

```
ubuntu@cookbook:~/puppet$ papply

Notice: /Stage[main]/Haproxy/Package[haproxy]/ensure: created

Notice:
/Stage[main]/Haproxy/File[/etc/default/haproxy]/ensure:
defined content as '{md5}ba6d6a5a15e8ddc7a9bbe3f91fb04a34'

Notice:
/Stage[main]/Haproxy/File[/etc/haproxy/haproxy.cfg]/ensure:
defined content as '{md5}84929f3207935b0c4338cfe5a7314ebe'

Notice: /Stage[main]/Haproxy/Service[haproxy]/ensure: ensure
changed 'stopped' to 'running'

Notice: /Stage[main]/Haproxy/Service[haproxy]: Triggered
'refresh' from 1 events

Notice: Finished catalog run in 5.14 seconds
```

7. Check the HAProxy stats interface on port `8080` in your web browser to make sure everything is OK (note that my backend servers are shown as down because those VMs aren't running; when I start them, HAProxy will detect this automatically and mark them up).

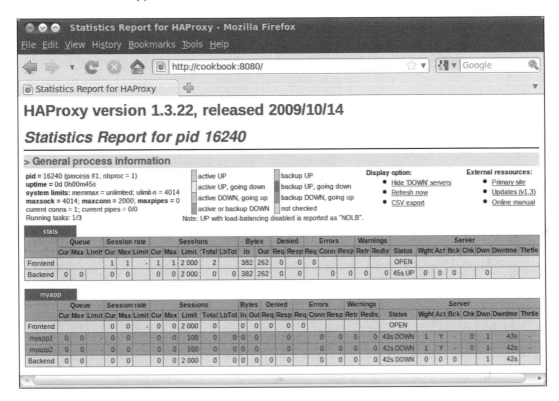

How it works...

The `haproxy` daemon listens for incoming requests and distributes them to the pool of backend servers (`myapp1` and `myapp2` in our example). If one backend server becomes overloaded, HAProxy will avoid sending it more traffic until it recovers. This helps prevent the drastic slowdown as a single web server becomes overloaded and queues up more and more requests that it can't serve. If a server fails altogether, HAProxy won't send it any more requests until it becomes available again.

The `stats` interface will show you how your backend servers are performing, how many sessions they are handling, whether HAProxy has marked them up or down, and so on.

There's more...

If you want to add more backends to handle the increased demand, just add more `server` lines to `haproxy.cfg`. If you find that the existing servers are getting swamped, try decreasing the per-server `maxconn` setting a little. HAProxy has a vast range of configuration parameters which you can explore; see the HAProxy website:

```
http://haproxy.1wt.eu/#docs
```

If you need SSL capabilities, you can put Nginx in front of HAProxy to handle this.

Although it's most often used as a web server, HAProxy can proxy a lot more than just HTTP. It can handle any amount of TCP traffic, so you can use it to balance the load of MySQL servers, SMTP, video servers, or anything you like.

Managing firewalls with iptables

As experienced system administrators know, security comes from defense in depth. It's not enough to stick a single firewall in front of your network and hope for the best. Every machine needs to be securely configured so that only the required network ports are accessible, and this means that every machine needs to have its own firewall.

Linux comes with its own industrial-strength, kernel-based packet filtering firewall, **iptables**. However, it's not particularly user-friendly, as a typical `iptables` rule looks something as follows:

```
iptables -A INPUT -d 10.0.2.15/32 -p tcp -m tcp --dport 80 -j
ACCEPT
```

It would be nice to be able to express firewall rules in a more symbolic and readable way. Puppet can help, because we can use it to abstract away some of the implementation detail of `iptables`, and create `roles` based on the services the machine provides:

```
firewall::role { 'webserver': }
firewall::role { 'dbserver': }
```

Getting ready...

You will need the `append_if_no_such_line` utility function we created in the *Making quick edits to config files* recipe in *Chapter 4, Working with Files and Packages*.

How to do it...

Here's what you need to do to manage `iptables` with Puppet:

1. Run the following commands:

   ```
   ubuntu@cookbook:~/puppet$ mkdir -p modules/firewall/manifests
   ubuntu@cookbook:~/puppet$ mkdir -p modules/firewall/files
   ```

2. Create the file `modules/firewall/manifests/init.pp` with the following contents:

   ```
   # Manage iptables firewall
   class firewall {
     file { ['/etc/firewall',
             '/etc/firewall/hosts',
             '/etc/firewall/roles']:
       ensure => directory,
     }

     file { '/etc/firewall/names':
       source => 'puppet:///modules/firewall/names',
       notify => Exec['run-iptables'],
     }

     file { '/etc/firewall/roles/common':
       source => 'puppet:///modules/firewall/common.role',
       notify => Exec['run-iptables'],
     }

     file { '/etc/firewall/iptables.sh':
       source => 'puppet:///modules/firewall/iptables.sh',
       mode   => '0755',
       notify => Exec['run-iptables'],
     }

     file { "/etc/firewall/hosts/${::hostname}":
       content => "export MAIN_IP=${::ipaddress}\nexport PRIVATE_
   IP=${::ipaddress_eth1}\n",
       require => File['/etc/firewall/hosts'],
       notify  => Exec['run-iptables'],
     }

     exec { 'run-iptables':
       cwd        => '/etc/firewall',
       command    => "/usr/bin/test -f hosts/${::hostname} &&
   /etc/firewall/iptables.sh && /sbin/iptables-save
   >/etc/iptables.rules",
   ```

```
      refreshonly => true,
    }


  append_if_no_such_line { 'restore iptables rules':
    file => '/etc/network/interfaces',
    line => 'pre-up iptables-restore <
/etc/iptables.rules',
    }
}
```

3. Create the file `modules/firewall/files/iptables.sh` with the following contents:

```
. `dirname $0`/names

export EXT_INTERFACE=eth0

# Flush and remove all chains
iptables -P INPUT   ACCEPT
iptables -P OUTPUT ACCEPT
iptables -F
iptables -X

HOST_RULES=`dirname $0`/hosts/`hostname -s`
[ -f ${HOST_RULES} ] && . ${HOST_RULES}

. `dirname $0`/roles/common

# Drop all non-matching packets
iptables -A INPUT -j LOG --log-prefix "INPUT: "
iptables -A INPUT -j DROP
iptables -A OUTPUT -j LOG --log-prefix "OUTPUT: "
iptables -A OUTPUT -j DROP
```

4. Create the file `modules/firewall/files/names` with the following contents:

```
# Well-known ports
export DNS=53
export FTP=21
export MYSQL=3306
export NRPE=5666
export NTP=123
export SMTP=25
export SSH=22
export WEB=80
export WEB_SSL=443
```

5. Create the file `modules/firewall/files/common.role` with the following contents:

```
# Allow all traffic on loopback interface
iptables -I INPUT 1 -i lo -j ACCEPT
iptables -I OUTPUT 1 -o lo -j ACCEPT

# Allow established and related connections
iptables -I INPUT 2 -m state --state ESTABLISHED,RELATED -j
ACCEPT
iptables -I OUTPUT 2 -m state --state ESTABLISHED,RELATED -j
ACCEPT

# Allow SSH and ping
iptables -A INPUT -p tcp -m tcp --dport ${SSH} -j ACCEPT
iptables -A INPUT -p ICMP --icmp-type echo-request -j
ACCEPT

# Allow common outbound ports
iptables -A OUTPUT -p tcp --dport ${SMTP} -j ACCEPT
iptables -A OUTPUT -p udp --dport ${NTP} -j ACCEPT
iptables -A OUTPUT -p tcp --dport ${NTP} -j ACCEPT
iptables -A OUTPUT -p udp --dport ${DNS} -j ACCEPT
iptables -A OUTPUT -p tcp --dport ${WEB} -j ACCEPT
iptables -A OUTPUT -p tcp --dport ${WEB_SSL} -j ACCEPT
iptables -A OUTPUT -p tcp --dport ${MYSQL} -j ACCEPT

# Drop some commonly probed ports
iptables -A INPUT -p tcp --dport 23 -j DROP # telnet
iptables -A INPUT -p tcp --dport 135 -j DROP # epmap
iptables -A INPUT -p tcp --dport 139 -j DROP # netbios
iptables -A INPUT -p tcp --dport 445 -j DROP # Microsoft DS
iptables -A INPUT -p udp --dport 1433 -j DROP # SQL server
iptables -A INPUT -p tcp --dport 1433 -j DROP # SQL server
iptables -A INPUT -p udp --dport 1434 -j DROP # SQL server
iptables -A INPUT -p tcp --dport 1434 -j DROP # SQL server
iptables -A INPUT -p tcp --dport 2967 -j DROP # SSC-agent
```

6. Create the file `modules/firewall/files/webserver.role` with the following contents:

```
# Access to web ports
iptables -A INPUT -p tcp --dport ${WEB} -j ACCEPT
iptables -A INPUT -p tcp --dport ${WEB_SSL} -j ACCEPT

# Send mail from web applications
iptables -A OUTPUT -p tcp --dport ${SMTP} -j ACCEPT
```

7. Create the file `modules/firewall/manifests/role.pp` with the following contents:

```
# Manage a specific firewall role
define firewall::role() {
  include firewall

  file { "/etc/firewall/roles/${name}":
    source  => "puppet:///modules/firewall/${name}.role",
    require => File['/etc/firewall/roles'],
    notify  => Exec['run-iptables'],
  }

  append_if_no_such_line { "${name} role":
    file    => "/etc/firewall/hosts/${::hostname}",
    line    => ". `dirname \$0`/roles/${name}",
    require => File["/etc/firewall/hosts/${::hostname}"],
    notify  => Exec['run-iptables'],
  }
}
```

8. Modify your `manifests/nodes.pp` file as follows:

```
node 'cookbook' {
  firewall::role { 'webserver': }
}
```

9. Run Puppet:

```
ubuntu@cookbook:~/puppet$ papply
Notice: /Stage[main]/Firewall/File[/etc/firewall]/ensure:
created
Notice: /Stage[main]/Firewall/File[/etc/firewall/names]/ensure:
defined content as '{md5}e792924596121c1e658765eed29c168b'
Notice: /Stage[main]/Firewall/File[/etc/firewall/roles]/ensure:
created
Notice: /Stage[main]/Firewall/File[/etc/firewall/roles/common]/
ensure:
defined content as '{md5}f8dc9e480c60fd0dd69532ad8562843b'
Notice:
/Stage[main]/Firewall/File[/etc/firewall/iptables.sh]/ensure:
defined content as '{md5}522fc7466a9b74479df698813595eaa7'
Notice:
/Stage[main]//Node[cookbook]/Firewall::Role[webserver]/File[/etc/
firewall/roles/webserver]/ensure: defined content as
'{md5}77d0e860fd8ebbe434b584e9ff025d42'
Notice:
/Stage[main]/Firewall/File[/etc/firewall/hosts]/ensure:
created
```

```
Notice:
/Stage[main]/Firewall/File[/etc/firewall/hosts/cookbook]/ensure:
defined content as '{md5}1dbf44f613a19f1f86c3e7bd63cef1bc'
Notice:
/Stage[main]//Node[cookbook]/Firewall::Role[webserver]/Append_if_
no_such_line[webserver role]/Exec[/bin/echo '. `dirname
$0`/roles/webserver' >>
'/etc/firewall/hosts/cookbook']/returns: executed successfully
Notice: /Stage[main]/Firewall/Exec[run-iptables]: Triggered
'refresh' from 6 events
Notice: /Stage[main]/Firewall/Append_if_no_such_line[restore
iptables rules]/Exec[/bin/echo 'pre-up iptables-restore <
/etc/iptables.rules' >> '/etc/network/interfaces']/returns:
executed successfully
Notice: Finished catalog run in 0.70 seconds
```

10. Run the following command to see the resulting firewall ruleset:

```
ubuntu@cookbook:~/puppet$ sudo iptables -nL
Chain INPUT (policy ACCEPT)
target      prot opt source            destination
ACCEPT      all  --  0.0.0.0/0         0.0.0.0/0
ACCEPT      all  --  0.0.0.0/0         0.0.0.0/0
state RELATED,ESTABLISHED
ACCEPT      tcp  --  0.0.0.0/0         0.0.0.0/0          tcp
dpt:80
ACCEPT      tcp  --  0.0.0.0/0         0.0.0.0/0          tcp
dpt:443
ACCEPT      tcp  --  0.0.0.0/0         0.0.0.0/0          tcp
dpt:22
ACCEPT      icmp --  0.0.0.0/0         0.0.0.0/0
icmptype 8
DROP        tcp  --  0.0.0.0/0         0.0.0.0/0          tcp
dpt:23
DROP        tcp  --  0.0.0.0/0         0.0.0.0/0          tcp
dpt:135
DROP        tcp  --  0.0.0.0/0         0.0.0.0/0          tcp
dpt:139
DROP        tcp  --  0.0.0.0/0         0.0.0.0/0          tcp
dpt:445
DROP        udp  --  0.0.0.0/0         0.0.0.0/0          udp
dpt:1433
DROP        tcp  --  0.0.0.0/0         0.0.0.0/0          tcp
dpt:1433
```

```
DROP          udp   --  0.0.0.0/0            0.0.0.0/0                 udp
dpt:1434
DROP          tcp   --  0.0.0.0/0            0.0.0.0/0                 tcp
dpt:1434
DROP          tcp   --  0.0.0.0/0            0.0.0.0/0                 tcp
dpt:2967
LOG           all   --  0.0.0.0/0            0.0.0.0/0                 LOG
flags 0 level 4 prefix "INPUT: "
DROP          all   --  0.0.0.0/0            0.0.0.0/0


Chain FORWARD (policy ACCEPT)
target        prot opt source               destination


Chain OUTPUT (policy ACCEPT)
target        prot opt source               destination
ACCEPT        all   --  0.0.0.0/0            0.0.0.0/0
ACCEPT        all   --  0.0.0.0/0            0.0.0.0/0
state RELATED,ESTABLISHED
ACCEPT        tcp   --  0.0.0.0/0            0.0.0.0/0                 tcp
dpt:25
ACCEPT        tcp   --  0.0.0.0/0            0.0.0.0/0                 tcp
dpt:25
ACCEPT        udp   --  0.0.0.0/0            0.0.0.0/0                 udp
dpt:53
ACCEPT        tcp   --  0.0.0.0/0            0.0.0.0/0                 tcp
dpt:80
ACCEPT        tcp   --  0.0.0.0/0            0.0.0.0/0                 tcp
dpt:443
ACCEPT        tcp   --  0.0.0.0/0            0.0.0.0/0                 tcp
dpt:3306
LOG           all   --  0.0.0.0/0            0.0.0.0/0                 LOG
flags 0 level 4 prefix "OUTPUT: "
DROP          all   --  0.0.0.0/0            0.0.0.0/0
```

How it works...

First, in the `firewall` class, we set up a basic directory structure for the firewall-related files and scripts to live in:

```
# Manage iptables firewall
class firewall {
  file { ['/etc/firewall',
```

```
        '/etc/firewall/hosts',

        '/etc/firewall/roles']:
    ensure => directory,
  }
```

We deploy a file called `names` that will set up a bunch of shell variables mapping user-friendly names to port numbers:

```
file { '/etc/firewall/names':
  source => 'puppet:///modules/firewall/names',
  notify => Exec['run-iptables'],
}
```

The `names` file consists of definitions like the following::

```
export WEB=80
```

We can then refer to these names in a readable way in firewall rules instead of using port numbers directly.

Next, we deploy a file called `roles/common` that contains rules common to all machines:

```
file { '/etc/firewall/roles/common':
  source => 'puppet:///modules/firewall/common.role',
  notify => Exec['run-iptables'],
}
```

Some of the rules in `common` (you'll probably want to modify these to suit your environment) look like the following::

```
# Allow SSH and ping
iptables -A INPUT -p tcp -m tcp --dport ${SSH} -j ACCEPT
iptables -A INPUT -p ICMP --icmp-type echo-request -j ACCEPT
```

Notice that we used the shell variable `$SSH` (defined in `names` as port 22).

Next up, the shell script, which actually loads and applies the firewall rules, as follows:

```
file { '/etc/firewall/iptables.sh':
  source => 'puppet:///modules/firewall/iptables.sh',
  mode   => '0755',
  notify => Exec['run-iptables'],
}
```

The `iptables.sh` script clears all existing firewall rules, loads the `common` and host-specific role files, and tells `iptables` to log and drop all packets not matched by any of its rules.

Next, the host-specific file, which sets the machine's public and private IP addresses (in case you need to refer to them), and any other variables you want:

```
file { "/etc/firewall/hosts/${::hostname}":
  content => "export MAIN_IP=${::ipaddress}\nexport
    PRIVATE_IP=${::ipaddress_eth1}\n",
  require => File['/etc/firewall/hosts'],
  replace => false,
  notify  => Exec['run-iptables'],
}
```

To actually make something happen, we need an `exec` resource to run the `iptables.sh` script when one of its dependent files changes:

```
exec { 'run-iptables':
  cwd          => '/etc/firewall',
  command      => "/usr/bin/test -f hosts/${::hostname} &&
    /etc/firewall/iptables.sh && /sbin/iptables-save
      >/etc/iptables.rules",
  refreshonly => true,
}
```

If the `iptables.sh` script succeeds (in other words, if there were no errors detected in the firewall rules) then the `iptables-save` command will save the ruleset to the file `/etc/iptables.rules` so that it can be reloaded when the machine boots.

The final bit of code adds a line to the `/etc/network/interfaces` file which performs this automatic ruleset reload on boot:

```
append_if_no_such_line { 'restore iptables rules':
  file => '/etc/network/interfaces',
  line => 'pre-up iptables-restore < /etc/iptables.rules',
}
```

At this point, we've set up a firewall that Puppet will install on each machine and configure to load the `common` role. However, we'd also like to be able to add specific roles, for machines which are `webservers`, for example. We do this with the `firewall::role` definition. In our example, we used:

```
firewall::role { 'webserver': }
```

So let's see how that works. The `firewall::role` code is as follows:

```
# Manage a specific firewall role
define firewall::role() {
  include firewall

  file { "/etc/firewall/roles/${name}":
    source  => "puppet:///modules/firewall/${name}.role",
    require => File['/etc/firewall/roles'],
    notify  => Exec['run-iptables'],
```

```
  }

  append_if_no_such_line { "${name} role":
    file    => "/etc/firewall/hosts/${::hostname}",
    line    => ". `dirname \$0`/roles/${name}",
    require => File["/etc/firewall/hosts/${::hostname}"],
    notify  => Exec['run-iptables'],
  }
}
```

Puppet will look for a file called `${name}.role` in the `modules/firewall/files` directory (in our example, this will be `webserver.role`). This file will be copied into `/etc/firewall/roles`, and the `append_if_no_such_line` resource adds a line to the host-specific firewall script which loads the role file.

There's more...

If you have certain specific machines which will be referenced in your rules (for example, your monitoring server) you can add it to the `names` file as follows:

```
MONITOR=10.0.2.15
```

Then in a suitable place (such as `common.role`) you can allow access from this machine to, for example, the NRPE port:

```
iptables -A INPUT -p tcp -m tcp -s ${MONITOR}   --dport ${NRPE} -j
ACCEPT
```

You can also do this anywhere you need to reference a specific address, network, or IP range in a role file.

Dynamically generating the firewall ruleset such as this can be very useful for cloud infrastructures, where the list of servers is constantly changing as new ones are created and destroyed. All you need to do to have any resource trigger a firewall rebuild, is to add:

```
notify => Exec['run-iptables'],
```

So you might have a **master server list** that you maintain in version control or update automatically from a cloud API such as Rackspace or Amazon EC2. This list might be a `file` resource in Puppet which can trigger a firewall rebuild, so every time you check in a change to the master list, every machine that runs Puppet will update its firewall accordingly.

Of course, such a high degree of automation means that you need to be quite careful about what you check in, or you might take your whole infrastructure offline by mistake!

A good way to test changes is to use a Git branch for your Puppet manifests which is only applied on one or two servers. Once you have verified that the changes are good, then you can merge them into the master branch and roll them out.

Managing EC2 instances

It doesn't make sense for many of us to own and host our own servers, in the same way as it doesn't make sense for us to generate our own electricity. Just like electricity, computing is now a utility. Utility computing (often called **cloud** computing, for no known reason) allows you to buy as much compute power as you need, for as long as you need it. This makes it easy and cost-efficient to scale your service in response to fluctuating demand.

Being able to create new cloud server instances, use them for a few minutes or hours, and then delete them also makes it a lot easier to test and experiment with new software or configurations. If you had to build the servers by hand every time, this process would be too lengthy to make it worthwhile, but with automated configuration management, it's a snap.

There are plenty of cloud service providers around, with Amazon's EC2 being one of the best-known and oldest-established. In this recipe I'll show you how to manage cloud instances using EC2, but the general principles and most of the code will be adaptable to any cloud provider.

Getting ready...

You'll need an **Amazon Web Services** (**AWS**) account if you don't already have one. Of course if you're using an EC2 instance to try out the recipes in this book, you'll already have everything you need, but otherwise you can sign up for an AWS account here:

```
http://aws.amazon.com/
```

You'll need the AWS access key ID and secret access key corresponding to your account. You can find these on the **Security Credentials** page of the AWS portal.

You'll also need your SSH keypair for accessing EC2 instances. To find this, log in to the AWS Management Console: `https://console.aws.amazon.com/ec2/home`.

Navigate to the **Amazon EC2** tab, and click **Key Pairs** under the **Network & Security** heading in the navigation section.

Click **Create key pair** and then download the `keypair` file when prompted. Save this somewhere safe, and set the file permissions to mode `0600`:

```
ubuntu@cookbook:~$ chmod 600 bitfield.pem
```

How to do it...

Follow these steps to start creating the AWS example:

1. Run the following commands:

```
ubuntu@cookbook:~/puppet$ mkdir -p modules/fog/manifests

ubuntu@cookbook:~/puppet$ mkdir -p modules/fog/files
```

2. Create the file `modules/fog/manifests/init.pp` with the following contents:

```
# Manage Fog and EC2 boot scripts
class fog {
  package { ['libxml2-dev','libxslt1-dev']: ensure =>
    installed }

  package { 'fog':
    ensure   => installed,
    provider => gem,
    require  => [Package['libxml2-dev'],Package['libxslt1-dev']],
  }

  file { '/usr/local/bin/boot-ec2':
    source => 'puppet:///modules/fog/boot-ec2.rb',
    mode   => '0755',
  }

  file { '/usr/local/bin/bootstrap-ec2':
    source => 'puppet:///modules/fog/bootstrap-ec2.sh',
    mode   => '0755',
  }
}
```

3. Create the file `modules/fog/files/boot-ec2.rb` with the following contents (change the `:private_key_path` argument to point to your own AWS private key file):

```
#!/usr/bin/ruby
require 'rubygems'
require 'fog'

HOSTNAME = 'devbox'
@server = '' # NB this is two single quotes, not a double
quote

def command( cmdline )
  puts "Running command: #{cmdline}"
  res = @server.ssh( "sudo #{cmdline}" )[0]
  puts res.stdout
  puts res.stderr
end

def create()
  puts "Bootstrapping instance..."
  connection = Fog::Compute.new( { :provider => 'AWS',
                                   :region   => 'us-east-1',
```

```ruby
                                           :aws_access_key_id
    => 'AKIAI5SGMC3JWRQAPO3A',
                                           :aws_secret_access_key
    => 'iygf2+KV/inG3XOlEyrh+otazeVXrQJYKx8E7Sf' } )
      @server = connection.servers.bootstrap( :private_key_path
    => '~/bitfield.pem',
                                                :image_id =>
    'ami-137bcf7a',
                                                :username =>
    'ubuntu' )
      @server.wait_for { print "."; ready? }
      @server.wait_for { !public_ip_address.nil? }
      @server.reload
      puts "Instance name: #{@server.dns_name}"
      puts "Public IP: #{@server.ip_address}"
      puts "Setting hostname..."
      @server.ssh( "sudo hostname #{HOSTNAME}" )
    end

    def copy_bootstrap_files()
      puts "Copying bootstrap files..."
      @server.scp( "puppet.tar.gz", "/tmp" )
      @server.scp( "/usr/local/bin/bootstrap-ec2", "/tmp" )
    end

    def bootstrap()
      puts "Bootstrapping..."
      command( "sudo sh /tmp/bootstrap-ec2" )
    end

    create()
    copy_bootstrap_files()
    bootstrap()
```

4. Create the file `modules/fog/files/bootstrap-ec2.sh` with the following contents:

```bash
#!/bin/bash
wget http://apt.puppetlabs.com/puppetlabs-release-precise.deb
dpkg -i puppetlabs-release-precise.deb
apt-get update
apt-get -y install puppet git
cd /etc
tar xzf /tmp/puppet.tar.gz
puppet apply --modulepath=/etc/puppet/modules
/etc/puppet/manifests/site.pp
```

5. Modify your `manifests/nodes.pp` file as follows:

```
node 'cookbook' {
  include fog
```

```
    }

node 'devbox' {
  file { '/etc/motd':
    content => "Puppet power!\n",
  }
}
```

6. Run Puppet:

```
ubuntu@cookbook:~/puppet$ papply
Notice: /Stage[main]/Fog/Package[libxslt1-dev]/ensure: ensure
changed 'purged' to 'present'
Notice: /Stage[main]/Fog/File[/usr/local/bin/bootstrap-ec2]/
ensure: defined content as '{md5}3780e9f5bd2252281729dc1706b01f14'
Notice: /Stage[main]/Fog/Package[fog]/ensure: created
Notice: /Stage[main]/Fog/File[/usr/local/bin/boot-ec2]/ensure:
defined content as '{md5}0cdba84340b1aedefffd0ed329784450'
Notice: Finished catalog run in 37.17 seconds
```

7. Create a Puppet tarball in your working directory for distribution to the EC2 instance. The simplest way to do this is to tar up your existing Puppet repo or checkout:

```
ubuntu@cookbook:~$ cd
ubuntu@cookbook:~$ tar czf puppet.tar.gz --exclude .git puppet
```

8. Run the `boot-ec2` script:

```
ubuntu@cookbook:~$ boot-ec2
Bootstrapping instance...
Instance name: ec2-107-20-59-174.compute-1.amazonaws.com
Setting hostname...
Copying bootstrap files...
Bootstrapping...
Running command: sudo sh /tmp/bootstrap.sh
sudo: unable to resolve host devbox
sudo: unable to resolve host devbox
...
notice: //Node[devbox]/File[/etc/motd]/content: defined
content as 'unknown checksum'
```

9. Log in to the instance to check whether your manifest has been applied properly:

```
ubuntu@cookbook:~$ ssh -i bitfield.pem ubuntu@ec2-107-20-59-174.
compute-1.amazonaws.com
Puppet power!
ubuntu@devbox:~$
```

How it works...

Fog is a Ruby library for managing cloud resources, including EC2 and other providers such as Rackspace. Although you can use Amazon's own `ec2-tools` scripts to start and manage instances, using Fog makes it much easier to move your instances to another provider, and you don't need to install Java or other dependencies for `ec2-tools`. Having built EC2 infrastructure both ways, I can confidently say that I prefer using Fog, despite the fact that it has almost no documentation (Amazon actually has too much).

In the `boot-ec2` script, we've used Fog to create a new EC2 instance using our credentials, and to transfer a copy of the Puppet manifest onto it. We then copy the `bootstrap-ec2` script which installs Puppet and applies the manifest.

In this example, the manifest is pretty simple:

```
file { '/etc/motd':
  content => "Puppet power!\n",
}
```

but you can easily change it to be, for example, the same as for your production app server. This would be a good way of quickly deploying a large pool of app servers behind a physical load balancer; for example, to handle a sudden spike in demand. Alternatively, you can use EC2 instances as test or staging servers—it's up to you.

There's more...

There's no limit to the number of instances you can deploy with EC2—except perhaps the limit imposed by your credit card. So you could try modifying the script shown here to start a number of instances, set by a command-line argument.

You might also want different types of instances—web servers and queue worker servers, for example. You could modify the boot script to take an argument specifying the instance type to start.

The script shown here has an important limitation, in that, it supplies the instance with a snapshot of your Puppet manifest, in the form of a tarball. Obviously as you make changes to your Puppet manifest, that won't be reflected on the instance. For the sake of simplicity, the recipe example just uses Puppet to build the server initially, and it doesn't check out a copy of your Git repo or regularly update the Puppet manifests.

This is often fine for EC2 instances that are short-lived and only spun up for specific purposes. If you need servers that run for a longer time or you need to be able to push changes out to them with Puppet, you'll need to modify the script to set up a Git checkout and regular updates like your other servers, as described in *Chapter 1, Puppet Infrastructure*.

You might also want to be able to use other cloud providers, such as Rackspace or Linode. To do this, you will need to make small modifications to the script. Consult the Fog documentation for more information on this at `http://fog.io`.

 You can also use Puppet's Cloud Provisioner extension to manage your EC2 instances; for more on this see the Puppet Labs page at:
`http://docs.puppetlabs.com/guides/cloud_pack_getting_started.html`

Managing virtual machines with Vagrant

While it's great to be able to deploy virtual machines in the cloud, running them on your own desktop is sometimes even more convenient, especially for testing. If every developer can have a clone of the production system in a VM on his/her own machine, he/she's less likely to run into problems when deploying for real. Similarly, if every sysadmin can test his/her configuration management changes on a private VM, it's a great way to catch issues before they affect customers.

For some years tools such as VirtualBox and VMware have been available to do this. However, desktop cloud has really taken off with the arrival of Vagrant, a tool for managing and provisioning VM environments automatically. Vagrant drives VirtualBox or another virtualization layer to automate the process of creating a VM, provisioning it with Chef or Puppet, setting up networking, port forwarding, and packaging running VMs into images for others to use.

You can use Vagrant to manage your development VMs on your own desktop, or on a shared machine such as a continuous integration server. For example, you might use a CI tool such as Jenkins to boot a VM with Vagrant, deploy your app, and then run your tests against it as though it were in production.

Getting ready...

In order to use Vagrant, you'll need to install VirtualBox (which actually runs the virtual machine) and Vagrant (which controls VirtualBox). Currently you can't run VirtualBox VMs on an EC2 instance (which is itself a virtual machine), so for this example I'm using my laptop.

1. Download and install VirtualBox for your platform here:
   `https://www.virtualbox.org/wiki/Downloads`

2. Download and install Vagrant for your platform here (use the latest available version). You'll need at least version 1.2 to use the configuration shown here (beware of installing Vagrant from Rubygems, as the latest gem version at the time of writing is 1.0.7, which won't work): `http://downloads.vagrantup.com/`

How to do it...

Follow these steps to create your Vagrant VM:

1. Create a directory for the VM on your machine:

   ```
   $ mkdir devbox
   ```

2. In this directory, check out or copy your Puppet repo into `puppet`:

   ```
   $ cd devbox
   git clone git@github.com:bitfield/puppet.git puppet
   Cloning into 'puppet'...
   remote: Counting objects: 41, done.
   remote: Compressing objects: 100% (31/31), done.
   remote: Total 41 (delta 2), reused 37 (delta 1)
   Receiving objects: 100% (41/41), 6.15 KiB, done.
   Resolving deltas: 100% (2/2), done.
   ```

3. In the `devbox` directory, create the file `Vagrantfile` with the following contents:

   ```
   Vagrant.configure("2") do |config|
     config.vm.box = "devbox"
     config.vm.box_url = "http://cloud-images.ubuntu.com/precise/
   current/precise-server-cloudimg-vagrant-amd64-disk1.box"
     config.vm.hostname = "devbox"

     config.vm.provision :puppet, :module_path =>
   "puppet/modules" do |puppet|
       puppet.manifests_path = "puppet/manifests"
       puppet.manifest_file  = "site.pp"
     end
   end
   ```

4. Modify your `manifests/nodes.pp` file as follows:

   ```
   node 'cookbook' {}

   node 'devbox' {
     file { '/etc/motd':
       content => "Puppet power!\n",
     }
   }
   ```

5. In the `devbox` directory, run the following command (it may take a while the first time, as Vagrant has to download the base Ubuntu image before booting it):

   ```
   $ vagrant up
   Bringing machine 'default' up with 'virtualbox' provider...
   [default] Box 'devbox' was not found. Fetching box from
   ```

specified URL for

the provider 'virtualbox'. Note that if the URL does not have
a box for this provider, you should interrupt Vagrant now and
add

the box yourself. Otherwise Vagrant will attempt to download
the

full box prior to discovering this error.

Downloading or copying the box...

Extracting box...

Successfully added box 'devbox' with provider 'virtualbox'!

[default] Importing base box 'devbox'...

[default] Matching MAC address for NAT networking...

[default] Setting the name of the VM...

[default] Clearing any previously set forwarded ports...

[default] Creating shared folders metadata...

[default] Clearing any previously set network interfaces...

[default] Preparing network interfaces based on
configuration...

[default] Forwarding ports...

[default] -- 22 => 2222 (adapter 1)

[default] Booting VM...

[default] Waiting for VM to boot. This can take a few minutes.

[default] VM booted and ready for use!

[default] The guest additions on this VM do not match the
installed version of

VirtualBox! In most cases this is fine, but in rare cases it
can

cause things such as shared folders to not work properly. If
you see

shared folder errors, please update the guest additions within
the

virtual machine and reload your VM.

Guest Additions Version: 4.1.12

VirtualBox Version: 4.2

[default] Setting hostname...

[default] Configuring and enabling network interfaces...

[default] Mounting shared folders...

[default] -- /vagrant

[default] -- /tmp/vagrant-puppet/manifests

[default] -- /tmp/vagrant-puppet/modules-0

[default] Running provisioner: puppet...

```
Running Puppet with site.pp...
stdin: is not a tty
warning: Could not retrieve fact fqdn
warning: Host is missing hostname and/or domain: devbox
notice: /Stage[main]//Node[devbox]/File[/etc/motd]/ensure:
defined content as '{md5}0bdeca690dbb409d48391f3772d389b7'
notice: Finished catalog run in 0.05 seconds
Log into the devbox VM to test your configuration:
$ vagrant ssh
Puppet power!
vagrant@devbox:~$
```

How it works...

When Vagrant boots the VM for the first time, it's configured to look in a subdirectory of the project directory named `puppet` for the Puppet manifest to provision the machine. This can be a symbolic link to your Puppet working copy, or a standalone Puppet manifest just for the devbox—whatever you like, so long as Vagrant can find it.

From that point, Puppet runs just as it would on a 'real' machine, and will apply the manifest you've provided, in this case, setting the `/etc/motd` file to display an encouraging message on login.

Once the VM has been provisioned and Puppet has completed its run, it's ready for use. Just run `vagrant ssh` to log into it, `vagrant halt` to stop it, and `vagrant up` to start it again.

There's more...

In this example we just configured `devbox` with a simple manifest that adds a message to the `/etc/motd` file. To make this more useful, have `devbox` pick up the same manifest as the real server you'll be deploying to. For example:

```
node 'production', 'devbox' {
    include myapp::production
}
```

Thus, any changes you make to the production server config will be reflected in the machine you run your tests on, so that you can pick up problems before deploying. Similarly, if you need to make a config change to support a new feature, you can test it on the VM first to see if anything doesn't work.

If you want to suspend or shut down your VM while you're not using it, run:

```
$ vagrant suspend
```

or

```
$ vagrant halt
```

To wipe the VM completely, so that you can test re-provisioning it, for example, run:

```
$ vagrant destroy
```

The Vagrant maintainers have done a great job at making it very straightforward to use, but you can read more about Vagrant if you need to at the documentation site:

```
http://docs.vagrantup.com/v2/getting-started/
```

8
External Tools and the Puppet Ecosystem

By all means leave the road when you wish. That is precisely the use of a road: to reach individually chosen points of departure.

—Robert Bringhurst, 'The Elements of Typographic Style'

In this chapter we will cover:

- ▸ Creating custom facts
- ▸ Adding external facts
- ▸ Setting facts as environment variables
- ▸ Importing configuration data with Hiera
- ▸ Storing secret data with hiera-gpg
- ▸ Generating manifests with puppet resource
- ▸ Generating manifests with other tools
- ▸ Testing your Puppet manifests with rspec-puppet
- ▸ Using public modules
- ▸ Using an external node classifier
- ▸ Creating your own resource types
- ▸ Creating your own providers
- ▸ Creating custom functions

Introduction

Puppet is a useful tool by itself, but you can get much greater benefits from using Puppet in combination with other tools and frameworks. We'll look at some ways of getting data into Puppet, including custom Facter facts, external facts, and Hiera databases, and tools to generate Puppet manifests automatically from existing configuration.

You'll also learn how to extend Puppet by creating your own custom functions, resource types, and providers; how to use an external node classifier script to integrate Puppet with other parts of your infrastructure; how to use public modules from Puppet Forge; and how to test your code with `rspec-puppet`.

Creating custom facts

While Facter's built-in facts are useful, it's actually quite easy to add your own facts. For example, if you have machines in different data centers or hosting providers, you could add a **custom fact** for this so that Puppet can determine if any local settings need to be applied (for example, local DNS servers or network routes).

How to do it...

Here's an example of a simple custom fact:

1. Run the following command:

   ```
   ubuntu@cookbook:~/puppet$ mkdir -p modules/facts/lib/facter
   ```

2. Create the file `modules/facts/lib/facter/hello.rb` with the following contents:

   ```
   Facter.add(:hello) do
     setcode do
       "Hello, world"
     end
   end
   ```

3. Modify your `manifests/nodes.pp` file as follows:

   ```
   node 'cookbook' {
     notify { $::hello: }
   }
   ```

4. Run Puppet:

   ```
   ubuntu@cookbook:~/puppet$ papply
   Notice: Hello, world
   ```

```
Notice: /Stage[main]//Node[cookbook]/Notify[Hello, world]/message:
defined 'message' as 'Hello, world'

Notice: Finished catalog run in 0.24 seconds
```

How it works...

The built-in facts in Facter are defined in the same way as the custom fact that we just created. This architecture makes it very easy to add or modify facts, and provides a standard way for you to read information about the host into your Puppet manifests.

Facts can contain any Ruby code, and the last value evaluated inside the `setcode do ...` `end` block will be the value returned by the fact. For example, you could make a more useful fact that returns the number of users currently logged in:

```
Facter.add(:users) do
  setcode do
    %x{/usr/bin/who |wc -l}.chomp
  end
end
```

To reference the fact in your manifests, just use its name like a built-in fact:

```
notify { "${::users} users logged in": }
Notice:  2 users logged in
```

You can add custom facts to any Puppet module. You might like to create a dedicated `facts` module to contain them, as in the example, or just add facts to whichever existing module seems appropriate.

There's more...

You can extend the use of facts to build a completely **nodeless** Puppet configuration; in other words, Puppet can decide what resources to apply to a machine, based solely on the results of facts. Jordan Sissel has written about this approach at:

```
http://www.semicomplete.com/blog/geekery/puppet-nodeless-
configuration.html
```

You can find out more about custom facts, including how to make sure that OS-specific facts work only on the relevant systems, and how to weight facts so that they're evaluated in a specific order, at the Puppet Labs website:

```
http://docs.puppetlabs.com/guides/custom_facts.html
```

See also

- ▸ The *Importing dynamic information* recipe in *Chapter 3, Writing Better Manifests*
- ▸ The *Importing configuration data with Hiera* recipe in this chapter

Adding external facts

The *Creating custom facts* recipe describes how to add extra facts to Puppet for use in manifests, but these won't show up in the command-line version of Facter. If you want to make your facts available to both Facter and Puppet, you can create **external facts** instead.

External facts live in the `/etc/facter/facts.d` directory, and have a simple `key=value` format, like this:

```
message="Hello, world"
```

Getting ready...

Here's what you need to do to prepare your system for adding external facts:

1. You'll need at least Facter 1.7 to use external facts, so run this command to check your Facter version:

   ubuntu@cookbook:~$ facter -v

   1.7.1

2. If your version is pre-1.7, you can install a more recent Facter version from the Puppet Labs APT repo. If you haven't already configured your system to use this repo, follow the instructions in the *Installing Puppet* recipe in *Chapter 1, Puppet Infrastructure*. Then, run the following commands:

   ubuntu@cookbook:~$ sudo apt-get update

   ubuntu@cookbook:~$ sudo apt-get install facter

3. You'll also need to create the external facts directory, using the following command:

   ubuntu@cookbook:~$ sudo mkdir -p /etc/facter/facts.d

How to do it...

In this example we'll create a simple external fact that returns a message, as in the *Creating custom facts* recipe.

1. Create the file `/etc/facter/facts.d/myfacts.txt` with the following contents:

   ```
   theanswer=42
   ```

2. Run the following command:

```
ubuntu@cookbook:~$ facter theanswer
42
```

Well, that was easy! You can add more facts to the same file, or other files, of course:

```
theanswer=42
world_population='7 billion'
breakfast=johnnycakes
```

But what if you need to compute a fact in some way; for example, the number of logged-in users? You can create **executable facts** to do this.

1. Create the file `/etc/facter/facts.d/users.sh` with the following contents:

```
#!/bin/sh

echo users=`who |wc -l`
```

2. Make this file executable with the following command:

```
ubuntu@cookbook:~$ sudo chmod a+x /etc/facter/facts.d/users.sh
```

3. Now check the `fact` value with the following command:

```
ubuntu@cookbook:~$ facter users
1
```

How it works...

1. Facter will look in `/etc/facter/facts.d` and parse any non-executable files there, as lists of `key=value` pairs, as in the `myfacts.txt` example. If it finds a key matching the one you requested, it will print the associated value:

```
ubuntu@cookbook:~$ facter theanswer
42
```

2. In the case of executable files, Facter will assume that their output is a list of `key=value` pairs. It will execute all the files in the `facts.d` directory and search their output for the requested key.

3. In the `users` example, Facter will execute the `users.sh` script, which results in the following output:

```
users=1
```

4. It will then search this output for `users` and return the matching value:

```
ubuntu@cookbook:~$ facter users
1
```

5. If there are multiple matches for the key you specified, Facter will return the one parsed first, which is generally the one from the file whose name is alphanumerically first.

There's more...

You're not limited to using the `key=value` format for text facts; you can also use YAML or JSON format, and Facter will detect the format based on the file extension. For example, here are some facts in YAML format:

```
---
robin: Erithacus rubecula
bluetit: Cyanistes caerulus
blackbird: Turdus merula
```

And here are the same facts in JSON format:

```
{
  "robin": "Erithacus rubecula",
  "bluetit": "Cyanistes caerulus",
  "blackbird": "Turdus merula"
}
```

Be careful with the file extension; for YAML files the extension must be `.yaml` (`.yml` won't work, for example). JSON files should have a `.json` extension.

For executable facts, however, the output has to be in `key=value` format. Facter can't auto-detect the format of executable facts (yet).

Debugging external facts

If you're having trouble getting Facter to recognize your external facts, run Facter in debug mode to see what's happening:

```
ubuntu@cookbook:~/puppet$ facter -d robin
```

```
Fact file /etc/facter/facts.d/myfacts.json was parsed but returned an empty data set
```

The `X was parsed but returned an empty data set` error means Facter didn't find any `key=value` pairs in the file or (in the case of an executable fact) in its output.

Note that if you have external facts present, Facter parses or runs all the facts in the /etc/facter/facts.d directory every time you query Facter. If some of these scripts take a long time to run, that can significantly slow down anything that uses Facter (run Facter with the −timing switch to troubleshoot this). Unless a particular fact needs to be recomputed every time it's queried, consider replacing it with a cron job that computes it every so often and writes the result to a text file in the Facter directory.

Using external facts in Puppet

Any external facts you create will be available to both Facter and Puppet. To reference external facts in your Puppet manifests, just use the fact name in the same way you would for a built-in or custom fact:

```
notify { "There are $::users people logged in right now.": }
```

Make sure you don't create facts with the same name as an existing or built-in fact, or strange and probably unwelcome things may happen.

See also

▶ The *Importing dynamic information* recipe in *Chapter 3, Writing Better Manifests*
▶ The *Importing configuration data with Hiera* recipe in this chapter
▶ The *Creating custom facts* recipe in this chapter

Setting facts as environment variables

Another handy way to get information into Puppet and Facter is to pass it in using environment variables. Any environment variable whose name starts with FACTER_ will be interpreted as a fact. For example, try the following command:

ubuntu@cookbook:~/puppet$ FACTER_moonphase=full facter moonphase

full

It works just as well with Puppet, so let's run through an example.

How to do it...

Follow these steps to see how to set facts using environment variables:

1. Modify your `manifests/nodes.pp` file as follows:

```
node 'cookbook' {
  notify { "The moon is $::moonphase": }
}
```

2. Run the following command:

```
ubuntu@cookbook:~/puppet$ FACTER_moonphase="waxing crescent"
puppet apply manifests/site.pp

Notice: The moon is waxing crescent

Notice: /Stage[main]//Node[cookbook]/Notify[The moon is waxing
crescent]/message: defined 'message' as 'The moon is waxing
crescent'

Notice: Finished catalog run in 0.06 seconds
```

Importing configuration data with Hiera

A key principle of good programming is to separate data and code. Many Puppet manifests are full of site-specific data that makes it hard to share and re-use the manifests. Grouping all such data into structured text files and moving it outside the Puppet manifests makes it easier to maintain, as well as easier to re-use and share code with other people.

Ideally, we'd not only be able to look up configuration parameters from a data file, but also choose a different data file depending on things like the environment, the operating system, and other facts about the machine. We'd also like to be able to organize the data hierarchically so that we can override certain values with other, higher-priority values.

Puppet has a mechanism named **Hiera** (as in 'hierarchy') to do just this. The `hiera` function lets you look up configuration data from within your manifest, and Hiera takes care of returning the correct value for the current environment.

Getting ready...

In this example we'll see how to set up a minimal Hiera data file, and read some information out of it. First, we need to configure Puppet to retrieve data from Hiera. Follow these steps:

1. Create the file `hiera.yaml` in your Puppet directory with the following contents:

```
:hierarchy:
    - common
:backends:
```

```
    - yaml
:yaml:
    :datadir: '/home/ubuntu/puppet/data'
```

2. Create the `data` directory in your Puppet directory:

    ubuntu@cookbook:~/puppet$ mkdir data

3. Modify your `modules/puppet/files/papply.sh` script as follows (if you don't have this yet, follow the *Writing a papply script* recipe in *Chapter 1, Puppet Infrastructure*). The `sudo puppet apply` command is all on one line.

    ```
    #!/bin/sh
    sudo puppet apply /home/ubuntu/puppet/manifests/site.pp
    --modulepath=/home/ubuntu/puppet/modules/ --hiera_config=/home/
    ubuntu/puppet/hiera.yaml $*
    ```

4. Make sure that your node includes the `puppet` module, as follows:

    ```
    node 'cookbook' {
      include puppet
    }
    ```

5. Run Puppet to update the `papply` script:

    ubuntu@cookbook:~/puppet$ papply

    Notice: /Stage[main]/Puppet/File[/usr/local/bin/papply]/content: content changed '{md5}171896840d39664c00909eb8cf47a53c' to '{md5}6 d104081905bcb5e1611ac9b6ae6d3b9'

    Notice: Finished catalog run in 0.26 seconds

How to do it...

We've now enabled Hiera, so we're ready to use it. Follow these steps to see how to read Hiera data into your Puppet manifest.

1. Create the file `data/common.yaml` with the following contents:

    ```
    magic_word : 'xyzzy'
    ```

2. Add the following to your manifest:

    ```
    $message = hiera('magic_word')
    notify { $message: }
    ```

3. Run Puppet:

    ubuntu@cookbook:~/puppet$ papply

    Notice: xyzzy

How it works...

1. When you look up a bit of data using the `hiera` function, Hiera has to do several things. First, it has to find its `data` directory, which is set in `hiera.yaml` here as `/home/ubuntu/puppet/data`.

2. Then it needs to know which data file to read. This is determined by the `hierarchy` setting, which in our example simply contains `common`. So Hiera will read `common.yaml` and look for the parameter `magic_word`. When it finds it, it will read the value (`xyzzy`) and return it to the manifest.

3. Finally, this value is stored in the `$message` variable and printed out for our enjoyment.

There's more...

Hiera is a very powerful mechanism for importing configuration data and we don't have space to explore all its possibilities here. But let's look at a simple improvement to our Hiera setup: adding node-specific settings.

Setting node-specific data with Hiera

In order to have Hiera read different data files depending on the name of the node, we need to make a couple of changes to the configuration in the previous example, as follows:

1. Modify your `hiera.yaml` file as follows:

```
:hierarchy:
    - %{hostname}
    - common
:backends:
    - yaml
:yaml:
    :datadir: '/home/ubuntu/puppet/data'
```

2. Create the file `data/cookbook.yaml` (if your machine is named `cookbook`; otherwise, name it after your hostname) with the following contents:

```
greeting : "Hello, I'm the cookbook node!"
```

3. Modify your `data/common.yaml` file as follows:

```
greeting : "Hello, I'm some other node!"
```

4. Modify your `manifests/nodes.pp` file as follows:

```
node 'cookbook', 'cookbook2' {
  $message = hiera('greeting')
  notify { $message: }
}
```

5. Run Puppet:

```
ubuntu@cookbook:~/puppet$ papply
Notice: Hello, I'm the cookbook node!
```

What's happening here? Recall that Hiera uses the `hierarchy` setting to determine which data files to search, and in which order. In our example, the first value of `hierarchy` is:

```
%{hostname}
```

This tells Hiera to look for a `.yaml` file matching the machine's hostname. If it can't find one, it will go on to the next value in the list:

```
common
```

So for all calls to the `hiera` function, Hiera will first look for `data/cookbook.yaml` (or whatever the hostname is), and then `data/common.yaml`. This allows us to set certain bits of data which are specific to a named node, in this case, `cookbook`:

```
greeting : "Hello, I'm the cookbook node!"
```

If Hiera can't find a data file matching the machine's hostname, it will look in `common.yaml` and use the value of the `greeting` parameter from that file. We can test this by temporarily setting the machine's hostname to something different as follows:

```
ubuntu@cookbook:~/puppet$ sudo hostname cookbook2
ubuntu@cookbook:~/puppet$ papply
sudo: unable to resolve host cookbook2
dnsdomainname: Name or service not known
dnsdomainname: Name or service not known
dnsdomainname: Name or service not known
Notice: Hello, I'm some other node!
Notice: /Stage[main]//Node[cookbook2]/Notify[Hello, I'm some other
node!]/message: defined 'message' as 'Hello, I'm some other node!'
Notice: Finished catalog run in 0.08 seconds
ubuntu@cookbook:~/puppet$ sudo hostname cookbook
```

The values you specify for `hierarchy` can include Facter facts (as in the `hostname` example) or even Puppet variables. For example, if you had a variable `$::vagrant` which is `true` on a Vagrant virtual machine and `false` otherwise, you could specify:

```
:hierarchy:
  - vagrant_%{::vagrant}
```

Depending on the value of `$::vagrant`, Hiera will either look for the data in `vagrant_true.yaml` or `vagrant_false.yaml`.

This is a great way to modify the node's configuration depending on some external factor without having to use lot of conditional statements and selectors in your Puppet code. Plus, you can store and version the Hiera data separately from your Puppet manifests (and for production use, this is a good idea; it means you can use different data depending on the Puppet environment setting).

Looking up data with Hiera

There are several ways to look up config data using Hiera: the `hiera` function, as we saw in the example, simply returns the first match found in the hierarchy for the specified key. However, you can also use `hiera_array` and `hiera_hash` to return multiple values. With these functions, Hiera will return all the matches found, including those at different levels of the hierarchy.

See also

- ▶ The *Importing dynamic information* recipe in *Chapter 3, Writing Better Manifests*
- ▶ The *Storing secret data with hiera-gpg* recipe in this chapter
- ▶ The *Creating custom facts* recipe in this chapter
- ▶ The *Adding external facts* recipe in this chapter
- ▶ The *Managing virtual machines with Vagrant* recipe in *Chapter 7, Servers and Cloud Infrastructure*
- ▶ To find out more about Hiera and explore some of its more advanced features, read the documentation on the Puppet Labs site:

`http://docs.puppetlabs.com/hiera/1/index.html`

Storing secret data with hiera-gpg

In *Chapter 4, Working with Files and Packages*, we looked at a way to store encrypted data in our Puppet manifest which can be decrypted only with the appropriate key (see the *Using GnuPG to encrypt secrets* recipe in *Chapter 4, Working with Files and Packages*).

If you're using Hiera to store your configuration data, there's a gem available called `hiera-gpg` which adds an encryption backend to Hiera to achieve the same result.

Getting ready...

To set up `hiera-gpg`, follow these steps:

1. Run this command to install `hiera-gpg`:

```
ubuntu@cookbook:~$ sudo gem install hiera-gpg --no-ri --no-rdoc
```

```
Fetching: json_pure-1.8.0.gem (100%)

Fetching: hiera-1.2.1.gem (100%)

Fetching: gpgme-2.0.2.gem (100%)

Building native extensions.  This could take a while...

Fetching: hiera-gpg-1.1.0.gem (100%)

Successfully installed json_pure-1.8.0

Successfully installed hiera-1.2.1

Successfully installed gpgme-2.0.2

Successfully installed hiera-gpg-1.1.0

4 gems installed
```

2. Modify your `hiera.yaml` file as follows:

```
:hierarchy:
    - secret
    - common
:backends:
    - yaml
    - gpg
:yaml:
    :datadir: '/home/ubuntu/puppet/data'
:gpg:
    :datadir: '/home/ubuntu/puppet/data'
```

How to do it...

In this example we'll create a piece of encrypted data and retrieve it using `hiera-gpg`.

1. Create the file `data/secret.yaml` with the following contents:

   ```
   top_secret: 'xyzzy'
   ```

2. If you don't already have a GnuPG encryption key, follow the steps in the *Using GnuPG to encrypt secrets* recipe in *Chapter 4, Working with Files and Packages* to create one.

3. Encrypt the `secret.yaml` file to this key using the following command (replace the `john@bitfieldconsulting.com` with the e-mail address you specified when creating the key). This will create the file `secret.gpg`:

   ```
   ubuntu@cookbook:~/puppet$ cd data
   ubuntu@cookbook:~/puppet/data$ gpg -e -o secret.gpg -r john@
   bitfieldconsulting.com secret.yaml
   ```

4. Remove the plaintext `secret.yaml` file:

   ```
   ubuntu@cookbook:~/puppet/data$ rm secret.yaml
   ```

5. Modify your `manifests/nodes.pp` file as follows:

```
node 'cookbook' {
  $message = hiera('top_secret')
  notify { $message: }
}
```

6. Now run Puppet:

```
ubuntu@cookbook:~/puppet$ papply

Notice: xyzzy

Notice: /Stage[main]//Node[cookbook]/Notify[xyzzy]/message:
defined 'message' as 'xyzzy'

Notice: Finished catalog run in 0.29 seconds
```

How it works...

When you install `hiera-gpg`, it adds to Hiera, the ability to decrypt `.gpg` files. So you can put any secret data into a `.yaml` file that you then encrypt to the appropriate key with GnuPG. Only machines that have the right secret key will be able to access this data.

For example, you might encrypt the MySQL `root` password using `hiera-gpg` and install the corresponding key only on your database servers. Although other machines may also have a copy of the `secret.gpg` file, it's not readable to them unless they have the decryption key.

There's more...

You might also like to know about `hiera-eyaml`, another secret-data backend for Hiera that supports encryption of individual values within a Hiera data file. This could be handy if you need to mix encrypted and unencrypted facts within a single file. Find out more about `hiera-eyaml` here:

```
https://github.com/TomPoulton/hiera-eyaml
```

See also

▶ The *Importing configuration data with Hiera* recipe in this chapter
▶ The *Using GnuPG to encrypt secrets* recipe in *Chapter 4, Working with Files and Packages*

Generating manifests with puppet resource

If you have a server which is already configured as it needs to be, or nearly so, you can capture that configuration as a Puppet manifest. The **puppet resource** command generates Puppet manifests from the existing configuration of a system. For example, you can have `puppet resource` generate a manifest that creates all the users found on the system. This is very useful for taking a snapshot of a working system and getting its configuration quickly into Puppet.

How to do it...

Here are some examples of using `puppet resource` to get data from a running system:

1. To generate the manifest for a particular user, run the following command:

   ubuntu@cookbook:~/puppet$ puppet resource user ubuntu

   ```
   user { 'ubuntu':
     ensure  => 'present',
     comment => 'Ubuntu',
     gid     => '1000',
     groups  => ['adm', 'dialout', 'cdrom', 'floppy', 'audio', 'dip',
   'video', 'plugdev', 'netdev', 'admin'],
     home    => '/home/ubuntu',
     shell   => '/bin/bash',
     uid     => '1000',
   }
   ```

2. For a particular service, run the following command:

   ubuntu@cookbook:~/puppet$ puppet resource service ntp

   ```
   service { 'ntp':
     ensure => 'running',
     enable => 'true',
   }
   ```

3. For a package, run the following command:

   ubuntu@cookbook:~/puppet$ puppet resource package libxml2-dev

   ```
   package { 'libxml2-dev':
     ensure => '2.7.8.dfsg-5.1ubuntu4.4',
   }
   ```

There's more...

You can use `puppet resource` to examine each of the resource types available in Puppet. In the preceding examples, we generated a manifest for a specific instance of the resource type, but you can also use `puppet resource` to dump all instances of the resource:

```
ubuntu@cookbook:~/puppet$ puppet resource user
user { 'bin':
  ensure  => 'present',
  comment => 'bin',
  gid     => '2',
  home    => '/bin',
  shell   => '/bin/sh',
  uid     => '2',
}
user { 'daemon':
  ensure  => 'present',
  comment => 'daemon',
  gid     => '1',
  home    => '/usr/sbin',
  shell   => '/bin/sh',
  uid     => '1',
}
...
```

This will generate a lot of output!

Generating manifests with other tools

If you want to quickly capture the complete configuration of a running system as a Puppet manifest, there are a couple of tools available to help. In this example we'll look at Blueprint and Pysa, both designed to examine a machine and dump its state as Puppet code.

Getting ready...

Here's what you need to do to prepare your system for using Blueprint.

Run the following commands to install Blueprint:

```
ubuntu@cookbook:~/puppet$ sudo apt-get install python-pip
ubuntu@cookbook:~/puppet$ sudo pip install blueprint
```

How to do it...

These steps will show you how to run Blueprint:

1. Run the following commands:

```
ubuntu@cookbook:~/puppet$ cd puppet/modules/
ubuntu@cookbook:~/puppet/modules$ sudo blueprint create -P bp_test
# [blueprint] searching for APT packages to exclude
No packages found matching installation-report.
No packages found matching linux-generic-pae.
No packages found matching language-pack-en.
No packages found matching language-pack-gnome-en.
No packages found matching linux-server.
No packages found matching ubuntu-desktop.
# [blueprint] caching excluded APT packages
# [blueprint] searching for Yum packages to exclude
# [blueprint] parsing blueprintignore(5) rules
# [blueprint] searching for npm packages
# [blueprint] searching for Ruby gems
# [blueprint] searching for PEAR/PECL packages
# [blueprint] searching for Yum packages
# [blueprint] searching for Python packages
# [blueprint] searching for software built from source
# [blueprint] searching for configuration files
# [blueprint] /etc/ssl/certs/EBG_Elektronik_Sertifika_Hizmet_Sa\
xc4\x9flay\xc4\xb1c\xc4\xb1s\xc4\xb1.pem not UTF-8 - skipping it
# [blueprint] /etc/ssl/certs/NetLock_Arany_=Class_Gold=_F\xc5\
x91tan\xc3\xbas\xc3\xadtv\xc3\xa1ny.pem not UTF-8 - skipping it
# [blueprint] /etc/ssl/certs/T\xc3\x9cB\xc4\xb0TAK_UEKAE_K\xc3\
xb6k_Sertifika_Hizmet_Sa\xc4\x9flay\xc4\xb1c\xc4\xb1s\xc4\xb1_-_S\
xc3\xbcr\xc3\xbcm_3.pem not U
TF-8 - skipping it
# [blueprint] /etc/ssl/certs/AC_Ra\xc3\xadz_Certic\xc3\
xa1mara_S.A..pem not UTF-8 - skipping it
# [blueprint] /etc/ssl/certs/Certinomis_-_Autorit\xc3\xa9_Racine.
pem not UTF-8 - skipping it
# [blueprint] searching for service dependencies
bp_test/manifests/init.pp
```

2. Read the file `bp_test/manifests/init.pp` to see the generated code:

```
#
# Automatically generated by blueprint(7).   Edit at your own risk.
#
class bp_test {
  Exec {
    path =>
      '/usr/local/sbin:/usr/local/bin:/usr/sbin:/usr/bin:/sbin:/
bin',
  }
  Class['sources'] -> Class['files'] -> Class['packages']
  class files {
    file {
      '/etc':
      ensure => directory;
      '/etc/X11':
      ensure => directory;
      '/etc/X11/Xwrapper.config':
      content =>
        template('bp_test/etc/X11/Xwrapper.config'),
      ensure  => file,
      group   => root,
      mode    => 0644,
      owner   => root;
      '/etc/apache2':
      ensure => directory;
  ...
```

There's more...

It's worth saying that tools like Blueprint are probably a bit less helpful than you might think. I've heard people say things like, "Great! I don't need to know Puppet at all: I just have to set up my system manually, then Blueprint it."

While this is true as far as it goes, there are some problems with that approach. The first is that Blueprint is completely indiscriminate about what it captures, which is to say, everything: as you can see in the example, it adds things such as the `/etc/X11` directory to the manifest. In fact, this is completely unmodified from a standard Ubuntu install, so putting it in Puppet is pointless.

The result is a very large amount of Puppet code (nearly 1500 lines for my system), most of which is entirely irrelevant to your application or service. Blueprint also makes no attempt to separate its generated code into modules, so you get one huge source file, which is awkward to maintain.

As you can see, the generated code itself is not compatible with the Puppet style guide, so it won't match the rest of your manifest. It's more verbose than it needs to be, because there are no refactoring steps to group together similar resources in arrays or definitions. It's not object-oriented in any way and you end up with just a few unhelpfully-named classes such as `packages` and `files`.

All package versions are hard-coded to whatever happens to be currently installed; this means the manifest will stop working as soon as any package is updated in the Ubuntu repository, because the version it specifies will no longer be available.

Need I go on? I think you get the point. Blueprint and other automatic manifest-generating tools can be a helpful aid to a busy sysadmin, if used sparingly. You should also regard the resulting code as a starting point rather than something to plug straight into your production systems.

Frankly, in my Puppet consulting work, I don't use tools like this. I find it easier and quicker to write good code from scratch (and help my clients to do the same) rather than try to wrestle crummy auto-generated code into shape. I recommend you do the same. But if your boss suggests you stop wasting time using your brain and use Blueprint instead, simply direct her to this book.

Playing with Pysa

Pysa is a new tool inspired by Blueprint, and is in some ways smarter. However, it suffers from most of the generic problems with automatic manifest generation tools that I've described. Currently it's in alpha status, meaning that its functionality is not yet complete, and the manifests it produces don't always work. However, it's under active development, and looks to be a promising tool in the future.

You can find out more about Pysa at the website:

```
http://www.madeiracloud.com/blog/introducing-pysa-reverse-your-
servers-configurations
```

Conclusion

There's definitely a place for automatic manifest generation tools. The most useful, I think, is probably `puppet resource` because you can use it in a targeted way to quickly generate manifests for only those resources you're interested in. The resulting code is of good quality and you can add it straight into your manifests without too much tweaking.

There's no short-cut to good configuration management, though, and those who hope to save time and effort by cutting and pasting someone else's code wholesale (as with public modules) are likely to find that it saves neither.

Testing your manifests with rspec-puppet

It would be great if we could verify that our Puppet manifests satisfy certain expectations without even having to run Puppet. `rspec-puppet` is a nifty tool for doing this. Based on RSpec, a testing framework for Ruby programs, `rspec-puppet` lets you write test cases for your Puppet manifests that are especially useful for catching regressions (bugs introduced when fixing another bug) and refactoring problems (bugs introduced when reorganizing your code).

Getting ready...

Here's what you'll need to do to install `rspec-puppet`.

Run the following commands:

```
ubuntu@cookbook:~/puppet$ sudo gem install rspec-puppet
ubuntu@cookbook:~/puppet$ sudo gem install puppetlabs_spec_helper
```

How to do it...

Let's write some tests for our `admin::ntp` class.

1. Run the following commands:

    ```
    ubuntu@cookbook:~/puppet$ cd modules/admin/
    ubuntu@cookbook:~/puppet/modules/admin$ rspec-puppet-init
      + spec/
      + spec/classes/
      + spec/defines/
      + spec/functions/
      + spec/hosts/
      + spec/fixtures/
      + spec/fixtures/manifests/
      + spec/fixtures/modules/
      + spec/fixtures/modules/admin/
      + spec/fixtures/manifests/site.pp
      + spec/fixtures/modules/admin/manifests
      + spec/fixtures/modules/admin/files
      + spec/spec_helper.rb
      + Rakefile
    ```

2. Create the file `spec/classes/ntp_spec.rb` with the following contents:

```
require 'spec_helper'

describe 'admin::ntp' do
  it { should contain_package('ntp') }
  it { should contain_service('ntp').with(
    'ensure' => 'running'
  ) }
  it { should contain_file('/etc/ntp.conf') }
end
```

3. Run the following commands:

```
ubuntu@cookbook:~/puppet/modules/admin$ rake spec
/usr/bin/ruby1.8 -S rspec spec/classes/ntp_spec.rb
...


Finished in 0.46446 seconds
3 examples, 0 failures
```

How it works...

The `rspec-puppet-init` command creates a framework of directories for you to put your specs (test programs) in. At the moment, we're just interested in the `spec/classes` directory. This is where you'll put your class specs, one per class, named after the class it tests, for example, `ntp_spec.rb`.

The `spec` code itself begins with the following statement, which sets up the RSpec environment to run the specs:

```
require 'spec_helper'
```

Then there follows a `describe` block:

```
describe 'admin::ntp' do
  ..
end
```

`describe` identifies the class we're going to test (`admin::ntp`) and wraps the list of assertions about the class inside a `do .. end` block.

Assertions are our stated expectations of the `admin::ntp` class. For example, the first assertion is the following:

```
it { should contain_package('ntp') }
```

The `contain_package` assertion means what it says: the class should contain a package resource named `ntp`.

Next, we test for the existence of the `ntp` service:

```
it { should contain_service('ntp').with(
  'ensure' => 'running'
) }
```

The preceding code actually contains two assertions. First, that the class contains an `ntp` service:

```
contain_service('ntp')
```

Second, that the service has an `ensure` attribute with the value `running`:

```
with(
  'ensure' => 'running'
)
```

You can specify any attributes and values you want using the `with` method, as a comma-separated list. For example, the following code asserts several attributes of a `file` resource:

```
it { should contain_file('/tmp/hello.txt').with(
  'content' => "Hello, world\n",
  'owner'   => 'ubuntu',
  'group'   => 'ubuntu',
  'mode'    => '0644'
) }
```

In our `admin::ntp` example, we need to only test that the file `ntp.conf` is present, using the following code:

```
it { should contain_file('/etc/ntp.conf') }
```

When you run the `rake spec` command, `rspec-puppet` will compile the relevant Puppet classes, run all the specs it finds, and display the results:

```
ubuntu@cookbook:~/puppet/modules/admin$ rake spec
/usr/bin/ruby1.8 -S rspec spec/classes/ntp_spec.rb
...


Finished in 0.46446 seconds
3 examples, 0 failures
```

If one of the specs failed, you'd see an error message like the following:

```
/usr/bin/ruby1.8 -S rspec spec/classes/ntp_spec.rb
```

```
..F

Failures:

  1)  admin::ntp
      Failure/Error: it { should contain_file('/etc/ntp.conf') }
        expected that the catalogue would contain File[/etc/ntp.conf]
      # ./spec/classes/ntp_spec.rb:8


Finished in 0.47529 seconds
3 examples, 1 failure
```

There's more...

You can find more information about `rspec-puppet`, including complete documentation for the assertions available, and a tutorial, at:

```
http://rspec-puppet.com/
```

See also

The *Checking your manifests with puppet-lint* recipe in *Chapter 2, Puppet Language and Style*

Using public modules

When you write a Puppet module to manage some software or service, you don't have to start from scratch. Community-contributed modules are available at the **Puppet Forge** site for many popular applications. Sometimes, a community module will be exactly what you need and you can download and start using it straight away. In most cases, you will need to make some modifications to suit your particular needs and environment.

In general, I would not recommend treating Puppet Forge as a source of "drop-in" modules, that you can deploy without reading or understanding the code. Rather, I would use it as a source of inspiration, help, and examples. A module taken from Puppet Forge should be a jumping-off point for you to develop and improve your own modules.

It's fine to start by using other people's modules, but if you don't learn the skills to extend them and write your own, you'll always be reliant on third-party code that may or may not be maintained in the future.

Be aware that a given module may not work on your Linux distribution. Check the README file that comes with the module to see if your operating system is supported.

How to do it...

In this example we'll use the `puppet module` command to find and install the useful `stdlib` module, which contains many utility functions to help you develop Puppet code.

1. Run the following command:

```
ubuntu@cookbook:~/puppet$ puppet module search stdlib
Notice: Searching https://forge.puppetlabs.com ...
NAME                            DESCRIPTION
AUTHOR            KEYWORDS
cek-fstdlib                     Fused additional "stdlib"
functions, types, facts and everything else.  @cek
standard-library fstdlib fused
juniper-netdev_stdlib_junos     Junos Provider code for
Networking Device (netdev stdlib) Library        @juniper
juniper netdevops junos networking
netdevops-netdev_stdlib         Type definitions for
Networking Device (netdev) Library               @netdevops
networking netdevops
aristanetworks-netdev_stdlib_eos Provider definition for
implementing Networking Device (netdev) Lib...
@aristanetworks   networking eos netdev arista
offline-stdlib                  Puppet Module Standard
Library                                          @offline
puppetlabs-activemq             ActiveMQ Puppet Module
@puppetlabs       java activemq amqp stomp stdlib
puppetlabs-java                 Manage the official Java
runtime                                          @puppetlabs
java stdlib runtime jdk jre
puppetlabs-stdlib               Puppet Module Standard
Library                                          @puppetlabs
```

2. There are several matching results, but the one we're looking for is `puppetlabs-stdlib`, so run the following commands to download this module and add it to your repo:

```
ubuntu@cookbook:~/puppet$ puppet module install -i /home/ubuntu/
puppet/modules puppetlabs-stdlib
Notice: Preparing to install into /home/ubuntu/puppet/modules
...
Notice: Downloading from https://forge.puppetlabs.com ...
Notice: Installing -- do not interrupt ...
/home/ubuntu/puppet/modules
└── puppetlabs-stdlib (v4.1.0)
```

3. The module is now ready to use in your manifests: most good modules come with a README file to show you how to do this.

How it works...

You can search for modules that match the package or software you're interested in with the puppet module search command. To install a specific module, use puppet module install with the -i option to tell it where your module directory is, as in the example.

You can browse the site to see what's available at

```
http://forge.puppetlabs.com/
```

There's more...

Not all publically available modules are on Puppet Forge. Some other great places to look are on GitHub:

 ▸ `https://github.com/camptocamp`
 ▸ `https://github.com/example42`

Though not a collection of modules as such, the Puppet Cookbook website has many useful and illuminating code examples, patterns, and tips, maintained by the admirable Dean Wilson:

```
http://www.puppetcookbook.com/
```

Using an external node classifier

When Puppet runs on a node, it needs to know which classes should be applied to that node. For example, if it is a web server node, it might need to include an apache class. The normal way to map nodes to classes is in the Puppet manifest itself, for example in a nodes.pp file:

```
node 'web1' {
   include apache
}
```

Alternatively, you can use an **external node classifier** to do this job. An external node classifier (**ENC** for short) is any executable program which can accept a node name and return a list of classes which should be applied to that node.

An ENC could be a simple shell script, for example, or a wrapper around a more complicated program or API that can decide how to map nodes to classes. In this example we'll build the most trivial of ENCs, a shell script which simply prints out a list of classes to include.

Getting ready...

An ENC has certain restrictions compared to a node declaration: for example, you can't declare individual resources, but can only include classes that already exist in your manifest. So for this example, we'll create a little `helloenc` class that the ENC will include.

1. Run the following command:

   ubuntu@cookbook:~/puppet$ mkdir -p modules/admin/manifests

2. Create the file `modules/admin/manifests/helloenc.pp` with the following contents:

   ```
   class admin::helloenc {
     notify { "Hello, I was included by your ENC!": }
   }
   ```

How to do it...

Here's how to build a simple external node classifier:

1. Create the file `/usr/local/bin/enc` with the following contents:

   ```
   #!/bin/bash
   cat <<"END"
   ---
   classes:
     admin::helloenc:

   END
   ```

2. Run the following command:

   ubuntu@cookbook:~/puppet$ sudo chmod a+x /usr/local/bin/enc

3. Modify your `/etc/puppet/puppet.conf` file as follows:

   ```
   [main]
     node_terminus = exec
     external_nodes = /usr/local/bin/enc
   ```

4. Run Puppet:

   ubuntu@cookbook:~/puppet$ papply

   Notice: Hello, I was included by your ENC!

   Notice: /Stage[main]/Admin::Helloenc/Notify[Hello, I was included by your ENC!]/message: defined 'message' as 'Hello, I was included by your ENC!'

   Notice: Finished catalog run in 0.29 seconds

How it works...

When an external node classifier is set in `puppet.conf`, Puppet will call the specified program with the node's hostname as the command-line argument. In our example script, this argument is ignored, and it just outputs a fixed list of classes (actually, just one class).

Obviously this script is not terribly useful; a more sophisticated script might check a database to find the class list, or look up the node in a hash or an external text file. Hopefully, this example is enough to get you started writing your own external node classifier.

There's more...

An ENC can supply a whole list of classes to be included on the node, in the following (YAML) format:

```
classes:
  CLASS1:
  CLASS2:
  CLASS3:
  ...
```

For classes that take parameters, you can use this format:

```
classes:
  mysql:
    package: percona-server-server-5.5
    socket:  /var/run/mysqld/mysqld.sock
    port:    3306
```

You can also produce top-scope variables using an ENC, with this format:

```
parameters:
  message: 'hello'
```

Variables that you set in this way will be available in your manifest using the normal syntax for a top-scope variable, for example `$::message`.

See also

See the Puppet Labs ENC page for more information on writing and using ENCs:

`http://docs.puppetlabs.com/guides/external_nodes.html`

Creating your own resource types

As you know, Puppet has a bunch of useful built-in resource types: packages, files, users, and so on. Usually, you can do everything you need to do by using either combinations of these built-in resources, or a custom `define` that you can use more or less in the same way as a resource (see *Chapter 3, Writing Better Manifests* for information on definitions).

However, if you need to create your own resource type, Puppet makes it quite easy. The native types are written in Ruby, and you will need a basic familiarity with Ruby in order to create your own.

Let's refresh our memory on the distinction between **types** and **providers**. A type describes a resource and the parameters it can have (for example, the `package` type). A provider tells Puppet how to implement a resource type for a particular platform or situation (for example, the `apt/dpkg` providers implement the `package` type for Debian-like systems).

A single type (`package`) can have many providers (`apt`, `yum`, `fink`, and so on). If you don't specify a provider when declaring a resource, Puppet will choose the most appropriate one given the environment.

How to do it...

In this section we'll see how to create a custom type that we can use to manage Git repositories, and in the next section, we'll write a provider to implement this type.

1. Run the following command:

   ```
   ubuntu@cookbook:~/puppet$ mkdir -p
   modules/custom/lib/puppet/type
   ```

2. Create the file `modules/custom/lib/puppet/type/gitrepo.rb` with the following contents:

   ```
   Puppet::Type.newtype(:gitrepo) do
     ensurable

     newparam(:source) do
       isnamevar
     end

     newparam(:path)
   end
   ```

How it works...

Custom types can live in any module, in a `lib/puppet/type` subdirectory and in a file named for the type (in our example, that's `modules/custom/lib/puppet/type/gitrepo.rb`).

The first line of `gitrepo.rb` tells Puppet to register a new type named `gitrepo`:

```
Puppet::Type.newtype(:gitrepo) do
```

The `ensurable` line automatically gives the type a property `ensure`, like Puppet's built-in resources:

```
ensurable
```

We'll now give the type some parameters. For the moment, all we need is a `source` parameter for the Git source URL, and a `path` parameter to tell Puppet where the repo should be created in the filesystem.

```
newparam(:source) do
   isnamevar
end
```

The `isnamevar` declaration tells Puppet that the `source` parameter is the type's **namevar**. So when you declare an instance of this resource, whatever name you give it will be the value of `source`, for example:

```
gitrepo { 'git://github.com/puppetlabs/puppet.git':
  path => '/home/ubuntu/dev/puppet',
}
```

Finally, we tell Puppet that the type accepts the `path` parameter:

```
newparam(:path)
```

There's more...

Once you're familiar with creating your own resources, you can use them to replace complicated `exec` statements and make your manifests more readable. However, it's a good idea to make your resources robust and reusable by adding some documentation and validating your parameters.

Documentation

Our example is deliberately simple, but when you move on to developing real custom types for your production environment, you should add documentation strings to describe what the type and its parameters do. For example:

```
Puppet::Type.newtype(:gitrepo) do
  @doc = "Manages Git repos"

  ensurable

  newparam(:source) do
    desc "Git source URL for the repo"
    isnamevar
  end

  newparam(:path) do
    desc "Path where the repo should be created"
  end
end
```

Validation

You can use parameter validation to generate useful error messages when someone tries to pass bad values to the resource. For example, you could validate that the directory where the repo is to be created actually exists:

```
newparam(:path) do
  validate do |value|
    basepath = File.dirname(value)
    unless File.directory?(basepath)
      raise ArgumentError , "The path %s doesn't exist" % basepath
    end
  end
end
```

You can also specify the list of allowed values that the parameter can take:

```
newparam(:breakfast) do
  newvalues(:bacon, :eggs, :sausages)
end
```

Creating your own providers

In the previous section, we created a new custom type called `gitrepo` and told Puppet that it takes two parameters, `source` and `path`. However, so far we haven't told Puppet how to actually check out the repo—in other words, how to create a specific instance of this type. That's where the provider comes in.

We saw that a type will often have several possible providers. In our example, there is only one sensible way to instantiate a Git repo, so we'll only supply one provider: `git`. If you were to generalize this type—to just `repo`, say—it's not hard to imagine creating several different providers depending on the type of repo, for example, `git`, `svn`, `cvs`, and so on.

How to do it...

We'll add the `git` provider, and create an instance of a `gitrepo` resource to check that it all works. You'll need Git installed for this to work, but if you're using the Git-based manifest management setup described in *Chapter 1, Puppet Infrastructure*, we can safely assume that Git is available.

1. Run the following command:

   ```
   ubuntu@cookbook:~/puppet$ mkdir -p
   modules/custom/lib/puppet/provider/gitrepo
   ```

2. Create the file `modules/custom/lib/puppet/provider/gitrepo/git.rb` with the following contents:

   ```
   require 'fileutils'

   Puppet::Type.type(:gitrepo).provide(:git) do
     commands :git => "git"

     def create
       git "clone", resource[:source], resource[:path]
     end

     def exists?
       File.directory? resource[:path]
     end
   end
   ```

3. Modify your `manifests/nodes.pp` file as follows:

   ```
   node 'cookbook' {
     gitrepo { 'https://github.com/puppetlabs/puppet.git':
       ensure => present,
       path   => '/tmp/puppet',
     }
   }
   ```

4. Run Puppet:

   ```
   ubuntu@cookbook:~/puppet$ papply

   Notice:
   /Stage[main]//Node[cookbook]/Gitrepo[https://github.com/
   puppetlabs/puppet.git]/ensure: created

   Notice: Finished catalog run in 10.76 seconds
   ```

How it works...

Custom providers can live in any module, in a `lib/puppet/provider/TYPE_NAME` subdirectory, in a file named after the provider (in our example, that's `modules/custom/lib/puppet/provider/gitrepo/git.rb`).

The first line of `git.rb` tells Puppet to register a new provider for the `gitrepo` type:

```
Puppet::Type.type(:gitrepo).provide(:git) do
```

When you declare an instance of the `gitrepo` type in your manifest, Puppet will first of all check whether the instance already exists, by calling the `exists?` method on the provider. So we need to supply this method, complete with code to check whether an instance of the `gitrepo` already exists:

```
def exists?
  File.directory? resource[:path]
end
```

This is not the most sophisticated implementation: it simply returns `true` if a directory exists matching the `path` parameter of the instance. A better implementation of `exists?` might check, for example, whether there is a `.git` subdirectory and that it contains valid Git metadata. But this will do for now.

If `exists?` returns `true`, then Puppet will take no further action, because the specified resource exists (as far as Puppet knows). If it returns false, Puppet assumes the resource doesn't yet exist, and will try to create it by calling the provider's `create` method.

Accordingly, we supply some code for the `create` method that calls the `git clone` command to create the repo:

```
def create
  git "clone", resource[:source], resource[:path]
end
```

The method has access to the instance's parameters, which we need to know where to check out the repo from, and which directory to create it in. We get this by looking at `resource[:source]` and `resource[:path]`.

There's more...

You can see that custom types and providers in Puppet are very powerful. In fact, they can do anything—at least, anything that Ruby can do. If you are managing some parts of your infrastructure with complicated `define` statements and `exec` resources, you may want to consider replacing these with a custom type. In fact, it's worth looking around to see if someone else has already done this before implementing your own.

Our example was very simple, and there is much more to learn about writing your own types. If you're going to distribute your code for others to use, or even if you aren't, it's a good idea to include tests with it. Puppet Labs has a useful page on the interface between custom types and providers:

```
http://docs.puppetlabs.com/guides/custom_types.html
```

on implementing providers:

```
http://docs.puppetlabs.com/guides/provider_development.html
```

and a complete worked example of developing a custom type and provider, a little more advanced than that presented in this book:

```
http://docs.puppetlabs.com/guides/complete_resource_example.html
```

Dean Wilson also has a very instructive example of a custom type to manage APT sources:

```
https://github.com/deanwilson/puppet-aptsourced
```

Creating your own functions

If you've read the recipe *Using GnuPG to encrypt secrets* in *Chapter 4, Working with Files and Packages*, then you've already seen an example of a custom function (in that example, we created a `secret` function, which shelled out to GnuPG). Let's look at custom functions in a little more detail now and build an example.

How to do it...

If you've read the recipe *Efficiently distributing cron jobs* in *Chapter 5, Users and Virtual Resources*, you might remember that we used the `inline_template` function to set a random time for cron jobs to run, based on the hostname of the node. In this example we'll take that idea and turn it into a custom function called `random_minute`.

1. Run the following command:

   ```
   ubuntu@cookbook:~/puppet$ mkdir -p
   modules/custom/lib/puppet/parser/functions
   ```

2. Create the file `modules/custom/lib/puppet/parser/functions/random_minute.rb` with the following contents:

   ```
   module Puppet::Parser::Functions
     newfunction(:random_minute, :type => :rvalue) do |args|
       lookupvar('hostname').sum % 60
     end
   end
   ```

3. Modify your `manifests/nodes.pp` file as follows:

```
node 'cookbook' {
  cron { 'randomised cron job':
    command => '/bin/echo Hello, world >>/tmp/hello.txt',
    hour    => '*',
    minute  => random_minute(),
  }
}
```

4. Run Puppet:

ubuntu@cookbook:~/puppet$ papply

Notice: /Stage[main]//Node[cookbook]/Cron[randomised cron job]/ ensure: created

Notice: Finished catalog run in 0.42 seconds

5. Check the crontab with the following command:

ubuntu@cookbook:~/puppet$ sudo crontab -l

 # HEADER: This file was autogenerated at Fri Jun 28 12:04:11 +0000 2013 by puppet.

 # HEADER: While it can still be managed manually, it is definitely not recommended.

 # HEADER: Note particularly that the comments starting with 'Puppet Name' should

 # HEADER: not be deleted, as doing so could cause duplicate cron jobs.

 # Puppet Name: randomised cron job

15 * * * * /bin/echo Hello, world >>/tmp/hello.txt

How it works...

Custom functions can live in any module, in the `lib/puppet/parser/functions` subdirectory, in a file named after the function (in our example, `random_minute.rb`).

The function code goes inside a `module ... end` block like this:

```
module Puppet::Parser::Functions
  ...
end
```

We then call `newfunction` to declare our new function, passing in the name (`:random_minute`), and the type of function (`:rvalue`):

```
newfunction(:random_minute, :type => :rvalue) do |args|
```

The `:rvalue` bit simply means that this function returns a value.

Finally, the function code itself is here:

```
lookupvar('hostname').sum % 60
```

The `lookupvar` function lets you access facts and variables by name: in this case, `hostname` to get the name of the node we're running on. We use the Ruby `sum` method to get the numeric sum of the characters in this string, and then perform integer division modulo 60 to make sure the result is in the range `0..59`.

There's more...

You can, of course, do a lot more with custom functions. In fact, anything you can do in Ruby, you can do in a custom function. You also have access to all the facts and variables that are in scope at the point in the Puppet manifest where the function is called, by calling `lookupvar` as shown in the example.

To find out more about what you can do with custom functions, see the Puppet Labs website:

```
http://docs.puppetlabs.com/guides/custom_functions.html
```

9
Monitoring, Reporting, and Troubleshooting

Show me a completely smooth operation and I'll show you someone who's covering mistakes. Real boats rock.

—Frank Herbert, 'Chapterhouse: Dune'

In this chapter, we will cover:

- ▶ Doing a dry run
- ▶ Logging command output
- ▶ Logging debug messages
- ▶ Generating reports
- ▶ Producing automatic HTML documentation
- ▶ Drawing dependency graphs
- ▶ Understanding Puppet errors
- ▶ Inspecting configuration settings

Introduction

We've all had the experience of sitting in an exciting presentation about some new technology, and rushing home to play with it. Of course, once you start experimenting with it, you immediately run into problems. What's going wrong? Why doesn't it work? How can I see what's happening under the hood? This chapter will help you answer some of these questions, and give you the tools to solve common Puppet problems. We'll also see how to generate useful reports on your Puppet infrastructure, and how Puppet can help you monitor and troubleshoot your network as a whole.

Doing a dry run

Sometimes your Puppet manifest doesn't do exactly what you expected, or perhaps someone else has checked in changes you didn't know about. Either way, it's good to know exactly what Puppet is going to do before it does it.

If it would update a `config` file and restart a production service, for example, this could result in unplanned downtime. Also, sometimes manual configuration changes are made on a server which Puppet would overwrite.

To avoid these problems, you can use Puppet's **dry run** mode (also called **noop mode**, for **no operation**).

How to do it...

Follow this step in order to do a dry run with Puppet. Run Puppet (or the `papply` script we wrote in *Chapter 1, Puppet Infrastructure*) with the `--noop` switch. The output will depend on whether Puppet has any changes to make to the machine. If there are resources to be applied, you'll see output similar to this (not the same, of course; the actual output will depend on your manifest):

```
ubuntu@cookbook:~/puppet$ papply --noop
Notice: /Stage[main]/Admin::Ntp/File[/etc/ntpd.conf]/ensure: current_
value absent, should be file (noop)
Notice: /Stage[main]/Admin::Ntp/Service[ntp]: Would have triggered
'refresh' from 1 events
Notice: Class[Admin::Ntp]: Would have triggered 'refresh' from 2 events
Notice: Stage[main]: Would have triggered 'refresh' from 1 events
Notice: Finished catalog run in 0.55 seconds
```

How it works...

In the `noop` mode, Puppet does everything it would normally, with the exception of actually making any changes to the machine (the `exec` resources, for example, won't run). It tells you what it would have done, and you can compare this with what you expected to happen. If there are any differences, double-check the manifest or the current state of the machine.

Note that Puppet warns us that it would have written the file `/etc/ntpd.conf`, and restarted the `ntp` service. This may or may not be what we want, but it's useful to know in advance. I make it a rule, when applying any non-trivial changes on production servers, to run Puppet in `noop` mode first, and verify what's going to happen.

There's more...

You can also use dry run mode as a simple auditing tool. It will tell you if any changes have been made to the machine since Puppet last applied its manifest. Some organizations require all config changes to be made with Puppet, which is one way of implementing a change control process. Unauthorized changes can be detected using Puppet in dry run mode and you can then decide whether to merge the changes back into the Puppet manifest, or undo them.

You can also use the `--debug` switch to Puppet (or `papply`) to see the details of every resource Puppet considers in the manifest. This can be helpful when trying to figure out if Puppet is loading a particular class, for example, or to see in what order things are happening.

See also

- ▸ The *Auditing resources* recipe in *Chapter 5, Users and Virtual Resources*
- ▸ The *Automatic syntax checking with Git hooks* recipe in *Chapter 1, Puppet Infrastructure*
- ▸ The *Generating reports* recipe in this chapter
- ▸ The *Testing your Puppet manifests with rspec-puppet* recipe in *Chapter 8, External Tools and the Puppet Ecosystem*

Logging command output

When you use the `exec` resources to run commands on the node, Puppet will give you an error message like the following if a command returns a non-zero exit status:

```
Notice: /Stage[main]//Node[cookbook]/Exec[this-will-fail]/returns:
/bin/cat: /tmp/missing: No such file or directory
Error: /bin/cat /tmp/missing returned 1 instead of one of [0]
```

As you can see, Puppet not only reports that the command failed, but shows its output:

```
/bin/cat: /tmp/missing: No such file or directory
```

This is useful for figuring out why the command didn't work, but sometimes the command actually succeeds (in that it returns a zero exit status) but still doesn't do what we wanted. In that case, how can you see the command output? You can use the `logoutput` attribute.

How to do it...

Follow these steps in order to log command output:

1. Define an `exec` resource with the `logoutput` parameter as shown in the following code snippet:

    ```
    exec { 'misbehaving-command':
      command   => '/bin/cat /etc/hostname',
      logoutput => true,
    }
    ```

2. Run Puppet:

    ubuntu@cookbook:~/puppet$ papply

    **Notice: /Stage[main]//Node[cookbook]/Exec[misbehaving-command]/
    returns: cookbook**

    **Notice: /Stage[main]//Node[cookbook]/Exec[misbehaving-command]/
    returns: executed successfully**

    Notice: Finished catalog run in 0.14 seconds

3. As you can see, even though the command succeeds, Puppet prints the output:

    cookbook

How it works...

The `logoutput` attribute has three possible settings:

- ▶ `false`: never print command output
- ▶ `on_failure`: only print output if the command fails (the default setting)
- ▶ `true`: always print output, whether the command succeeds or fails

There's more...

You can set the default value of `logoutput` to always display command output for all `exec` resources by defining the following in your `site.pp` file:

```
Exec {
  logoutput => true,
}
```

What's this `Exec` syntax? It looks like an `exec` resource, but it's not. When you use `Exec` with a capital `E`, you're telling Puppet to apply this to all `exec` resources anywhere in the manifest. It's a handy way of setting global defaults for a particular resource type.

If you never want to see command output, whether it succeeds or fails, use:

```
logoutput => false,
```

Logging debug messages

It can be very helpful when debugging problems if you can print out information at a certain point in the manifest. This is a good way to tell, for example, if a variable isn't defined or has an unexpected value. Sometimes it's useful just to know that a particular piece of code has been run. Puppet's `notify` resource lets you print out such messages.

How to do it...

Define a `notify` resource in your manifest at the point you want to investigate:

```
notify { 'Got this far!': }
```

How it works...

When this resource is applied Puppet will print out the message:

```
notice: Got this far!
```

There's more...

If you're the kind of brave soul who likes experimenting, and I hope you are, you'll probably find yourself using debug messages a lot to figure out why your code doesn't work. So knowing how to get the most out of Puppet's debugging features can be a great help.

Printing out variable values

You can refer to variables in the message:

```
notify { "operatingsystem is ${::operatingsystem}": }
```

And Puppet will interpolate the values in the printout:

notice: operatingsystem is Ubuntu

The double colon (::) before the fact name tells Puppet that this is a variable in top scope (accessible to all classes) and not local to the class. For more about how Puppet handles variable scope, see the Puppet Labs article:

```
http://docs.puppetlabs.com/guides/scope_and_puppet.html
```

Checking when a resource is applied

If you want to find out when a particular resource has been applied, you can have your notify resource require it. That way, when you see the notify, you can be sure that the dependent resource has already been applied:

```
notify { 'Resource X has been applied':
  require => Exec['X'],
}
```

Generating reports

If you're managing a lot of machines, Puppet's reporting facility can give you some valuable information on what's actually happening out there.

How to do it...

To enable reports, just add this to a client's puppet.conf:

```
report = true
```

How it works...

With reporting enabled, Puppet will generate a report file, containing data such as

- ▶ The date and time of the run
- ▶ Total time for the run
- ▶ Log messages output during the run
- ▶ List of all resources in the client's manifest

- ▶ Whether Puppet changed any resources, and how many
- ▶ Whether the run succeeded or failed

By default, these reports are stored on the node in `/var/lib/puppet/reports` in a directory named after the hostname, but you can specify a different destination using the `reportdir` option. You can create your own scripts to process these reports (which are in the standard **YAML** format).

There's more...

If you just want one report, or you don't want to enable reporting all the time, you can add the `--report` switch to the command line when you run Puppet manually:

```
ubuntu@cookbook:~/puppet$ papply --report
Notice: Finished catalog run in 0.17 seconds
```

You won't see any output, but a report file will be generated in the `report` directory.

You can also see some overall statistics about a Puppet run by supplying the `--summarize` switch:

```
ubuntu@cookbook:~/puppet$ papply --summarize
Notice: Finished catalog run in 0.19 seconds
Changes:
Events:
Resources:
             Total: 11
           Skipped: 6
Time:
         Filebucket: 0.00
               Cron: 0.00
               File: 0.01
   Config retrieval: 0.17
              Total: 0.18
           Last run: 1364230708
Version:
             Config: 1364230706
             Puppet: 3.2.2
```

If you want to collate Puppet reports centrally, one way to do this is to have Puppet write its reports to the node's syslog, and use a distribution mechanism such as `rsyslog` to send these logs to a central machine.

See also

- The *Auditing resources* recipe in *Chapter 5, Users and Virtual Resources*
- The *Doing a dry run* recipe in this chapter

Producing automatic HTML documentation

Like most engineers, I never read the manual, unless and until the product actually catches fire. However, as your manifests get bigger and more complex, it can be helpful to create HTML documentation for your nodes and classes using Puppet's automatic documentation tool, `puppet doc`.

How to do it...

Follow these steps to generate HTML documentation for your manifest:

1. Run the following command:

   ```
   ubuntu@cookbook:~/puppet$ puppet doc --all --outputdir=/home/
   ubuntu/puppet/doc --mode rdoc --manifestdir=/home/ubuntu/puppet
   ```

2. This will generate a set of HTML files in `/home/ubuntu/puppet/doc`. Open the top-level `index.html` file with your web browser, and you'll see something like the following screenshot:

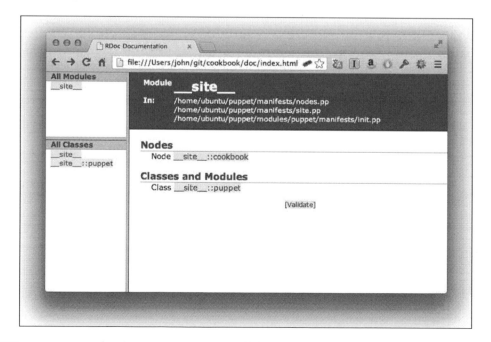

How it works...

puppet doc creates a structured HTML documentation tree similar to that produced by **RDoc**, the popular Ruby documentation generator. This makes it easier to understand how different parts of the manifest relate to one another, as you can click on an included class name and see its definition, for example.

There's more...

puppet doc will generate basic documentation of your manifests as they stand, but you can include more useful information by adding comments to your manifest files, using the standard RDoc syntax. Here's an example of some documentation comments added to a class:

```
# == Class: puppet
#
# Everything required to run Puppet automatically on a client.
#
# === Parameters
#
# No parameters.
#
# === Variables
#
# No variables used.
#
# === Examples
#
#   include puppet
#
# === Authors
#
# John Arundel <john@bitfieldconsulting.com>
#
# === Copyright
#
# Copyright 2013 Bitfield Consulting Ltd.
class puppet {
    ...
}
```

Your comments are added to the documentation for each class in the resulting HTML files, as shown in the following screenshot:

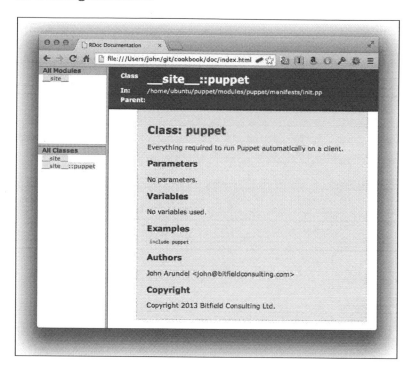

See also

The *Checking your manifests with puppet-lint* recipe in *Chapter 2, Puppet Language and Style*

Drawing dependency graphs

Dependencies can get complicated quickly, and it's easy to end up with a **circular dependency** (where A depends on B, which depends on A) that will cause Puppet to complain and stop working. Fortunately, Puppet's `--graph` option makes it easy to generate a diagram of your resources and the dependencies between them, which can be a big help in fixing such problems.

Getting ready...

Install the `graphviz` package for viewing the diagram files:

```
ubuntu@cookbook:~/puppet$ sudo apt-get install graphviz
```

How to do it...

Follow these steps to generate a dependency graph for your manifest:

1. Create the directories for a new `admin` module:

   ubuntu@cookbook:~/puppet$ mkdir modules/admin

   ubuntu@cookbook:~/puppet$ mkdir modules/admin/manifests

   ubuntu@cookbook:~/puppet$ mkdir modules/admin/files

2. Create the file `modules/admin/manifests/ntp.pp` with the following code containing a deliberate circular dependency (can you spot it?):

   ```
   # Manage NTP
   class admin::ntp {
     package { 'ntp':
       ensure  => installed,
       require => File['/etc/ntp.conf'],
     }

     service { 'ntp':
       ensure  => running,
       require => Package['ntp'],
     }

     file { '/etc/ntp.conf':
       source  => 'puppet:///modules/admin/ntp.conf',
       notify  => Service['ntp'],
       require => Package['ntp'],
     }
   }
   ```

3. Copy your existing `ntp.conf` file into Puppet:

   ubuntu@cookbook:~/puppet$ cp /etc/ntp.conf modules/admin/files

4. Include this class on a node using a snippet like the following:

   ```
   node cookbook {
     include admin::ntp
   }
   ```

5. Run Puppet:

```
ubuntu@cookbook:~/puppet$ papply
Error: Could not apply complete catalog: Found 1 dependency cycle:
(File[/etc/ntp.conf] => Package[ntp] => File[/etc/ntp.conf])
Try the '--graph' option and opening the resulting '.dot' file in
OmniGraffle or GraphViz
Notice: Finished catalog run in 0.18 seconds
```

6. Run Puppet with the `--graph` option as suggested:

```
ubuntu@cookbook:~/puppet$ papply --graph
Error: Could not apply complete catalog: Found 1 dependency cycle:
(File[/etc/ntp.conf] => Package[ntp] => File[/etc/ntp.conf])
Cycle graph written to /var/lib/puppet/state/graphs/cycles.dot.
Notice: Finished catalog run in 0.14 seconds
```

7. Check the graph files have been created:

```
ubuntu@cookbook:~/puppet$ sudo ls -l /var/lib/puppet/state/graphs
total 20
-rw-r--r-- 1 root root  121 Mar 26 13:34 cycles.dot
-rw-r--r-- 1 root root 4785 Mar 26 13:34 expanded_relationships.
dot
-rw-r--r-- 1 root root 2258 Mar 26 13:34 relationships.dot
-rw-r--r-- 1 root root 2927 Mar 26 13:34 resources.dot
```

8. Create a graphic using the `dot` command as follows:

```
ubuntu@cookbook:~/puppet$ dot -Tpng -o relationships.png /var/lib/
puppet/state/graphs/relationships.dot
```

9. The graphic will look something like the following:

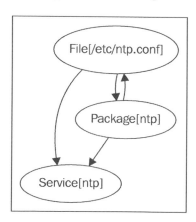

How it works...

When you run `papply --graph` (or enable the `graph` option in `puppet.conf`) Puppet will generate three graphs in DOT format (a graphics language):

▶ `resources.dot`: showing the hierarchical structure of your classes and resources, but without dependencies

▶ `relationships.dot`: showing the dependencies between resources as arrows, as shown in the preceding screenshot

▶ `expanded_relationships.dot`: a more detailed version of the relationships graph

The `dot` tool (part of the `graphviz` package) will convert these to an image format such as PNG for viewing.

In the relationships graph, each resource in your manifest is shown as a balloon, with arrowed lines connecting them to indicate the dependencies. You can see that in our example, the dependencies between `File['/etc/ntp.conf']` and `Package['ntp']` form a circle.

To fix the circular dependency problem, all you need to do is remove one of the dependency lines and to break the circle. The following code fixes the problem:

```
# Manage NTP
class admin::ntp {
  package { 'ntp':
    ensure  => installed,
  }

  service { 'ntp':
    ensure  => running,
    require => Package['ntp'],
  }

  file { '/etc/ntp.conf':
    source  => 'puppet:///modules/admin/ntp.conf',
    notify  => Service['ntp'],
    require => Package['ntp'],
  }
}
```

There's more...

Resource and relationship graphs can be useful even when you don't have a bug to find. If you have a very complex network of classes and resources, for example, studying the resources graph can help you see where to simplify things. Similarly, when dependencies become too complicated to understand from reading the manifest, the graphs can be a useful form of documentation.

See also

The *Using run stages* recipe in *Chapter 3, Writing Better Manifests*

Understanding Puppet errors

Puppet's error messages can sometimes be a little confusing. Here are some of the most common errors you might encounter, and what to do about them.

How to do it...

Often the first step is simply to search the web for the error message text and see what explanations you can find for the error, along with any helpful advice about fixing it. Here are some of the most common puzzling errors, with possible explanations:

```
Could not retrieve file metadata for XXX: getaddrinfo: Name or service
not known
```

Where XXX is a `file` resource, you may have accidentally typed `puppet://modules...` in a file source instead of `puppet:///modules...` (note the triple slash).

```
Could not evaluate: Could not retrieve information from environment
production source(s) XXX
```

The source file may not be present or may not be in the right location in the Puppet repo.

```
Error: Could not set 'file' on ensure: No such file or directory XXX
```

The file path may specify a parent directory (or directories) that doesn't exist. You can use separate file resources in Puppet to create these.

```
Could not parse for environment production: Syntax error at end of file
at line 1
```

You may have mistyped some command line options (particularly, using a single hyphen instead of a double hyphen).

change from absent to file failed: Could not set 'file on ensure: No such file or directory

This is often caused by Puppet trying to write a file to a directory that doesn't exist. Check that the directory either exists already or is defined in Puppet, and that the file resource requires the directory (so that the directory is always created first).

undefined method 'closed?' for nil:NilClass

This unhelpful error message is roughly translated as "something went wrong". It tends to be a catch-all error caused by many different problems, but you may be able to determine what is wrong from the name of the resource, the class, or the module. One trick is to add the --debug switch, to get more useful information:

ubuntu@cookbook:~/puppet$ papply --debug

If you check your Git history to see what was touched in the most recent change, this may be another way to identify what's upsetting Puppet.

Could not parse for environment --- "--- production": Syntax error at end of file at line 1

This can be caused by mistyping command line options; for example, if you type puppet -verbose instead of puppet --verbose. That kind of error can be hard to see.

Duplicate definition: X is already defined in [file] at line Y; cannot redefine at [file] line Y

This one has caused me a bit of puzzlement in the past. Puppet's complaining about a duplicate definition, and normally if you have two resources with the same name, Puppet will helpfully tell you where they are both defined. But in this case, it's indicating the same file and line number for both. How can one resource be a duplicate of itself?

The answer is if it's a definition (a resource created with the define keyword). If you create two instances of a definition, you'll also have two instances of all the resources contained within the definition, and they need to have distinct names. For example:

```
define check_process() {
  exec { 'is-process-running?':
    command => "/bin/ps ax |/bin/grep ${name} >/tmp/pslist.${name}.
txt",
  }
}

check_process { 'exim': }
check_process { 'nagios': }
```

```
ubuntu@cookbook:~/puppet$ papply
```

Error: Duplicate declaration: Exec[is-process-running?] is already
declared in file /home/ubuntu/puppet/modules/admin/manifests/broken.pp at
line 5; cannot redeclare on node cookbook.compute-1.internal

Error: Duplicate declaration: Exec[is-process-running?] is already
declared in file /home/ubuntu/puppet/modules/admin/manifests/broken.pp at
line 5; cannot redeclare on node cookbook.compute-1.internal

Because the `exec` resource is named `is-process-running?`, if you try to create more than one instance of the definition, Puppet will refuse because the result would be two `exec` resources with the same name. The solution is to include the name of the instance (or some other unique value) in the title of each resource:

```
exec { "is-process-${name}-running?":
  command => "/bin/ps ax |/bin/grep ${name} >/tmp/pslist.${name}.txt",
}
```

Every resource must have a unique name, and a good way to ensure this with a definition is to interpolate the `${name}` variable in its title. Note that we switched from using single to double quotes in the resource title:

```
"is-process-${name}-running?"
```

The double quotes are required when you want Puppet to interpolate the value of a variable into a string.

See also

- The *Generating reports* recipe in this chapter
- The *Doing a dry run* recipe in this chapter
- The *Logging debug messages* recipe in this chapter

Inspecting configuration settings

You probably know that Puppet's configuration settings are stored in `puppet.conf`, but there are lots of parameters, and those that aren't listed in `puppet.conf` will take a default value. How can you see the value of any configuration parameter, regardless of whether or not it's explicitly set in `puppet.conf`? The answer is to use the `puppet config print` command.

How to do it...

Run the following command. This will produce a lot of output (it may be helpful to pipe it through `less` if you'd like to browse the available configuration settings):

```
ubuntu@cookbook:~/puppet$ puppet config print |less

agent_catalog_run_lockfile = /home/ubuntu/.puppet/var/state/agent_
catalog_run.lock

agent_disabled_lockfile = /home/ubuntu/.puppet/var/state/agent_disabled.
lock

allow_duplicate_certs = false

allow_variables_with_dashes = false

...
```

How it works...

`puppet config print` will output every configuration parameter and its current value (and there are lots of them).

To see the value for a specific parameter, add it as an argument to the `puppet config print` command:

```
ubuntu@cookbook:~/puppet$ puppet config print noop

false
```

See also

The *Generating reports* recipe in this chapter

Index

A

a2ensite command 148
Amazon EC2 tab 188
Amazon Web Services (AWS) 188
Apache servers
  about 144
  managing 144, 145
Apache virtual hosts
  creating 145-147
  custom domains 149
  docroots 149
  working 148, 149
APT package framework 106
arguments
  passing, to shell commands 84, 85
array iteration
  using, in templates 96, 97
arrays
  about 45
  creating 45
  creating, with split function 46
  hashes, using 46
  using 45
  working 45
arrays, of resources
  using 58
audit metaparameter 140
Augeas tool
  about 87
  automatically editing config files with 89, 90
auto_failback setting 171
automatic syntax checking
  Git hooks, used 29
AWS Management Console
  URL 188

B

Blueprint
  installing 214
  running 215, 216

C

case statements
  about 50, 52
  default value, specifying 52
  examples 50
  working 51
CentOS 8
changes parameter 90
check_syntax.sh script 32
circular dependency
  about 245
  fixing 248
class inheritance
  extra values, adding using +> operator 78
  using 75, 76
cloud computing 188
command output
  logging 237, 238
  working 238
community Puppet style
  about 34
  indentation 34
  parameters 35
  quoting 34
  symlinks 36
  using 34
  variables 35
conditional statements
  comparisons 48
  elsif branches 48

example 47
expressions, combining 48
working 47
writing 47
config files
building with snippets 91- 93
editing automatically with Augeas 89-91
adding lines to 88, 89
configuration data
importing, with Hiera 206-208
configuration settings
inspecting 251
contain_package assertion 220
cron
Puppet, running from 18, 19
cron jobs
distributing 126-128
cross-platform manifests
writing 79
custom facts
creating 200, 201

D

Dean Wilson
example, URL 231
debug messages
logging 239
resource, checking 240
variable values, printing 240
decentralized Puppet architecture
creating 14, 16
definitions
creating 59
using 59
working 60
dependencies
using 61- 64
dependency graphs
drawing 245-247
directory trees
distributing 135, 136
DocumentRoot parameter 150
dotfiles 121
DOT format, graphs
expanded_relationships.dot 247

relationships.dot 247
resources.dot 247
dry run mode
using 236, 237
dynamic information
importing 83

E

EC2 instances
AWS example, creating 188-193
managing 188
ENC. *See* **external node classifier**
environment variables
facts, setting as 205
ERB (embedded Ruby) syntax 94
ERB templates
using 94, 95
exec resource 186
dependencies 61
quoting command line for 84
replacing with custom types 230
running only when notified 93
scheduling 129
executable facts
creating 203
external facts 202-205
external node classifier 223

F

Facter
about 81
using 82
working 82
facts
setting, as environment variables 205
facts.d directory 203
file
shares, managing 171-174
firewall class 184
firewalls
managing, with iptables 178-187
functions
creating 231, 232

G

generate function 83
Git
  used, for managing manifests 11-13
Git hooks
  used, for automatic syntax checking 29-31
gitrepo 228
GnuPG
  used, for encrypting secrets 98-101
grep command 89

H

HAProxy
  using, to load-balance multiple web servers
    174-177
haproxy daemon 177
Heartbeat
  installing 169
  used, for building high-availability services
    166-171
Hiera
  configuration data, importing with 206, 208
  looking up with 210
  node-specific data, setting 208, 209
hiera-gpg
  secret data, storing with 210, 212
  setting up 210, 211
high-availability services
  building, Heartbeat used 166-171
host resources
  using 132
HTML documentation
  generating 242, 243

I

inherited attributes
  removing 77
inline_template function 126
inline templates
  using 44
  working 44
in operator
  about 53
  using 53

installation
  Puppet 8
ipaddresses array 97
iptables
  firewalls, managing with 178-187
isnamevar declaration 227

L

lenses 90
Linux distributions 8
Load balancing 174-177
logoutput attribute 237, 238
lookupvar function 233

M

managehome parameter 120
manifests
  about 58
  checking, with puppet-lint 36-38
  creating 10, 11
  generating, with other tools 214- 217
  generating, with puppet resource 213
  making, portable 79, 80
  managing, Git used 11, 13
  testing, with rspec-puppet 218-220
master server list 187
metaparameter 70
module
  about 38
  custom facts 41
  custom functions 41
  custom types 41
  module layout, autogenerating 41
  organizing 41
  providers 41
  template, using 40, 41
  third party modules 41
  using 38, 39
  working 40
multiple file sources
  using 133, 134
multiple items
  iterating over 45

MySQL
about 153
managing 153-155
working 156, 157
MySQL databases
creating 157, 158

N

--noop switch 139
Network File System (NFS)
servers, managing 171-174
nfs class 174
Nginx 150
Nginx virtual hosts
creating 150-152
working 152, 153
node inheritance
using 71, 72
nodeless configuration, Puppet 201
node-specific data
setting, with Hiera 208, 209
noop metaparameter 140
using 141
noop mode 236

O

old files
cleaning up 137, 138
options parameter 174

P

packages
building, from source 106, 107
installing, from third-party repository 103-105
package versions
comparing 108, 109
papply script
about 207
writing 16-18
parameters
passing, to classes 73, 74
providers
about 226
creating 228-230

implementing 231
public modules
using 221, 223
pull-updates script 23
Puppet
configuration settings, inspecting 251
errors 248-250
installing 8-10
running, from cron 18-22
puppet apply command 14
puppet config print command 251, 252
Puppet Labs official style guide
reference link 34
Puppet Labs
URL 201, 233
puppet-lint
installing 37
URL 37
used, for checking manifests 37
Puppet manifests . *See* manifests
puppet module command 222
puppet module search command 223
puppet resource 214
manifests, generating with 213
puppet resource command 213
Pysa
about 217
URL 217

R

Rake
about 22
used, for bootstrapping Puppet 26-28
used, for deploying changes 22, 23
rbenv
about 163
installing 163
RDoc 243
realize function 113
recurse parameter 135
Red Hat 8
refreshonly parameter 93
regsubst function 54
regular expression
about 49

pattern, capturing 50
syntax 50
using, in conditional statement 49
using, with selectors and case statements 52
regular expression substitutions
using 54, 55
working 55
reports
generating 240, 241
resources
auditing 139, 140
disabling 78
disabling, temporarily 140, 141
scheduling 129, 131
overriding 75
resource types
creating 226, 227
documentation 228
validation 228
reusable manifest
writing 79
root parameter 150
rspec-puppet
manifests, testing with 218-220
rspec-puppet-init command 219
Ruby
about 158
managing 158, 160
working 161
ruby-build
about 161
installing 161, 162
Ruby regular expression syntax
reference link 50
run stages
creating 68, 69
using 68-70

S

schedule metaparameter
used, for limiting resources within specified
period 129-131
secret data
storing, with hiera-gpg 210-212
secret function 102

selector
about 51
default value, specifying 52
examples 50
using 50
working 51
shellquote function 84
source parameter 133
spec code 219
standard naming conventions
using 42, 43
stats interface 177
stdlib module 222
sum method 233

T

--timing switch 205
tags
about 65
using 65-67
third-party repository
packages, installing from 103-106
tmpfile definition 60
type 226

U

Ubuntu 8
unless parameter 88
user customization files
managing 121-125
users
managing, virtual resources used 115-117
users SSH access
managing 118-121
user::virtual class
creating 116
Utility computing 188

V

Vagrant
documentation site, URL 197
downloading 193
installing 193

  used, for managing virtual machines 193
  VM, creating 194, 196
versioncmp function 108
vhost_domain parameter 149
vhost_root parameter 149
virtual IP (VIP) 166
virtual machines
  managing, with Vagrant 193
virtual resources
  about 112
  used, for managing users 115-117
  using 112-115

Y

YAML format 241

Thank you for buying
Puppet 3 Cookbook

About Packt Publishing

Packt, pronounced 'packed', published its first book "*Mastering phpMyAdmin for Effective MySQL Management*" in April 2004 and subsequently continued to specialize in publishing highly focused books on specific technologies and solutions.

Our books and publications share the experiences of your fellow IT professionals in adapting and customizing today's systems, applications, and frameworks. Our solution based books give you the knowledge and power to customize the software and technologies you're using to get the job done. Packt books are more specific and less general than the IT books you have seen in the past. Our unique business model allows us to bring you more focused information, giving you more of what you need to know, and less of what you don't.

Packt is a modern, yet unique publishing company, which focuses on producing quality, cutting-edge books for communities of developers, administrators, and newbies alike. For more information, please visit our website: www.packtpub.com.

About Packt Open Source

In 2010, Packt launched two new brands, Packt Open Source and Packt Enterprise, in order to continue its focus on specialization. This book is part of the Packt Open Source brand, home to books published on software built around Open Source licences, and offering information to anybody from advanced developers to budding web designers. The Open Source brand also runs Packt's Open Source Royalty Scheme, by which Packt gives a royalty to each Open Source project about whose software a book is sold.

Writing for Packt

We welcome all inquiries from people who are interested in authoring. Book proposals should be sent to author@packtpub.com. If your book idea is still at an early stage and you would like to discuss it first before writing a formal book proposal, contact us; one of our commissioning editors will get in touch with you.

We're not just looking for published authors; if you have strong technical skills but no writing experience, our experienced editors can help you develop a writing career, or simply get some additional reward for your expertise.

Puppet 3 Beginner's Guide

ISBN: 978-1-78216-124-0   Paperback: 204 pages

Start from scratch with the Puppet configuration management system, and learn how to fully utilize Puppet through simple, practical examples

1. Shows you step-by-step how to install Puppet and start managing your systems with simple examples

2. Every aspect of Puppet is explained in detail so that you really understand what you're doing

3. Gets you up and running immediately, from installation to using Puppet for practical tasks in a matter of minutes

4. Written in a clear, friendly, jargon-free style which doesn't assume any previous knowledge and explains things in practical terms

Puppet 2.7 Cookbook

ISBN: 978-1-84951-538-2   Paperback: 300 pages

Build reliable, scalable, secure, high-performance systems to fully utilize the power of cloud computing

1. Shows you how to use 100 powerful advanced features of Puppet, with detailed step-by-step instructions

2. Covers all the popular tools and frameworks used with Puppet: Dashboard, Foreman, MCollective, and more

3. Written in a simple, practical style by a professional systems administrator and Puppet expert, every recipe has detailed step-by-step instructions showing you the exact commands and configuration settings you need

Please check **www.PacktPub.com** for information on our titles

[PACKT] open source *
PUBLISHING community experience distilled

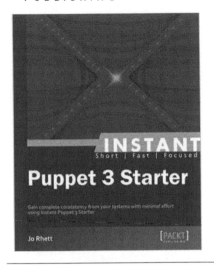

Instant Puppet 3 Starter

ISBN: 978-1-78216-174-5 Paperback: 50 pages

Gain complete consistency from your systems with minimal effort using Istant Puppet 3 Starter

1. Learn something new in an Instant! A short, fast, focused guide delivering immediate results

2. Learn how deterministic results can vastly reduce your workload

3. Deploy Puppet Server as a Ruby-on-Rails application to handle thousands of clients

4. Design your own module for complex configurations

OpenStack Cloud Computing Cookbook

ISBN: 978-1-84951-732-4 Paperback: 318 pages

Over 100 recipes to successfully set up and manage your OpenStack cloud environments with complete coverage of Nova, Swift, Keystone, Glance and Horizon

1. Learn how to install and configure all the core components of OpenStack to run an environment that can be managed and operated just like AWS or Rackspace

2. Master the complete private cloud stack from scaling out compute resources to managing swift services for highly redundant, highly available storage

3. Practical, real world examples of each service are built upon in each chapter allowing you to progress with the confidence that they will work in your own environments

Please check **www.PacktPub.com** for information on our titles

Made in the USA
Lexington, KY
26 January 2014